Y0-EBO-670

Corporate Revolution

Corporate Revolution

New strategies for executive leadership

ROGER HAYES
and
REGINALD WATTS

NICHOLS PUBLISHING COMPANY : NEW YORK

First published in the United States of America in 1986 by
Nichols Publishing Company,
Post Office Box 96
New York, N.Y. 10024

Library of Congress Cataloging-in-Publication Data

Watts, Reginald, 1932–
Corporate revolution.
1. Industry—Social aspects. 2. Organizational change. 3. Leadership. I. Hayes, Roger. II. Title.
HD60.W38 1986 658.4'06 86–12499
ISBN 0–89397–255–X

Printed in Great Britain

'It is all very well to write a book but can you waggle your ears?'

J. M. Barrie who could
to H. G. Wells who couldn't

Acknowledgements

We would like to thank Karen Block, Kep Simpson, Jacquetta Pease, Penny Cooper and above all our agent Carolyn Whitaker, for their ideas, the patient hours of reading, proofing or word processing and for their general encouragement.

Contents

An introduction

'If you keep your head when all about you are losing theirs, it's just possible that you haven't grasped the situation.'

– Jean Kerr,
'Please Don't Eat The Daisies'

Large hierarchical structures are becoming outdated in an information environment. Speed, synthesis and flexibility are the critical factors – not order, repetition and stability. In his book *The Search for New Values*, Daniel Yankelovich said of the U.S., but he could as well have been writing about any post-industrial society, 'We now find our nation hovering midway between an old post-war faith in expanding horizons and a newer sense of lowered expectations, apprehension about the future, mistrust of institutions and a growing sense of limits'. Add to this the question posed in a Young & Rubicam published monograph commenting on current changes in society: 'What will we do with all the new well-educated indians with chief-like tendencies in the classical hierarchical organizations' and you get the theme of this book. Change is upon us. Are we moving fast enough in business to keep up? For too long we've measured *things* – now we need to measure *knowledge* – the skills, training and performance of people. Managements which accept that change is not a new piece of gloomy hardware perched on their secretaries' desk will be those which move into the Hall of Fame for the 1990s. It is not just a proliferation of more data and more information, with an expectation of faster responses, that signifies the onslaught of the new technologies on management thinking. It is about something more fundamental. It is about new ways of tackling problems, new sets of values and above all, new learning and training processes that will ultimately generate a new type of man and woman for leadership, who as Benedetti of Olivetti has achieved, can mix human creativity and financial resources to add value and grow those around them.

In general, business has been remarkably slow to respond to social change – although those nearest to the communications industries have fared better than most. Business systems tend to be resistant to change and the only data they accept is of the quantitative, financial and economic variety. Yet, as Peter Drucker says 'None of the headline makers . . . nor (economic) crises are nearly as important, let alone as real as the changes taking place in population structure and dynamics.' The determinants of a society's structures and dynamics are the values, the beliefs, the attitudes and the concerns of its members. Ultimately, changes in individual values and attitudes as manifest in the home, workplace and the community, are what will change the structure and systems in use within our business organizations. If we fail to see this we fail to understand why our corporate objectives are not being met, our mission-statements are rejected and why our sense of direction is diffuse and misunderstood by managers and workers alike.

The purpose of this book is to force the reader to fasten his eyes firmly on the future, not in a futurologist sense but with a new set of parameters, viewing the world with a new conceptual lens, using a new route map. To so impregnate him with a sense of forwardness that his management decisions will be taken against a backcloth of – How will things be this time next year and the year after? – It is often said that Japanese economic success lies in their ability to think in the long-term. While the American and European manager is concerned with his year-end figures (and half-yearly and even quarterly), the Japanese equivalent thinks decade-end. Whether this is completely true is difficult for the Westerner to ascertain. One thing is clear however. If we compare the slant of British newspapers with those published in Japan, there is a reversal of the timeframe. British papers are full of the past. Whether it is royalty or residences, people or policies, the tendency is to emphasize past connections, historic precedents and how they compared with one hundred years before. Perhaps it is because of a wish to forget the past, blot out the horrors of atomic blasts and avoid concern for what went wrong in the forties that causes Japanese newspapers to constantly harp on about the future. They describe what will be happening next year, next decade, next century. They talk about new technologies and create, in doing so, an attitude of mind that accepts the new, that welcomes change and organizes itself to work towards new horizons of advance and achievement. We very much doubt whether techno-fear or risk-aversion exists within the Japanese culture. Certainly it is less apparent in France and Germany than it is in the U.K.

The very attributes that make the British islands such a pleasant place in which to live – environment, courtesy (football hooligans apart) and stability – can also become restrictive pressures leading to an inability to achieve economic growth. As nations, the British and Europeans need to learn from the Japanese and the Americans. They need to know how to graft enterprise, entrepreneurial skills and attitudes and above all, hard work, onto a social structure that personifies the British way of living.

The signs are that the 'mad period' of education which has reduced standards over the past two decades is now being reversed. The removal of state cushioning is forcing more and more companies to be aggressively competitive, and merit is seen increasingly as a qualification for the boardroom rather than the right school or the right family. There is still much to be done but the direction being taken by the British is the right one.

The questions we shall be asking in this book are whether British managers and to a lesser extent, their European and American counterparts, are now ready to intensify the rate of change and pass through a process that we can only call metamorphosis. (We *talk* of Britain partly because we know it well and partly because many of its corporations and managers are classic illustrations of this book's theme.) A change that is not in this case into a Kafkaesque insect but into a type of manager who is capable of leading and organizing the corporation that will be upon us within the next two decades. We are not concerned here with futurology. Future shock is here already.

A week spent working within one of the modern, successful high-tech companies within the Silicon belt of Scotland or the area west of London towards Bristol will provide a flavour of how all successful companies will be run within five or ten years. To work for even a few days within, say, the Digital Equipment Company at Reading, and then to up roots and work within one of the more traditional low-tech manufacturing operations on Tyneside or the Wirral is like moving through a time-warp. A time-warp that carries you from the late twentieth century back into the Belle Epoch of 1890, only there isn't much Belle about it. The computer company in Reading marks you with its culture within only a few hours. Its style, attitudes, non-hierarchical management, customer-driven philosophy, its dress codes, the quality of its thought processes are just a few of the attributes that will hit even a casual visitor on his first day.

The changes we are discussing therefore are already with us. The first signs are being flown at the masthead of many successful companies of today, but in the words of one Hollywood actor, 'We ain't seen nuttin' yet'. Before moving forward, some facts and comments should be noted about Britain's failure so far to accept these new options. Some managers – we fear the proportion is all too high – still fail to accept the extent of Britain's decline. If they do, they frequently blame it onto a range of factors which includes trade union power, the effect of the Common Market, even the aftermath of the war, without seeing that all too frequently, the causes can be found within the leadership of our many industrial giants. When we consider that even in the late 1950s Britain was still one of the richest nations in Europe. Today, her standard of living is under half of France or Germany's and she is seen as the poor man of Europe. On a world scale, using World Bank figures, she is in the third division of nations in income per head. She rubs shoulders with Puerto Rico, the Soviet Union and Yugoslavia.

If we compare the position in 1900 when Britain ruled a fifth of the world's land surface, her navy was twice as powerful as the next two combined and even the merchant fleet was bigger than the rest of the world's put together. Consider the quality of life then, the average Briton enjoyed a standard 40% higher than her next rival, Germany.

In a period of only eighty years, Britain has seen her share of world trade fall from 33% to less than 10%. During the past decade this decline has accelerated, often as a result of poor competitiveness and a process of de-industrialization that has started but is destined to gather speed in the years ahead. Famous names like Triumph motor cycles, Imperial Typewriter, Garrard record decks and Hornby toys are now almost forgotten. As traditional manufacturing collapses, there is a knock-on effect as supporting companies and suppliers also die – what is called the downward multiplier effect. As the infrastructure decays, then investors look elsewhere to invest, usually abroad. The fact is, British industry started falling behind American competition over a hundred years ago. In the 1870s, people were complaining then about the high prices and outdated design in British goods.

The decision-making process of Britain's top management has been at fault for more than one generation. The National Economic Development Office, in a series of reports in the early nineteen-eighties, listed the following seven failures of management:

i Too little spent on research compared with competition;
ii Too many big defence contracts have made large corporations fat and unwilling to fight in the marketplace;
iii Product innovation has been poor and design even worse;
iv British executives prefer to stay at home rather than export (even the word 'export' reflects a myopia);
v Late deliveries;
vi The least well-trained workforce in Europe;
vii 'The amateur tradition' of managers dies too hard, with the result that missed opportunities abound, from robotics and biotechnology to soft and hardware provision.

This last point is where we need to stop and take the message forward. Corelli Barnett and Martin J. Weiner in their book *The Collapse of British Power* (1972) suggest that the rot really started to set in during the nineteenth century even while the industrial revolution was in progress. The aristocratic tradition in Britain was so strong and so unbroken because neither revolution nor war had destroyed its social structure. The class structure with its accepted – or unaccepted – social values was becoming more, not less, ingrained.

Possibly the most significant and certainly obvious aim of anyone who was successful was to emulate the upper class in life-style and attitudes.

The governing classes in Britain, whether they were politicians or industrialists, never took to busness as a preference. Once they were settled or they reached their pinnacles of success, they preferred to assume the life of the country squire. Many in fact still do. Traipsing down to their country houses for long weekends, they try to think as countrymen for two and a half days rather than put in those long and intensive hours that a German or American businessman would take as the norm.

The British industrialist still has generations of forebears who think that gentlemen don't dirty their hands and that the professions of the law or even the army are preferable to manufacturing. This is an attitude which developed and continued into this century until it permeated every level of the commercial world. For a hundred years, industry was left to the traders and practical men who were never truly accepted into high society. The successful manufacturer could hope to become, in later life, a member of the gentry or even a peer, have a country seat, ride to hounds and leave the family business to trundle downhill back to the 'smoke'. His sons would do the right thing: a profession, the army or navy, the Civil Service or politics.

This potted history of British decline may seem irrelevant in a book which stakes its claim for attention on the need to gaze into the future on a global stage. Yet this short description of a social attitude which leads towards an antagonism towards the commercial process, highlights the need to look beyond the immediate, easily accessible factors in management if we want to understand and respond to change. John Eatwell, a Cambridge economist, speaking in a 1982 television series called 'Whatever Happened to Britain?' said then that 'A reconstruction of the British economy will require, as much as anything, a change in intellectual perspectives and prejudices. It is the economic ideas of the past which need to be overthrown before any straight thinking can be done'. Think how much more accurate is this statement when we start to construct our route map into the 1990s.

How then will the executives running or aspiring to run companies in the next two decades differ from you, the reader? Will their job be harder or easier? In later chapters we discuss the attitudes, training and values they will need to apply to their jobs. At this stage we should simply lay down the ground rules. What are likely to be the hard facts, as opposed to the softer responses of opinion and guesstimate? A survey carried out by *Chief Executive* magazine in June 1985 included 900 named Managing Directors in its list, of which 209 produced responses. If anyone wanted to look forward to some basic trends one would think we are unlikely to get a better informed group of people to make such a projection than 200 chief executives. However, we must remember that in the year 2000, the generation of CEOs who will be in power will have begun their careers after the advent of the computer as a normal part of business life.

Drawing extensively upon this *Chief Executive* Survey, we summarize here some of their findings:

i Over 50% expect the demand of the top job to be less, due to computer aids;

ii A majority (62%) think that the spread of information technology will force the Managing Director to be more democratic in management style. He also expects society to demand a higher standard of conduct from him.

iii Attitudes to women, wives and female business colleagues are ambivalent. A majority expect their jobs to be done by women and they see this as an impediment of their own development as males. They see the demand of their jobs leading to more failed marriages.

iv At least three out of four of today's CEOs are confident that their successors will do a better job than they themselves do now.

In terms of the impact of advances in information technology on the top job, this is how the respondents rated the improvements:

	Yes(%)	*No(%)*
Able to make decisions more quickly and with greater certainty	82	18
Better understanding of what competitors are doing and likely to do	68	32
Better equipped to anticipate economic and other changes which could put their company at risk	77	23
Tighter control of all corporate activities	83	17

What is so amazing is that there is a substantial body of computer sceptics (1 in 7) who foresee no extra help in top management from computers. Equally worrying is the number of respondents who put more weight on internal controls than on competitive strategy and development of policies aimed at the anticipation of external pressures.

Nearly half the MDs thought there will be less travelling and a third expect the future MD to do more work at home.

On the all-important question of managerial training there was still a belief that an arts degree would be more use than a science degree. This despite the fact that more and more personnel managers handling graduate trainees for managerial vacancies prefer the discipline that a degree in science produces over an arts subject. Fortunately business degrees showed a high rating as does post-experience training. Most of the respondents foresee a weakening of the old boy network and only one in twenty put much store on family connections – a good sign.

Nine out of ten of the respondents think that future executives will gain their experience in several companies and over half think that they will move from a specialist job into one of general management. The favoured specializations were seen as:

Marketing	66%
Production	27%
Computers	10%
Legal	4%
Personnel	1%
Other	27%

(N.B. Some respondents gave an equal rating to 2 or more specializations)

Possibly of most relevance to the hypothesis we propound were the personal skills the future MD will be expected to need. They were, in order of magnitude:

	Points
Numeracy	4.2
Literacy	4.2
Computing	4.1
Time Management	4.0
Marketing	4.0
Selection	3.9
Selling	3.8
Industrial Relations	3.8

Public Relations	3.7
Public Speaking	3.5
Team Building	3.1
Speed Reading	3.1
Languages	3.0
Typing	1.4

The last skill is an interesting one. Five years ago the tendency was to argue that computers should spill out the data and the senior executive then looks at it in hard copy form. Today the trend is towards a personal computer on every desk. To use it, typing skills are necessary. However, it is a matter of terminology. Many executives learn to type by the simple process of repetitive work on their computer.

Three out of five of those who replied expect formal management training to play a bigger part in education for leadership and equal proportions see more emphasis being placed on such training after reaching a senior level. Only two out of five see the traditional leadership qualities as being important for the future. Interestingly enough, the issue of social responsibility came very low on everyone's priorities despite the comment earlier that CEOs expect they will have to maintain higher ethical standards in the future.

There is a danger in treating research of this type taken among senior executives as a real guide for the future. 'After all', you may say, 'Who better to know what is going to happen in the office of the future'. In fact, it is no more than a reflection of the attitudes held today by a sample of chief executives about business and the direction it is likely to take over the next few years. As such, it is a particularly worrying reflection on the ability of senior managers to clear their minds and think forward. Their attitudes towards automation and information technology is reinforced by research carried out by many other organizations such as Booz Allen and PA Management Consultants. They all came up with the same responses. They show that few senior managers are at all computer literate and tend, because of their backgrounds and upbringing during the 1960s and 1970s, to misunderstand the size and impact of the computer/high technology revolution on their business lives. Having in their youth studied the industrial revolution as part of history at school, possibly considered the same subject under economic history at university or business school, they have grown up perpetuating a belief that the computer is no more than an up-to-date version of the technologies that changed the face of Europe in the nineteenth century.

The fact is, that revolution was a revolution of muscle, the computer revolution one of brains and they bear no relationship to each other in terms of their impact. Because the labouring process was carried out by the less intelligent and lower social stratas of society, it was natural that the managers of companies saw new engineering processes that replaced human labour as an area they need only view from afar. Their concern was with the intellectual aspects of the new inventions. What would be the capital costs, how much saving, would the workers strike and so on? They didn't have to worry about handling the new equipment themselves.

The new revolution is about the extension of brain power. It is not an area where managers can stand off and treat the hardware like a lathe. The computer is a mental appendage – a second or third brain attached to their desk. As such they have to use it themselves, understand it and invest time on its application if they are to utilize its potential to the full and keep up with those managers who can. The chief executive who remains aloof and asks only for hard copies of data will not gain from the new revolution. He will simply edge slowly but surely into a backwater, all the time convincing himself that he's keeping up with the stream and that his company's decline is due to outside forces beyond his control. He will not blame himself, only acts of God. In fact, he is subconsciously resisting the changes which are happening about him – or as we saw in the survey, he is *consciously* unaware of the extent of the change. He is a latter-day Luddite, sipping his even drier Martinis before lunch while the corporate ship lurches from one iceberg to another. Today's country squire sits in a soft carpeted boardroom suite where the buzz of computer hardware never disturbs the calm – unless of course, he has given his secretarial assistant a treat by buying her a word-processor. If he's heard of electronic mail, it's something to be relegated to the telex room, not an item to spoil his own leather-topped desk. Even if he's out of touch, he should at least have the foresight to insist on training for his subordinates and we don't just mean at the college of hard knocks either. A society changing as fast as this one poses many problems for its leaders. This book suggests that solutions will depend on changing the attitudes and skills of our leaders and a greater ability to communicate. As Anthony Jay said in *Management and Machiavelli*, industry desperately needs senior managers who can take on highly verbal politicians at their own game, can see the other point of view, have a mastery of words and arguments and apply the techniques and strategies vital to change behaviour in an evolving environment, an information and knowledge-based environment. The competitive edge will go to those who understand that people are the key and who place a higher value on creativity, the soft skills and a change in the language we use to break the mould?

This book will deal with three important and interlinked themes:

- Corporations which fail to adapt fossilize and die;
- Managers are frequently out-of-date in their attitudes and skills by the time they assume senior office. They seldom recover (though there are notable exceptions);
- Few senior managers recognize the raison d'etre of the modern company has so changed that it's now a different type of institution to its predecessors and therefore requires a different shape and thrust.

We quote from a British Institute of Management Report (1983) *Profits from Change*:

> 'Industrial organizations should be seen as an integral part of the overall social system, not isolated and independent but essentially responding to a variety of pressures and influences, meeting material needs and providing the work environment of a large proportion of the population.'

The corporation survives or dies depending on its ability to marshall all its talents to shape the future rather than be swamped by it. The pace of change and the sheer complexity of tasks and ideas in a turbulent worldwide business environment requires a new kind of business leader – a 'philosopher entrepreneur', who can above all, handle people and communicate effectively to internal as well as external audiences.

The catalyst to success or failure, particularly in the technology age is leadership. In the information society brought about by the 'chip', a direct correlation exists between leadership and image. Leadership is based on good communications. So often it is lacking in modern chief executives who think they do it well and don't hire the right advice or do it badly because their advisers are not up to the task.

Managing a business is one dimension, but orchestrating change by communicating the changing nature of the business and its needs to stakeholders is a more important factor in longer-term management. This change in the skills needed by management, especially in reaching the internal constituency makes an anachronism of so many managers. They are often out-of-date before they assume office because their training and learning experience took place during formative years that are two decades away. Some gather their strength through post-graduate mature student business studies at the middle manager level, but the majority – like all human beings – stop the learning process at thirty.

Many CEOs and their advisers are unable to chart the future because their training and experience was set in an environment that was so different that it might as well have been on another planet.

Corporate leadership is often taken by production engineers turned managers, who because of this give insufficient weight to social, political and personal lifestyle factors. This makes their quantitative approach almost instantly out-of-date. The same applies to accountants and economists turned chief executives.

The qualitative and quantitative man/woman is difficult to find. That is because our education system – despite C. P. Snow's lifetime crusade – still divides early into humanities or science. It's difficult to generalize but this is also true throughout most of Europe.

Education, in rational scientific thinking rather than communications and people handling, has ill-prepared the modern CEO or his executive suite to see the wood for the trees and adapt to the new inter-dependence of institutions, horizontal networking and the business integration that derives from two-way communications. The post-industrial society, the demassification of the media which reflects the increasingly 'inner directed' attitude of consumers and the values of employees who were brought up in a new age, are all affecting the ability of companies to adapt to the market around them. They must reach the new market now or their companies will certainly fail to reach the even faster changing markets of the future.

The pre-requisite for success is for management to provide leadership, not authoritarianism, internally – to generate commitment and motivation – and externally to build bridges towards collaboration and interaction. What has been called 'social management' with other organizations such as universities, government and pressure groups, creates a need to avoid confrontation. There is a need to accept the fact that corporations will be expected to be accountable to other audiences than the traditional shareholder. The power of government and the community to provide a thumbs-up or down, like Nero at the Coliseum, has become almost absolute. The life or death of the corporation now rests on new groups of people, people whose sympathies and understanding are quite out of tune with the old-style corporate manager. This shows up alarmingly in television confrontations on issues from smoking to South Africa.

Business education is a factor, as are new skills in training. In particular, there is a need for more credibility for the role of the communications adviser in monitoring, counselling and implementing communications policy as an integral part of corporate strategy. Aside from the CEO, it may be that only the specialist in communications skills is sufficiently broadly trained. This is the function of analyzing so many variables in the decision-taking process and can thus help to interpret them.

Currently the PRO is rarely more than a technician lacking an authoritative intellectual basis for the advice he should be giving. To be acceptable he must become accountable and identify with corporate priorities.

The leadership that is required to place the new style of corporation onto a higher plane means equating human with business values and assuming social responsibility by achieving a more politicized role in society. This is dependent on sound, open communications. Both the CEO and communications adviser need to have a more solid base of training and education if they are to become 'polymaths'. They must be able to interpret all the issues impacting the corporation. New technologies and the hardware of communications have blinded them to the software implications.

Like culture, communication should be inbred in the strategy which should be based on less hide-bound, narrow attitudes. To achieve the necessary shift requires enlarging what is often called 'the response repertoire'.

1

Future shock is here

'Like many machines of the smokestack era, our intellectual tools, too, are ready for the museum.'

Alvin Toffler.

If we are to create, like the Japanese, a new cast of mind by which we think forward rather than backwards, we must be prepared to contemplate our children's future style of life. A child entering secondary school today could be a manager in fifteen years time. Management and its application to corporate life is not a thing apart from daily living. Books on business studies talk about new techniques and disciplines as if they operated in a vacuum. A corporation reflects the values, attitudes and lifestyles of its staff. Each acts and reacts on the other, but essentially the changing mores of society change the mores of business life too. We cannot begin to understand what is happening within our companies unless we view them as a group of people that reflect a sample of society. Sometimes it is a sample of the local community, sometimes a class or an intellectual segment, more often it is a fair breakdown of all society, especially if it is in the manufacturing sector.

Managers must start by understanding the future if they want to make decisions for the present. The past too will play its part in emphasizing why employees and colleagues think as they do. To plan for the future, therefore, we need to understand the ground on which we are planting our seeds, and this means accepting the past and not rejecting it. T. S. Eliot, the poet, may have worked in a bank but he would never describe himself as a manager. Yet, in the poem from the *Four Quartets*, 'East Coker', he sums up the process of management decision-making so accurately when he wrote '. . . at the still point, there the dance is, but neither arrest nor movement. And do not call it fixity, where past and future are gathered.'

According to management consultants McKinsey, by the year 2000 AD 5% of the European population will be producing all the agricultural products needed for Europe, 20% of the working population will be involved in manufacturing industries, 25% will be in manual services and 50% in some form of what they term 'brainwork'. They believe (according to an address given by Henry Strange, a senior director at the London office of McKinsey) that although Britain can lay claim to fame as having invented 55% of the significant inventions in the world since 1945, on being the only major free-world country self-sufficient in energy, and to a high quality education system, there are three underlying problems for the future of the British economy.

First, British managers and workforce lack commitment; second, their scientific inventions occur almost by accident and third, management is *unstructured, disorganized* and *badly trained*. Britain spends approximately half the amount on vocational training that every other European country does, while her expenditure on higher education is half the OECD average. West German productivity is 63% higher than Britain's, due, they claim, to the fact that 100% of West German foremen possess higher craft qualifications, whereas only 12% of U.K. foremen have qualifications. This may, on the surface, sound like an over-simplistic answer to Britain's decline. Yet it is a symptom, a symptom of Germany's (and other countries) greater acceptance of the fact that the intellectual revolution is upon us. Knowledge and skill in using our brains is rapidly becoming the lodestar of success for a national economy. Consider therefore what this may mean one or two decades from now. The need for intellectual excellence will be that much more intense. What is more, it will be a thread, a necessity, that will run through every sector of society down to the lowest level. Already we suffer from the problem among housewives of a failure to understand modern computerized cooking equipment, and many men have a similar difficulty with advanced hi-fi equipment, video recorders, and many of the so-called extra aids offered in popular automobiles. Class structures and union luddism will have to go, if countries like Britain are not to become holiday camps for the Japanese (and the new Gang of Four).

If this is a problem today for the less intelligent stratas of society we can expect it to become truly serious if our educational systems are not prepared to re-adapt to those new demands. There is little point in teaching an understanding of why Henry VIII had six wives if the pupils are unable to work household appliances when they get home. Even worse, the opportunities for work, already more complex, will become tougher as structural unemployment rises in line with new technology.

The question of how societies in the Western world will adapt to these changes will become the great issue of the next decade. Alvin Toffler, the futurologist, writing in the *Sunday Times* (17/2/85) said that he expects democracies to become involved in a great macro-conflict of ideas. A conflict that will shake the roots of the political party systems and cause new groupings in some countries. On the one side will be those dedicated to mass manufacturing, centralized political control, heavy government bureaucracy, urban concentration, equality and uniformity, standardized compulsory education, and a belief that if the economy can be made to work the rest will take care of itself. On the other side '. . . of the super-struggle are an as yet unorganized array of political forces which represent the emerging economy based on de-massified, computer-based custom production, decentralization and privatization of many central government functions, educational diversity and choice, on shorter working hours, on flexible hours, work-at-home, and employee participation in decision making'.

Toffler argues in many of his books, especially *The Third Wave*, that post-industrial society is not really on us yet, only its first signs have emerged in the U.S. particularly around Silicon Valley. One of its most evident symptoms will be, in his view, the decline in mass manufacturing as a factor in the total economy. Having said that, however, he quickly makes the point that no modern nation can live on services and information flow alone. 'It is quite true', he said in his *Sunday Times* article, 'that a country cannot survive economically by taking in washing, barbering, making telephone calls, and going to meetings. But robots, automation, new materials, and new organizational and distributional systems now make it possible for factories to turn out even more goods than before with far fewer workers . . . there is no technological reason to prevent 5% of workers turning out all the material goods people need. This suggests a work force in which as many as 90% are engaged in services, information and communications activities.' He goes on to say that the great issue of the next decade will not be the clash between rich and poor, between black and white, but between all these factors as personified by a battle between the enemies and the advocates of post-industrial society. It will be a protracted war between industrial and post-industrial society. Ahead we are seeing the first signs of this war, albeit hidden under various trade union cloaks. Highly paid dockers who are earning very high sums from containerization, will strike for more pay despite the fact they are earning incomes well in excess of non-unionized office workers, many of whom work for the greatest part of their life as clerks. This latter group are those who suffer from techno-fear, resist new office technologies and despite their white shirts, dark suits and ties will be the truly deprived of the new age. The new demassification of the old society will create more diversity and a growing demand for individual treatment. In place of the large voting blocks organized under party banners to deliver votes for a central bland manifesto, we are likely to see an increasingly fragmented electorate made up of thousands of transitory groupings.

These changes are slow, and to those concerned with the next general election or tomorrow's financial report it may appear as if enthusiasm for a brave new world is taking over. In fact the speed of change is such that people pass it by unrecognized. Some try to avoid it altogether and insist on equipment and methods they feel comfortable with. Others draw round them a cloak of past values where life continues almost without visible change. The products of the top private schools can, if their parents wish it, move from their school sixth-form to Oxbridge, and then to a bank in the City of London. There is hardly a hitch in their transition from parents' sunny home to their own parentally subsidized house and a season ticket to Waterloo station. This situation is changing but the opportunities for a family connection to open a door and then hold it open are still sufficiently strong to ensure there are enough declining companies to keep the take-over specialist in business.

The mid-eighties are likely to be seen as the period when telecommunications and computing merged. The high-tech advances of the last twenty years in microprocessors, integrated circuits, fibre-optics and software, are becoming as integral to the new functions offered by transmission facilities as they are to word-processors, mainframe computers, and today's office equipment.

This equipment, once developed for, and employed in, stand-alone work-station environments has now become transmission-orientated, capable of networking information centres that are geographically dispersed. For the first time, offices which process data are no longer bound to the point where this data originates. They include claims offices for insurance companies, reservation centres for hotel chains and airlines, remote newspaper printing plants, data processing, credit card billing, coupon redemption centres and bank and broker back-office facilities. All have several characteristics in common: substantial employment levels with potential for lower wages in remote locations, pressure for building space, facilities located outside metropolitan areas, heavy volumes of data flow, and little need for direct person-to-person contact with headquarters or with the sources of these data.

The options available for servicing and managing information needs have never been greater. Microcomputers are no longer employed only in the office, but are found in third generation PBXs which merge voice and data communications and provide the most striking examples of the new interdependence of data processing and communications.

Storage and retrieval systems are becoming increasingly more attractive to the business manager. It has been estimated that 35% of the paper information in a company's files is never accessed and 90% can be discarded after one year. Twelve-inch optical discs are available, which can store digital data, equivalent to one million pages of full text on a single side of the disc. On-line services are available to connect business managers to data bases offering a wide range of professional subject material which would be extremely expensive to create in the office.

Time-sharing services, developed to answer business needs to access software without having to make extensive capital investments or to use extra computer capacity, have been one of the fastest growing services. Cellular radio, the new mobile telephone and paging technology, are already having an impact on the way business people communicate, increasing their productivity and availability.

Satellite teleconferencing, world networking, electronic mail, and computer conferencing, are but a few of the additional options available to the corporation in its effort to remain viable and competitive in an environment of growing dependence on information management techniques and systems.

Outside the office, in the home, information can be received, generated, stored, edited – and in some instances, transmitted in new ways. VCRs, the hottest thing since television, are the first of a series of black boxes conveying information into the home. Already retailed media, purchased over the counter for use in these machines, are producing a threatening alternative to the electronic media that beams out signals to a broader audience.

Videotext and teletext – two generic terms which cover the system, that control large quantities of information through the use of equipment such as the telephone, the television receiver, and a control pad – are now available and are expected to influence purchasing habits by offering home purchasing through catalogues and home bank facilities.

Work in the home, using electronic equipment, is also on the rise. Word-processing centres, software development, and data base consulting, will turn the home into an electronic cottage. Increasingly as information becomes the same as for offices and factories, the home will become an attractive alternative to today's workplace for some, capable of changing the economics of the corporation's operations and the employment of the workforce.

All of these subjects – satellites, electronic mail, telecommunications, computers, videotext, data bases – are the components of the largest industry in the world, the information technology industry. It is, however, an industry in continual transition. A potential glut of transmission capacity, brought about by improvements in satellite and fibre-optics technologies, has the potential to exacerbate the competitive situation. Nowhere is the competition within the industry more visible than among computer manufacturers. Each year Wang, IBM, DEC and other vendors produce cheaper versions of their current product lines having increased features and functions. New products emerge while others 'cool down'. The video revolution in the home appears to be flattening out, at the same time that video-conferencing in the business community may be on the upswing once its de-personalized atmosphere can be fine-tuned. Two years ago cable was the media superstar; today it is satellites for business applications – despite the fact that the direct-broadcast-to-home satellite market has not yet matured. For the time being, in Europe at least, it will be beamed via cable. But already the implications for cross-cultural penetration, quality of information and choice of entertainment given the sheer size of the satellite footprint – are immense.

Corporations are now heavily immersed in the technologies, services, systems and business aspects of information as a factor of production. In an effort to control costs, to exploit the opportunities associated with information-related options and to cope with the continual restructuring of the industry, these organizations are turning more and more to an examination of their intellectual and technical resources. This is because the ultimate goal of information, in a corporate setting, is to extend the capabilities and potential of human minds for improved business performance.

Having outlined the massive hardware changes that are just commencing their journey through our daily agendas we must accept that their impact will to a large extent be controlled by the human factor. Later we discuss this, but as Robert Tyrell, director of social forecasting at the UK Henley Centre for Forecasting says, 'companies have got to take a broader perspective than simply economic change. What you're interested in as a business employing people is the consumer and people at work.' One of the themes of this book is emphasized by Christine MacNulty, programme manager of the US SRI International Strategic Environment Centre, who says that 'economists keep getting it wrong because the relationships they build into the huge econometric models they construct are yesterday's relationships, not tomorrow's.' Changes in social attitudes affect the products people buy, their behaviour at work, how the public perceives a corporation and its relationship with its environment. It is interesting to draw from the Henley Centre for Forecasting their glimpse of the future in social terms, as they were described in an article in *International Management* (April 1981). It is relevant to look at this set of forecasts, made a few years ago, in order to gauge and understand some of the underlying pressures that they envisaged at that time. Forecasting of this type is not a quantifiable art. It is a discipline more like philosophy, where a total understanding of the logic as well as the strands of individual change have to be merged. With that understanding it then becomes possible to use the knowledge as an indicator for the interpretation of change as it takes place around us. Here then are Henley's glimpses of the future as they saw them in 1981.

- An increase in the number of people seeking self-sufficiency life styles, but economic realities will cause the traditional view of what constitutes the good life to remain largely unaltered.
- The notion that technology and progress are synonymous will be resisted. This is linked in some ways to a questioning of secular society and the possibility of a resurgence of orthodox religion in the West.
- Pressures for the preservation and improvement of the environment will be sustained. But the costs of environmental protection are being recognized, causing the pressures to slow down.
- As unemployment rises and the bargaining power of labour is eroded, there will be some easing in the pressures to improve working conditions and the quality of working life. The pressures will not vanish altogether, however.
- The retreat of the state from the economy will continue and governments will become more like umpires in society's affairs. This reflects evolving social attitudes towards the role of the state. However, the state will in any case be less well-equipped to take a more activist role. Single-issue politics will be on the ascendant with a corresponding decline in the cohesion of the old political groupings. Issues will transcend party lines and the enforcement of party discipline will be more difficult.
- There will be a decline in respect for, and effectiveness of, authority. This will start to affect the middle classes, where the restraint exercised by traditional moral precepts will be less effective.
- Xenophobic tendencies will increase. The alien will become a more frequent scapegoat for economic and social problems. Nationalist inclinations in the industrialized world will, in part, be a reaction to Third World nationalism.
- Women's relative educational attainment and aspiration levels will continue to rise. They will represent a more significant threat to males in their traditional job preserves.
- Attitudes to business will remain demanding. However, the notion of business as a social trustee (with formal accountability to

'stakeholders' other than shareholders, such as consumers, workers, minorities, local communities, and ecologists) will not become a *de jure* reality. At most, in one or two of the larger Western countries – probably the U.S. and West Germany – it will begin to become more of a *de facto* reality, with stakeholders joining forces on a single issue.

- Several significant developments indicate that the Western world is on the threshold of the post-industrial society. Among them are a shift of employment to service industries; evacuation of the inner cities by private families and industry; a halt in population growth but an increase in longevity; and a low-growth, if not no-growth future.

Christine MacNulty sums up the importance of thinking and debating these future trends when she says we need to 'change managers' mental maps. Managers on the whole might be very good at managing their organizations, but essentially they live in the past. They expect things to continue as they've always been.' In plotting a route through these maps it is important to consider alternative roads. Shell has been using such concepts for many years so that when they consider their corporate plans they can develop alternative social scenarios. They are not always different. In some cases they can be a matter of degree, in others more of speed or timing. For example, they believe that Western societies may either go for radical change as new generations shake off the values of their parents or they may, in the more stable societies, simply tinker at the edges. Shell calls the first scenario the 'New New World' and the second, the 'New Old World' and they look in value system terms something like this:

NEW OLD WORLD	NEW NEW WORLD
Confidence in technology (but not at any price)	The price of progress is too high
Wealth creation	Wealth distribution
'Stand on my own feet'	'Stand up for my rights'
Old institutions can do a good job if modified	Old institutions have failed and need replacing

Business aims give main priority to growth and profit	Business aims give main priority to social contribution
Participation mainly up and down 'the line'	Participation mainly through industrial economy
Work is necessary but needs to give satisfaction	Work an unfortunate necessity, leisure is 'really living'
Flexible hierarchies acceptable as one possible organization form	Formal authority resented – power diffused widely and deeply

Some people believe that these changes are happening in parallel with each other, and are not alternatives but different strands that will be balanced out as one generation moves into positions of influence and alters imperceptibly the values of their predecessors. Michael G. Royston, faculty member of the International Management Institute in Geneva, writing in the May 1984 issue of the *International Public Relations Association (IRPA) Journal* said:

'My own experience in the classroom suggests that there is an age group of managers, now joining the ranks of senior executives, whose liberal, some would say "soft" outlook, puts them philosophically and perhaps managerially at odds not just with their superiors but with their subordinates as well. If this conflict moves out of the classroom and into the corporate corridors of power it could throw up all sorts of problems.

'Older managers today find these junior colleagues hard to understand and difficult to communicate with. They appear to be undisciplined, less motivated by company goals, less concerned by the hard economic facts of life. They are nice people, socially oriented, but "soft". Equally, these junior managers find the "old guard" too narrow in their thinking, cramped in their outlook, and enemies of change.

'One could elaborate on this somewhat over-simplified picture. But it is perhaps more interesting to dwell on the question of whether this disparity – if it really exists – is simply due to difference in age and responsibility, in which case the "young Turks" will cool down in time, or are there outside factors that make the problem permanent?

'The answer could be that there *are* such factors. Senior

managers are by and large those who could be called the "wartime" generation. They remember the Second World War and the immediate post-war period, when life was serious – even tough. The issue was simple – survival. The response was equally simple – obey orders and work hard.

'Some of our senior managers even remember the pre-war days of the Great Depression, when these lessons were even more heavily reinforced. If the first seven years of life are the formative years, anyone who was seven in 1945 or before is likely to be oriented towards discipline and growth. So there might be "environmental" factors governing the attitude of today's managers who are over 45 years old.

'On the other hand, those managers born in 1950 knew nothing about the war. They were born into a world of continuous growth, expansion and consumption, to a degree when guilt started to appear.

'Their early readings might have included Vance Packard's *Waste Makers* and Rachel Carson's *Silent Spring.* At 18 they were at university, where in May 1968 riot and revolt were universal and took precedence over the academic life, and the "flower power" hippy movement was in full bloom.

'They were soon avidly reading Dennis Meadow's *Limits to Growth* and thinking about the post-industrial society and expressing growing concerns for society, the environment and ecology.

'Today, those managers are typically 33 years old and moving into important subordinate positions. They are the ones who find it difficult to live with the old guard – and vice versa. There can be a genuine "generation gap" here. But more, these managers are likely to carry their "environmental" attitudes with them right through their careers. If this is the case, one would expect a continuation of the generation problem until the older generation retires, and a progression to a more people-oriented, society-oriented management style.

'Now a slight problem occurs. I used to see this as a two-generation problem. Now there is a third generation arising to complicate the issue. These are the graduates of the oil crisis in 1973, born after 1955, now in their upper 20s and moving into junior and middle management positions. They tend to be task-

> oriented and technology-oriented and in their personal style, distinctly tough, goal-driven, self-promoting and even aggressive.
>
> 'The old guard find it easier to relate to these newcomers to the managerial ranks than to many of their colleagues who are 30 to 40 years old.
>
> 'If such a "three-generation problem" exists, even marginally, then it is likely to present a new problem for companies. The soft, people-oriented group will be sandwiched between the old guard and the "new conservatives". Even more important is the fact that the conventional, stern father–creative son balance typical of most senior-junior management relations will become upset as the environmental generation reach senior management positions, only to be continuously challenged by their younger, more result-oriented and task-oriented colleagues.'

Sir Ieuan Maddock FRS, one-time chief scientist at the Department of Industry and today a director of International General Electric U.S.A. Ltd., writing in the *New Scientist* (11/12/82) said, 'The ability to forget – to shed past habits, attitudes, techniques and capital resources is often at least as important as the ability to learn . . . the forgetting curves – how are old or outdated skills shed, old attitudes discarded, old plant scrapped and old traditions rejected? . . . experience shows that forgetting curves are much gentler than learning curves, yet success in a rapidly changing industry is largely determined by the interplay between the two. Failures can be caused not so much because the learning curves are not steep enough but because the forgetting curves are too gentle.' He expands on his theme:

> 'Here we are dealing with a natural human trait – a desire to cling to what is familiar – to the areas where experience lies. In many fields of human endeavour this is an attractive quality – to cherish traditions, old buildings, ancient cultures and graceful lifestyles is a worthy aspiration. In the world of technology it is a prescription for suicide. To cling to outmoded methods of manufacture, old product lines, old markets or old attitudes among both management and workers is to let the newcomers race away. Alas, to acquire the ability to forget is a long and difficult process, often

spanning the entire working lifetime of the generation which experienced the ascent of the technology.

'In all kinds of activities all over the world people stick to the old ways. Even in America – that apparently natural home of change – it was not the great companies traditionally linked with radio valves that made the great success of semiconductors, but small companies that were almost complete strangers to the field. It was not the great electronic companies that made the conquest of computers possible, but companies that were working in different areas. This was not through lack of knowledge and skill on the part of the original companies, nor indeed lack of enterprise, but because their forgetting curves were too long. The newcomers quite simply had nothing to forget.

'This is the irony and the threat. A new company that has full access to latest technology – in whatever country – will immediately acquire the most up-to-date equipment, will train staff to the optimum level, will build up staff to the minimum level needed to work the equipment and will not be burdened by surplus plant, buildings and stockholdings. A long-established business will have old plant, probably the wrong mix of skills in the work force, surplus machinery and buildings and will carry stock no longer relevant to the business. These constraints will be compounded by old-style attitudes towards management methods, a trade union structure inherited from earlier and different times, and an ethos ill-suited to the changing world. Forgetting curves persist for several reasons. The most prominent are:

Attitudes. Dedication to past traditions, habits of thinking, pride, arrogance or just plain obstinacy are invariably present when forgetting curves are long. These characteristics are human and it would be wrong to regard them as failing. The same qualities can be a source of strength under different circumstances. But people must be aware of their existence so they can decide whether they are a help or hindrance and resolve to do something about the latter. But the cures must be as human as the characteristics that create the need for them. Education, indoctrination, changing responsibilities, new people, early retirement and re-structuring of firms are all methods that need to be considered and acted upon.

> **Structure.** An organization that has evolved successfully around one type of product or market environment can rarely change rapidly. Yet all too often, new firms merely graft opportunities or challenges onto existing structures rather than take bold steps into the future. The reluctance to change comes in part from the attitudes I have described already but it is also due to too slow a pace of change. People who can recognize the foothills of some dramatic change rather than merely seeing them as perturbations in the normal run of business are vital to innovation.'

Despite this, Tom Peters of Stanford University and co-author of *In Search of Excellence* says, 'big organizations are incredibly dumb. If you want to put over something new within them, you have to say things over and over again in a credible way.' Interestingly, this need to keep repeating ideas over and over again in order to achieve management change was brought out at the annual conference of the Strategic Management Society in Montreal (October 1982). Speakers said that the best way to accomplish strategic change was not to change the management team but to keep it. The permanence of key executives was seen as crucial, a view which flies very clearly in the face of conventional corporate wisdom in most American companies. It all depends, as Sir Ieuan Maddock would say, on their forgetting curves.

In conclusion we would suggest that any manager trying to find principles or themes that appear to be consistent over a time span of two or three decades, would do well to note the classification originally drawn up by Stanford Research Institute International back in the 1960s. We make no apologies for quoting *in extenso* from the attached description of these typologies listed in *International Management* (April 1981):

> 'In the mid-1960s the U.S. research group SRI International started to develop a programme to measure social indicators.
>
> 'It identifies nine basic groups of people based on Maslow's hierarchy of needs. This is a theory developed by U.S. behaviourist Abraham Maslow which says that people go through life aspiring to satisfy successively higher levels of needs.
>
> 'Once such basic needs as hunger, security and sex are satisfied, people move on to higher-level needs, eventually arriving at the

"self-actualization" stage. This is the desire for self-fulfilment at the summit of Maslow's hierarchy.

'Following this basic principle, SRI classified people as Survivors, Sustainers, Belongers, Emulators and Achievers. But research in 1968 identified 2% of the U.S. population that did not conform to the conventional Maslow hierarchy. By 1978 this minority had risen to 17% and by 1988 it is expected to be 27%. In fact, according to SRI, it is the fastest growing group of people.

'SRI has classified this category of people as the inner-directed group. It differs fundamentally from the rest of the population – the outer-directed group. The latter are generally concerned with externals. They do things as a response to the outside world. They follow fashions and strive for acquisitions that reflect their social status.

'Inner-directeds, on the other hand, are motivated by their own inner wants and desires, instead of responding primarily to the norms of others.

'Explains Christine MacNulty, programme manager of SRI's Strategic Environment Centre: "There's a lot to be said for the inner-directed groups. They are much more concerned about other people, the physical environment, conservation and that sort of thing."

'At work, for example, inner-directeds are not motivated by traditional incentives such as money, power, ambition or success. They want to have rewarding, fulfilling jobs.

' "Since this is the best educated group, it would traditionally have been the one from which leaders in management the professions and politics were drawn," explains MacNulty. "Now the real question is: How can business and the professions attract such people? What conditions can they be offered? Or will an increasingly larger segment of industry and government be deprived of this resource?"

'More recent research by MacNulty has established that the inner-directed segment of the population is growing just as rapidly in Europe as in the U.S., and in some European countries indications are it is growing even faster.

' "We're using this as the means for forecasting change, because looking at these groups and the way they behave in the market-place and through social pressures on government,

> hence on legislation we feel we're getting a very good picture of what social trends are developing," she says.
>
> 'The rapid growth in the numbers of inner-directed people tends to confirm the growing conviction among SRI researchers that the world is undergoing what in the jargon of the experts is known as "a shift in paradigm".'

There's likely to be social upheaval probably as great as the change from the Aristotelian to Newtonian world or the Middle Ages to the Renaissance. In 30 or 40 years' time most of the population will have the attitudes and values of these inner-directed people. These are the people at the leading edge of this paradigm shift.

2

The corporate Hampton Court

'Organizations as systems composed of ideas the meaning of which must be managed.'

Martin.

It is impossible to survey the management literature available today without gaining the distinct impression that employees, staff and workers have suddenly had the spotlight turned on them, as though corporations have functioned quite smoothly without them until now. Described in terms of the two phrases 'commitment' and 'culture', this new breed are finding a myriad of books written about how to motivate them, speeches from politicians extolling their virtues in improving productivity, and seminars riding on the wave of 'Excellence' being held on how to marry corporate goals with individual needs. In fact a veritable industry has grown around the people who have always made the wheels turn. Anyone would think that employees have never been communicated to and their cultures left in the closet to collect dust and, presumably, wilt.

Can we be sure that all this talk about business versus human values. The creation of healthy corporations around the work spirit – a knee-jerk reaction to obvious internal pressures for change – is not throwing the baby out with the bathwater? After all, despite the undoubted changes in the value systems and expectations of many employees, as well as the relationships of the individual to the corporation, staff continue to do what they have always done, namely work for reward and sometimes fulfilment in return for higher productivity and profitability. We would answer that this is not so.

In the last chapter we discussed the social, economic, political and technological pressure affecting corporations. The pace of change appears to be accelerating, the problems are becoming more complex and institutions more interdependent. Customers have become sophisticated and demanding, and shareholders more vociferous in their demand for more accountability. Margins and profits are subject to intense pressure from international competition, deregulation and rising costs. Product life-cycles are shortening, and changes in technology are bringing about changing patterns of work. In addition, changing patterns of employment and retraining requirements have sent a shudder around even the most solid of business establishments.

We are seeing a move from the mechanical to the communicative era. People are beginning to realize that the information being dispersed is not enough. Communication is about getting through, and this has brought employees and their relationship with their company to the forefront of management thinking. Just as the global village is surrounded by an invisible network of pulsing social information spreading like bushfire round the planet, so too in microcosm are company infrastructures being radically altered. The knowledge industry has led to increasing democratization and consumer decision-making. Its growing complexity has created as much interdependence between organizations as between corporate departments themselves. The advent of laser discs which have increased one hundred fold in capacity, and decreased by an equivalent amount in their storage costs, have triggered an upheaval in the way we handle information. There is a domino effect on the structure of companies, departmental interrelationships and the people in them. All of whom can communicate more directly and informally with each other horizontally as well as vertically from their desk. Authoritarianism thrives on ignorance. We are now in a post-autocratic society because of this information flow. In lateral structures feedback is essential and information is power. As we become more reliant on the expert, leadership will not remain fixed on one individual. Teams of professionals cause an assignation of authority and responsibility to different members of the staff as the nature of tasks change. It is difficult to divide and rule any more. The dominance of major corporations will also decline as they become more devolved into small work units and are penetrated by horizontal networks of specialists and consumer groups, thus increasing transactions at global and local level. As the electronic mail technology improves, more and more people will work on a consultancy basis, part home, part office.

So information and information technology has changed not only the nature of the firm but also the value systems of the individuals within the firm. The pace of change has led to cults and eccentricities from LA to Tehran, and economic forces are changing the shape of the culture. Not only have there been changes in the attitudes towards patriotism, sexism and the family but also towards the work ethic itself. Next century it will be our psychological well-being that is the key. Who knows what after that. In the previous chapter we described the growth in importance of the inner-directed person and how it was creating a shift from a materialistic, status orientated society to spiritual, ecological, inner-directed value systems where life style and work fulfilment are more important than reward for overworking until the inevitable coronary. Maslow's research into the 'hierarchy of human needs' supports the power of this argument.

Although we must be cautious, Maslow's theory is an artefact of Western cultures. The existence of an organization depends on an ability to motivate all employees, from whatever culture. People from the U.S. are achievement dominated whereas those from Brazil are more affiliation orientated. Even in Japan women's expectations and values are reshaping corporations.

Information is power, and it is so pressing on our bureaucracy, on our systems, our work patterns and its structures that an injection of new thinking is needed to defuse it. Interlocking communication networks and 'positive-sum', participatory democracy will be the order of what after all is a 24-hour day.

But how do we get senior management to shift from the production focus of the mechanical era, and then to switch their conceptual lens from purely material goals to more holistic human goals? Currently most managements are locked in paradigm paralysis, awash in an outmoded sea of knowledge.

The whole business environment has altered and employees (as employees and individuals) living in society have not been sheltered from it. The external changes have impact not just in markets and products but on the attitudes and values of staff. They have ricocheted around the corporation, leading to cracks in the traditional hierarchical structure. The horizontal networking that has been made possible by travel and the electronic village has led to a penetration of the corporation's shell by new allegiances and by loyalties which flatten both the traditional, vertical pyramid and change, like an amoeba, the shape of the company. In future global may not necessarily mean gigantic! The evolving cellular organization, where rank and role are sharply defined to cope with the interdisciplinary nature of today's business and core satellite businesses are differentiated to allow for more individual needs and for venture-capital requirements. Work will be undertaken in small, semi-autonomous, task-orientated units linked by computers to a central base. These small units, like atoms, will not be bouncing around in blind chaos but bonded like molecules into a strong corporate entity via carefully nurtured cultural bonds.

If such an era of rapid technological advance into the post industrial society is not to lead to the disintegration of giant companies, then the cement that holds the organizational bricks together must become softer, more flexible to the needs not just of the market place, but of the new emerging employee.

External pressures impact on the individual who works in the corporation as much as on the corporation's other resources. Employees in turn exert their own pressure on the corporation. The trick for managers is to match changing individual expectations and values with the need for the corporation to adapt to the market's wishes.

This chapter will discuss the inter-relationship between externalities and internalities together with the strain on internal relationships and organizational structures that is implicit in constant adaptation. The company is after all more than an infrastructure, it is a living/evolving creature with its own myths and rituals. In short there will be a looser, more dynamic, corporate environment in future if the company is not to become a beached whale. The culture will have to adapt to this. We will discuss corporate culture in more depth in the next chapter. This Hampton Court maze called the corporation is a vulnerable nervous system in need of care and attention if it is not to breakdown from excessive stress.

Without resorting to some of the wilder flights of fancy, debate on this soft, what we call 'high-touch' subject is taking place on the fringes of academe and the management consultancy world. The chief executive officer, his corporate communications and personnel advisers, need to come out from behind their closed doctrines and gain greater knowledge on how to use corporate culture for the benefit not only of the market place but also the employee, who is at present taking the strain of change. There are some positive signs of a new realism but the attitudes, judgement and welter of information required by CEOs on which to base decision are growing by the day.

If we were to undertake a matrix of external and internal issues affecting the corporation, we would find a growing convergence. The pace of change, the microelectronic revolution, the shift to service industries, the global village, have all impacted the corporation and the human mixture that comprises the cement between the corporate bricks. There is no doubt also that this, as yet unquantifiable area of analysis can impact the bottom line and affect survival more dramatically than other costs. By far the closest link between external and internal pressures has been the impact of technology on the skills requirement and the content of the workforce. For example why is it that unemployment continues to soar in Europe when job creation schemes are successful in the U.S.? It is worth examining this phenomenon if only to set the scene for how these changes are working on the employee in the context of the corporation in which he or she works.

Europe is a contrast not only to the U.S. but also to Japan, which unlike the U.S. has no real domestic market or raw materials. There is a far more favourable background for innovation in these two countries and there is a vigorous life of small companies. Europe certainly is a laggard in the current post-industrial revolution. With the East Asia edge taking on the world economically, will Europe ever develop a new lease of life and emerge from its current Eurosclerosis?

Obviously there are supply-side constraints such as employment and competitive protection. But it is to the dynamism of the U.S. and Japanese economies, for different reasons, that Europe should turn in order to learn some noteworthy lessons. The U.S. is market-driven and risk-orientated while Japan is long-term and initiative-driven with a built-in system of rewards making large corporations more flexible.

In Europe the trade unions are a constraint as is the greater attachment to the local community, a factor that helps cause structural unemployment. But while Europe lost two million jobs last decade, the U.S. added 20 million in the service industries.

Women have compensated by supplying much of the new-type labour required in new manufacturing as well as in low and 'high-tech' industries. In the U.S. two-thirds of new jobs in the last decade were filled by women. The answer is in the dynamic character of the U.S. labour market identified by its questing, restless and changing energy. It is arguable however whether such a fecundity of services that has helped U.S. job creation can continue, given the inter-relationships and interdependence of the emerging global village.

With such a backdrop let us look at some of the factors that are upsetting the internal structure of companies. The flood of new technologies that has burst upon the industrialized world is forcing increasingly rapid change in the skills requirements of many jobs whether they are located in factory, office or other environment. Chief among these is a blurring of the distinction between jobs. Because of the word-processor there is a shift from 'hand' to 'head' due to the interdependence of systems, especially in the CAD/CAM area. There is a trend towards the multiskilled tradesman and the rise of the 'mecatronic'. Japan's Nippon Co. combines mechanical with electronic skills. Daimler Benz in Germany is 'shaping hybrids' – operatives who deal with programming, loading and maintenance of machines. The educational system needs to watch out; it is rapidly falling further and further behind the manpower needs of the marketplace.

The traditional method of organizing production by splitting up jobs into low-grade repetitive components is proving inefficient when applied to office automation.

Roy Grantham, of APEX, the U.K. staff union, says the need is for group work and job enrichment programmes, which are low specialist, and more involvement based. Robots versus robotics is an important debate for the future of trade unions, which need to look beyond traditional attitudes to new technology and the nature of work itself.

A recent report by the U.K. Department of Employment talks of the need for greater flexibility and decentralization in company agreements as well as for union and employee involvement at plant level in final decision making which affects their department.

Despite the media attention devoted to the U.K. miners' strike, there is a new realism growing which is based on changes in the structuring of industry, the composition of its workforce, the organization within the work places, and the institutions of collective bargaining and joint consultation that have evolved. These trends are encouraging because it gives an incentive to the Japanese to invest in the U.K., so long as they obtain an open-union, no-strike deal. Many managements believe that unions have a favourable impact on plant operations, particularly in the newer industries. The U.K. registers well in strike performance compared to some of its European neighbours, where not only politics but even religion is part of the tapestry.

People like Sir Peter Parker, chairman of Rockware and former chairman of British Rail, attest to the reality that if management is first class, and the workforce is well led, with an element of identity with the company and its competitive position created among the employees, then only the headlines which concentrate on the pathology of industrial relations will destabilize the climate. It all depends on improved consultation and communication over a wider range of issues which should include marketing and work organization as well as the more immediate needs of remuneration and reward.

In the R and D environment, classical management structures will not work, says Gordon Edge of PA Technology, because the hierarchical approach is inconsistent with the needs of modern industrial scientists and engineers. The central point is the distinction between rank and role, the latter having nothing to do with status. Not all scientists can be good managers let alone marketeers.

The entry of women into the job market will undoubtedly have a major impact on the structure and value system of corporations. It is anticipated by the year 2000 women will earn up to 74% of male wages. Even so this reflects the fact that attitudes are still lagging behind and that even then there will not be parity of women lawyers, bankers and business women opportunities. This previously 'wasted' resource will have a profound effect on the corporation of the future. It is certain that the structure of most companies still does not adequately reflect changes in demographics and social trends and does not allow for a true climate of innovation. You can have ideas that fit within existing rules but the company can still die.

Does the improving European economy herald a new era of high productivity and profitability or will it signal a return to aggressive pay demands and conflict rather than cooperation and a continuation of the argument between 'them' and 'us'? The paradigm shift should be from control to commitment in the workplace.

The symptoms are familiar. Good strategies are badly executed. Costs rise out of all proportion to gains in productivity. High rates of absenteeism persist, and a disaffected work force, taking little pride or pleasure, retards innovation. To those at the top it seems if they are the captains of a ship in which the wheel is not connected to the rudder. Only lately have managers themselves begun to take responsibility for these symptoms and for the approach to work-force management out of which they grow. Only belatedly have they begun to see that workers respond best and more creatively, not when they are tightly controlled, or placed in narrowly defined jobs, but when they are given broader responsibilities, encouraged to contribute and helped to find satisfaction in their work. It should come as little surprise that eliciting worker commitment and providing an environment in which it can flourish, pays tangible dividends for the individual and for the company. How can we match individual with corporate goals. Can a company handle its key resource – human capital?

So far corporations have not handled their human capital very effectively, or certainly not during the last two decades. That is why Bullock sprouted in the U.K., and Vredeling in the European community. Both were unsuccessful attempts to saddle employers with legally enforceable disclosure requirements and two-tier boards aimed to ensure 'real' participation in decision making. The fact that these politically inspired bureaucratic initiatives were publicized as a panacea almost ensured that they could not work. Effective arrangements for employee involvement will only develop on a voluntary, mutual and flexible basis. They should not hide the fact that they were policies designed to fill a vacuum. If management had spent more time getting the climate right earlier they would have had to spend less time through the 1970s when company law directives were spewing out of the Brussels sausage machine, fighting off potential legislation which would have crippled them in the market-place. This was a classic example of failing to reconcile external and internal pressures. It is to be hoped that the new EEC initiatives which it is said could 'radically alter the concept of employee information and consultation procedures', will be negotiated by employers with the wisdom of hindsight, a greater empathy with their human asset and more understanding of the changing nature of the values and attitudes of a modern work force. We include middle and senior management under this heading.

Bullock may be dead and buried but there are two irreversible trends left behind. First there is likely to be an enhancement of employees' statutory or property rights, such as portable pensions, maternity leave and discrimination rights. The EEC is likely to initiate statutory upper limits on working hours for all categories of employees (except managers of course!). The second will be the extension of workplace participation both in decision-making and financial ownership. Employee share schemes and joint works councils are examples of this. Some companies include comment on 'involvement' in their annual report. A further expression of 'democracy' at the workplace is the progressive devolution of collective bargaining from national to local level, thus altering the union base from the leadership to grass roots. This has implications not only for understanding changing attitudes but for more accurate targetting of its communications. However, the conventional urging that *maximum* communication among individuals is necessary must be replaced by a more reasoned search for *optimum* communications. Managers who are anxious about communications can clog up the channel with noise by issuing too much. At other times they do not listen. Then they communicate information that either baffles employees or raises their hackles. Relevance and research to obtain feedback is key.

Most managers are totally a-political, with private lives and views separated from managerial action. As we discuss later, this is inadequate. The rise of new stakeholders – public interest groups in particular – can be traced partly to the ideological abdication of managers. The vacuum has been filled by others who do not understand or wish to understand the nuances of business activity. This can include employees who have different objectives for their working day than those of their management.

Another internal imperative in recent years is the corporate mythology that gives rise to the elusive go-getter sometimes called the 'intrapreneur' – an in-house entrepreneur primed for innovative action within a large company. Business is after all sustained not only by management backing alone, it needs to find new ways to spawn fresh ideas inside the old ones. It is in effect an attempt to reach beyond the common limitations of a company's existence. How does this rare species survive the hierarchical constraints of traditional bureaucratic organizations? At 3M for example intrapreneurs have to scramble for 'intra capital' at the same odds as the entrepreneur. They succeed sometimes because of the powerful culture rather than the formal organization. There are stories of fired people persisting with their ideas within the same company. Ironically the best breeding ground for such creative action is often the large company. Intrapreneurship is in many ways a description of the organization, not the person. With corporate culture descending from the top, the entrepreneurial spirit must be accepted by the CEO and encouraged to flourish. But a prerequisite is to identify and foster those individuals who will carry the torch. In all probability the intrapreneur will be a major element of the business system of the future. All the implications for absorbing and motivating them need to be thought through. We have to take on board the question of equity possibilities, of spin-off and satellite companies, and of the role of a 'mentor', which is critical for support and motivation.

'The challenge', as PA Management Consultants have stated in their management journal *Issues*, 'For tomorrow's CEO is how to harness that drive and energy within the mainstream corporate structure. It usually requires a radical reshaping of the corporate culture. It can possibly mean that the CEO may himself have to be one.'

Obviously evolution, not revolution in structures is critical. Flexible management processes and broader management perspectives is the common thread of our argument in this book. If management can design information systems, train personnel with the right attitudes and vision to bridge the global and local balance, then the right climate will evolve. But the emphasis must be on interdisciplinary teams and task forces on the creation of decision-making forums, with flexibility as the main ingredient. A word of warning should be interjected however.

Most recent contributions to theory on the firm as a concept have centred upon the interaction between corporate state and entrepreneurship and the quality of management performance. The structural scaffolding of corporate life must be recognized as independent factors which bely the traditional assumption that all businessmen seek to maximize profits. Whereas economists stress economies of scale and adaptation to market forces, we should not forget the diseconomies of coordination that accompany size, particularly in a period of economic discontinuity and the changing values of employees.

Following the Second World War, the excellent track record of large corporations was based on their effective integration of mass production with mass markets. In this new era of volatile mass segmented markets, of slow growth rates and of customization, the corporation needs to restructure to meet the changed situation. The mechanisms needed to direct the work of their managerial fiefdoms and the relations between divisional managers and corporate HQ are now wanting. The winners and losers in management are always played out internally and are based on the lack of structure and on the type of environment the corporation maintains.

Without organization, structure and a series of decision-making rules, no corporation can function. But only human beings, not the structures around them, can act. By the time employees take their first job, their psychological values, attitudes and behaviours have already become fixed. Many corporations fail to take this into account. They try to mould people when it is too late. They refuse to make changes in their structure, their decision-making, and personnel policies, in the face of significant changes in attitude and values by a new labour force. This is particularly noticed among the more educated type of employee now entering the market place and on whom the new corporation will rely. Professor Warren Bennis of the University of Southern California begged the question when he wrote that 'there is a commitment gap . . . rather than an erosion of the work ethic'.

There has been an inevitable clash between the rising expectations and career options of graduates wanting self-fulfilment and the choice to pursue a life-style of *their* choosing, and on the other hand the slowing up of the economy and the maturity of markets which has eroded sales, thus giving companies limited room for manoeuvre. The underlying pressures can be seen in the slowness with which many corporations are adjusting their structures and human resource policies to what are obviously changed conditions.

Over the past decade we have seen in more and more multinational companies a diffusion of responsibility and a fragmentation of authority. This creates the preconditions for power – determined behaviour among major business/staff units which has precious little to do with the corporation's overall goals. Managers soon learn how to survive in this power game and their career ambitions start to alter as they take account of their corporate responsibilities within a changed power structure. When such behaviour becomes pervasive, the corporation is genuinely at risk because the hidden symptoms become inbred. Sometimes a corporation is actually better run by these symptoms and perceived to be better run, than its own management self-criticism would accept. Even so the corporation must endeavour, as a matter of priority, to realign its structure to meet these new needs and ambitions of its staff.

Twenty years of intensive management education has permeated the thinking of the majority of the modern manager. If he didn't attend business school himself he certainly read books, articles and lecture notes that always seemed to reduce his complicated ideas about the running of a company to diagrams, flow charts and meticulous management structures. So long as the classic 'tree' with its neat boxes housing each department could be drawn then all things were well in the best of all possible management worlds. When the flow charts have been assembled, drawn and agreed, it appears to the managers that decisions have now become logical and by implication right. The mass of ideas from some previous meeting or the views expressed at a recent confrontation with staff have all been analyzed and now a solution has been found. All is well, or is it? We live in the age of management by diagram. If it fits the plan it works, if it doesn't, it fails.

Yet, is the drawn structure really the equivalent of a completed building, or is it only the bricks and the girders? Perhaps something is missing. We would argue that it is the cement and bricks of human reaction, of staff aspirations and sheer barrack-room bloody-mindedness that actually make the total structure work and come alive. These boxes won't interact on their own. It is how people who inhabit these boxes react that will determine the plan's success or its failure.

It is here in this often less quantifiable area that the best laid boardroom plans, assembled with all the skills acquired from two years at business school, can come awry. In this extraordinary area of human frailty so many management decisions, whether they are made by unit and department heads or by the CEO himself, fail to produce the right response and sink not with a bang but a whimper.

Strangely it is an area that occupies little time at business school and seldom appears at all in the lower levels of management training. Lip service is frequently paid to the skills of leadership and employee motivation. The Confederation of British Industry publishes worthy pamphlets on how to involve staff in setting individual objectives. Many books have been written on the psychology and purpose of participative management and variously titled 'group interaction' training sessions rise and fall in popularity like the fashionable height of women's skirts.

Yet these attempts, all worthy in themselves, are concerned with the micro, the one-to-one situation. It is like running a country with a cabinet composed of psychoanalysts. The manager may well be dealing with one executive (or maybe a small group) at any one time. A corporation, however, is composed of all those people interacting, responding and interpreting for every minute of their working day, and even at times beyond working hours as they retire to a nearby hostelry. Most managers see their decision-making in two parts. The planning – impersonal production of an objective response to a complex problem, and the job aspects. Then there is a softer, more subjective range, of dealings between themselves and individual staff, the people aspects. Between these extremes of cold diagrammatic planning on the one hand and the warm human relations (some managers, often with accounting backgrounds, even manage to turn the latter into the former) lies a real company, an actual living corporation that responds effectively, efficiently and quickly, or as the case may be more sluggishly, slowly, and with considerable distortion to each command given by management. The bridge between people is communication (information and persuading), motivation and above all, leadership.

If we consider a normal large corporation in visual terms it is an ant-hill. There are thousands of relationships going on every minute of the day between each ant. If we continue the analogy we begin to understand why the financial pages of newspapers are littered with the debris of unsuccessful companies.

The complexity of all those interactions, of all those ants moving and contacting, swerving and bumping into one another, minute after minute, hour after hour, is enough to make the head of even a computer on a chip pause for a microsecond of contemplation.

The inter-personal communications of one executive with another are like the contacts of one ant on a hill with another. Immediately after contact each ant goes on its way and makes another hundred, even thousand, contacts with other ants. There are differences of course. Corporations have a hierarchy of contacts supported by hardware which ranges from paper to computers. This ensures the message communicated has some permanent life, even if it is only the time it takes to read and dispatch to the waste bin. Unfortunately this last comment is not made in a spirit of levity. Many executives, especially when under pressure from home life or work, will consign messages, especially ones they don't like, to the nearest waste-paper basket. It is an easy way of reducing extra pressures on an already overcrowded mentality.

Another difference between a corporation and the metaphoric ant-hill is the fact that human beings carry an ability to receive, interpret and emotionally distort every message they receive. Decisions and commands often communicated in a cloudy, indecisive style will be absorbed in different ways by different people. Different backgrounds and emotional problems will set their own parameters and govern which parts of the command they will or will not respond to. They will act as a filter through which only some messages are allowed to pass. Having processed the message in this fashion a recipient executive meets other people who again affect and adjust their views on the message. Until, one hour later, we have a section of the ant-hill acting upon one single message in a multitude of different ways. From there the ants continue their journey, fanning outwards into other departments and subsidiaries, disturbing more and more of the original concept the further they travel from the source.

The old game of whispering a message down a line of children to see how it comes out at the end is possibly one of the most important management games we should play. If the phrase 'send reinforcements, we are going to advance' becomes in the children's game 'send three and fourpence, we are going to a dance', imagine how quite complex inter-managerial commands are altered in the process of a single day. The message is altered even before the staff have had the advantage of a discussion back at home with wives or husbands or with colleagues in the pub down the street. How expert systems will impact this progress we can only hazard a guess.

Some of this may seem an obvious fact of life, something we must learn to live with. But is it simply a built-in hazard on the corporate golf course, a water-soaked bunker lying beside some boardroom green, annoying, but put there by God to try us?

The answer is of course 'no'. There are route maps that can help us understand more clearly why these distortions take place. If we study the maps and begin to understand them, we can show how individual companies control the range of reactions that follow the receipt of a command, or an internal message. We can even study what happens to the well-constructed and carefully thought out message that is supposed to emanate from a carefully prepared company event.

On the one side we have a body of research available. We can learn from it because it outlines the processes by which attitudes and opinions are transferred in everyday life. Research has been developed in the U.S. and U.K. on the processes by which messages are communicated. They are based around certain concepts and these hypotheses seem to show varying degrees of influence by one person upon another according to the esteem and the respect that one person holds for the other. What is important is that the research also shows people are listened to with more or less respect by other people within their circle according to how they are judged by previous contacts they have had with each other. Sometimes they are what one researcher calls 'specific influencers' and sometimes they are 'general influencers'. The former are people that are listened to by their intimate groups – known usually as their primary group – on one subject only, while general influencers carry weight on a broader front due to their intelligence, education, wider experience or simply style in putting across views.

All the members of primary units are themselves moving around within wider secondary groupings. A secondary group can be circumscribed by common bonds such as their trade union, employer associations or by the accident of geography where a town may create a closely knit community linked through history or common tragedy. Membership of a profession, a leisure activity, or a large corporation, can all exert specific, usually coherent influence on its members' ideas, attitudes, even values for life or philosophy. It is a reinforcing process that has to be noted and examined so that its dynamics, as well as its mores, are understood.

Within such an interactive environment people belong to more than one primary and usually more than one secondary unit.

For example most people have a primary unit that consists of their immediate relatives, another their friends at home, and others drawn from friends at work or their departmental associates. Among this range of different primary units there will tend to be one which is the most important to them personally. This one is usually known as their 'reference group' and it is to this group that they most frequently refer for their important opinions, attitudes and values. It will be the group that shapes their basic drives, mores and enthusiasms in life.

The process of communication takes place through a sieve or selection process that is set up informally by opinion-leaders who have assumed their function unconsciously. They have become opinion-leaders within small primary units almost by the accident of balances and strengths of personality. They are themselves influenced by a broader secondary group. We begin now to see that the apparent anarchy of corporate attitudes and responses to management decisions operates within a sequence of quite firm constraints. The effectiveness of a command structure is thus mitigated by the respect with which the recipient is held within a particular primary group. If that respect is high then the next link in the communication chain may be strong. If it is low, the recipient, when passing on views, will have them corrupted and interpreted by a stronger personality or opinion-leader within his or her group.

Richard Giordano, the most famous American running a British based company, BOC, has come up with the concept of 'horizontal networking' in a highly task-oriented organization, where ideas move quickly because managers are encouraged to make contact – irrespective of official channels and hierarchy – with those who have the necessary knowledge or resources to help them accomplish the task. In this way the classic compartments which don't communicate, line/staff confusions and boss/subordinate conflicts are avoided. In this process incidentally, oral communication is favoured over lengthy reports and 'protect your flank' memos. The key values here are trust and cooperation tinged with carrot and stick.

We have discussed form, now let us consider the changing content. The values of employees may be creating a fault line that will cause a cracking at the very foundation of corporate life. There is a marked shift from the acceptance of worker alienation to worker self-realization. Naturally some employees are more sensitive to particular values than others and some companies as we shall see, have less or more highly developed value systems. But if management would look beyond their hidebound attitudes and interrogate the future they will see a cooperative and less conflictional mode, a desire for participation rather than limited work-interest. A desire also for more leisure and a horizontal approach to life fulfilment. The new manager will put an emphasis on health and wellness in work as well as outside. Yet the tendency is still to think top down for changing the value system (if indeed it can be identified) rather than learn from the feedback received. The new attitude to authority and the wish for greater flexibility in organizational structure also needs to be brought into the equation. This is best reflected in the U.S. with the 56 million new 'Baby Boomers' (the 25- to 34-year-olds) who are pushing for power and nudging not so gently the generation stasis and self-perpetuating oligarchy which exists in many senior management structures.

As someone once said 'the fostering of the individual is not an act of corporate do-goodism and "Recapturing the Vitality of Work".' This title of a New York seminar was not off-the-wall spiritualism that had no bearing on corporate reality. As in science and spiritualism, ultimate perfection is reached where high performance individual conviction is aligned with the shared articulate purpose of the organization. Work spirit means a more holistic approach to solving employee problems.

The locus for this new thinking resides in a network called the 'Aquarian Conspiracy'. In her book of that name Marilyn Ferguson talks of a leaderless, non-political network which seeks only to disperse power. Many such networks are in corporations where they are examining old assumptions, looking anew at their work relationships and reconsidering so-called experts' goals and values. Central to the book is a conspiracy of men and women whose perspective will trigger a critical re-appraisal of change.

Many studies confirm the importance of 'multiple linkages' within an organization, of the development of innovative approaches and a willingness to accept change. Multiple linkages concern not only work but also social/cultural and personal links too. With so much external uncertainty and the willingness to take more risks, reducing uncertainty internally is vital to facilitate discussion of new ideas. Innovative ideas are not usually forthcoming from those in an organization who distrust one another. In Japan the emphasis on teamwork increases peer and mixed status communication in the service of product quality, and competitive edge.

A paradigm shift is making people realize that they have been leading needlessly circumscribed lives in a society whose so-called rational social structure has failed to produce harmony between men and nature. This is all too apparent in the questions being asked today in the work environment.

What do we mean by rich and poor, bosses and workers, growth versus no growth, work versus leisure, control versus commitment? Making a life more than a living is essential to spiritual wholeness, say the benign conspirators. When individual needs change so too do economic patterns affect buying, selling, owning, saving and sharing. In some minds materialism is being replaced by a desire for quality of life, although the distinction is often more analytic than real. So in theory at least the workplace could be transformed with evolving lifestyles that take advantage of synergy, sharing, co-operation and creativity. It has its practical application in the use of that new breed of entrepreneur discussed earlier, and the search for 'appropriate technology'.

It is high costs, resource scarcities, inflation and unemployment which have led to the ecology movement. A belief held by this loose network (which is penetrating every company, often internationally thanks to information technology) structures our ideas about work, money, profit and management. Old ideas grew out of an old stable social order which is outmoded. The truth is there are no facts about the future.

Although this philosophy questions whether materialism of a capitalist or socialist kind is relevant to human need and as such has an ideological content, it has nevertheless influenced many individual values. Values summed up in the phrase we used earlier: 'inner directed values'. Management and corporations should not ignore them just because the baby boomer generation in the U.S. is pushing for power with the very values the benign conspirators are seeking to eradicate.

As Ilya Prigogine, the Nobel Prize winner pointed out, the complexity of our modern pluralistic society and the increasingly autonomous values of its people have created vast economic uncertainty. The new paradigm can be summed up as jobs to fit people, in a more flexible, creative manner rather than people to fit jobs. Equally in management, the implications are clear that employees want shared values, they want consensus and self-actualization rather than top-down imposition and hierarchical structure.

In the corporation of the future, individual identity, even within a new capitalist environment, will transcend normal job descriptions, the company and loyalty to one's own profession. Spiritual values will be as important as material needs, the context of a problem will be as vital as its content. Above all, goals will be shared rather than polarized. The heart of entrepreneurial thinking must be to engage staff as part of a process of marrying corporate to individual values. All of this has profound implications for industrial relations, short-term stock market valuations, business strategy, competition policy and the political time-frames which are governed by the tyranny of elections. The classic report issued by SRI in 1972 *Changing Image of Man* described a new transcendental social and business ethic characterized by self-determination, concern for the quality of life and for decentralization. The report urged a rapid corporate understanding of this new emergent order. But it has not happened yet, over a decade later. There has been little if any public debate on the subject.

Just as the worker has a new vision, so too will the working machine. The corporation has to find a different organizational structure. Will senior management have the necessary traits to ask the right questions, to move from a control to a commitment mode?

Employee commitment is paramount. As employees' expectations rise, more vigorous involvement and communications practices are needed. Commitment stems from feelings of confidence, respect and personal recognition, which means direct involvement rather than consultative committees or trade unions. This is a whole world of difference from efforts made to fend off the EEC's fifth Directive. Involvement does not mean management relinquishing authority (which anyway is based on consent).

The larger shape of institutional change is always difficult to recognize when one stands in the middle of it. Significant change in patterns of organization and the management of work systems are under way in the U.S.

Since the early 1970s General Foods, General Motors and Proctor & Gamble among others have begun to remove levels of plant hierarchy, increase managers' spans of control and open up new career possibilities. Some corporations have even begun to chart organizational renewal for the entire company, encouraging participation, responsibility, flexibility and communication – not just informing but actually getting through. Sadly this is the exception rather than the rule.

With management hierarchies becoming relatively flat and status differences minimized, control and lateral coordination is depending increasingly on shared goals and expertise rather than on formal positions to determine influence. At the People's Express airline for example, everyone is a 'manager' and performance standards are designed to provide 'stretch objectives'. They are 'market driven', with scope for equity sharing and retraining. In these settings, the additional tasks include making relations less adversarial. There is a broadening of the agenda for joint problem solving and the facilitation of conciliation. But there must be genuine desire embodied in a published statement of mission acknowledging the legitimate claims of all shareholders, not least employees, if it is to work. This attitude change has major implications for employee participation. It includes a wide range of issues which have to be debated at boardroom level. Interestingly, as technology becomes less hardware dependent and more software intensive and as costs decline, so too can technology reinforce this commitment strategy rather than have unions resisting it. All is well so long as the unions participate in the debate, come out from behind their closed doctrines and are encouraged when they do.

It is important not to shift from control to commitment overnight. The system won't cope. Only a small fraction, even of U.S. workplaces, can today boast a comprehensive commitment strategy. But the rate of transformation continues to accelerate, partly because of economic necessity. This new body of knowledge needs to be codified and tested for future generations to mull over. Human values have traditionally been outside the corporate paradigm. Now there are signs that this is changing.

Of course bold policies of share ownership, as in the case of home ownership, could bring its own rewards as British Telecom have found, so long as they use communications (hardware and software) effectively, of course. Share options blur the old shareholder/ employee distinction. Indeed the new small shareholder of the future is in fact likely to be a junior employee as opposed to a senior manager.

One of the biggest modern challenges to management is to bring engineers and marketeers together. Quality circles have helped in this and these are now being used in 90% of the biggest *Fortune* 500 companies. But its limits are being recognized as it extends beyond the fad stage, to being a catalyst for a more participative task-force management style. Team briefing is the order of the day. We must not lose sight of what it is for – more efficient, competitive and wealth creating corporations.

To survive in today's onrushing change brought on by external and internal pressures, management must reconsider the very models on which obsolete organizations are based. Instead of rigid, conventional departments, the firm will in the future be divided into a highly flexible structure composed of a framework with modules within it. Instead of being treated as an isolated unit, it is likely, according to Toffler in his *The Adaptive Corporation*, to occupy a position at the centre of a shifting constellation of related companies, organizations and agencies. The framework is the thin coordinative wiring that strings together a set of temporary or changing modular units. The constellation consists of the company and the independent, semi-autonomous outside organizations on which it relies.

The super industrial revolution will of necessity require basic changes in the structure of its organizations. Classical industrial bureaucracies are pyramidal in structure, with a small control group at the top and an array of permanent, functional departments below. The replacement model should, if it adapts properly, consist of a slender, semi-permanent framework from which a variety of small, temporary modules can be suspended. They move or can be spun off in response to changes in the market, government or supply situation. The emphasis is on flexibility. This approach is being witnessed to some extent in the growth of industrial holding companies where at the centre these are bankers of last resort. The biggest constraint to change is organizational mismatch, where the new range of problems are not easily solved within traditional departments such as manufacturing and finance. Problems tend to be bent out of shape to fit pre-existing organizational lines. This is why organization charts have such low life expectancy. 'One time' problems require temporary ad hoc organizations to solve them.

Another constraint is vertical hierarchy, where because of the radically diversifying economic, technological and social environment within which the corporation functions, a more varied and rapid response is required. As a consequence of this, effective decisions today must be taken lower and lower down the organization. Thirdly, there exists the constraint of scale or flab, as Toffler terms it. It seems possible that a good many of the largest companies have exceeded optimum size.

In Search of Excellence identifies a strong 'productivity through people' orientation in the U.S. companies it examined. This was also evident in the British companies surveyed in *The Winning Streak*. Many successful companies show a high profit orientation. The workforce are informed about costs, profit and loss, and accord a high priority to what surplus is all about. Concentration on profitability helps employees identify with overall corporate marketing goals. *The Winning Streak* itemized several common factors that lead to involvement and pride in ownership. They were a high degree of communication, high pay/incentives, promotion from within, stress on training, recognition of the 'social' side of work, and a genuine respect for the individual.

Senior management may need to adapt to the possibility of blue jeans ousting the business suit in some types of organization, as Ray Kassar, the then President of Atari, found to his cost. He treated a group of dissident young designers of video games, who wanted royalties for their ideas, with disdain, so they set up their own company in competition. Others soon copied them. Look what happened to Atari. Dress codes are not about Levis versus Lazenfeld or Armand versus Anoraks. They are about attitudes, values and how a person perceives himself.

Recently several professors at Carnegie Mellon University in Pittsburgh decided to start their own artificial intelligence company rather than make a free gift of their ideas to the college. Such new breeds of employees could be called 'grass roots capitalists'. They could soon be the norm in certain situations. Salaried workers are coming to view themselves as individual businesses with assets to be utilized. Each person becomes his or her own entrepreneur.

These people are recognizing that they must protect their investment from exploitation even from their own firms. This becomes especially important with the onset of artificial intelligence. Knowledge workers are becoming a scarce resource. As the demand increases so firms will have to grant new freedoms. Until recently investors considered the quality of management. Now they also need to assess the fundamental intelligence and values of the workforce. When knowledge workers become a majority of the workforce and computers can replicate decisions, managers will either become Luddites or they will adapt to the new age of learning by using smart people and smart machines over which they exert increasingly less control.

Most modern books on management which discuss the 'involvement factor', have given information about successful companies that shows how their staff are instinctively drawn into something greater than themselves. It is bound up with integrity, leadership and individual autonomy. Many companies however having decided to involve employees at all levels using similar techniques and communication methods, fail to succeed because their employees en masse do not identify with the overall culture of the company.

This leads us full circle back to the link between culture and structure, culture and strategy. Unless new missions for old cultures are found, the company will be unable to find new market niches to keep them competitive.

3

New missions for old cultures

'Any organization, in order to survive and achieve success, must have a sound set of beliefs on which it premises all its policies and actions . . . in other words, the basic philosophy, spirit and drive of an organization have far more to do with its relative achievements than do technological or economic resources, organizational structure, innovation and timing.'

Thomas Watson, Jnr.

The preceding pages are a fleeting description of a complex communication web. It is a backcloth upon which we can now paint what is known glibly as the corporate culture. We can begin at last to assess the complexities of that non-organizational structure which exists within every company and frequently constitutes the hidden agenda of daily discussion. It exists alongside the diagrams and charts that litter the pages of the CEO's management strategy. Culture is what differentiates one company from another. A corporation does not bear the cumulative weight of the past in the same way as society. It is more limited in size. Technically it is freer to adapt to a changing world. But will it and does it? What is this thing called culture?

The CEO is the living symbol and trustee of the corporate culture and as such he and his managers must communicate messages that foster a good organizational climate, particularly developing policies that add values and beliefs. Why then has corporate culture become such an obsession with business writers and academics over the last decade?

In the 1950s the focus was on an indefinable 'feeling in the air' of a company and in the 1960s it became known as the 'organizational climate'. The growth of the subject into a sub-discipline of its own reflects the need to strengthen corporate entities for reasons discussed earlier. Corporate culture gurus began to appear in the late

1970s claiming that by creating a good culture, a company can gain as much as one or two hours of productive work per employee per day. Now it is talked about as an identifiable and quantifiable management tool to be mastered in creating, to quote the vogue phrase, 'quality and excellence'. *Business Week*, in discussing the merger of the American Broadcasting Corporation and Capital Cities Corporation, said 'A Star is Born . . . blending two very different corporate cultures will be tough'. We have come a long way from a 'feeling in the air'.

The environment in which the business operates, the pressures we have discussed, and the interrelationships between home and the workplace are arguably the most significant element of organizational culture. These factors are the building blocks of the value systems. In accounting and management consulting firms for instance, quality, independence, objectivity and client service are the prime forces. Of course, many firms have a variety of cultures but hopefully some 'shared values'.

Values and beliefs are the currency of culture, an unwritten set of guidelines for employees to follow. At 3M Corporation where innovation is a core value, employees are told 'never kill an idea', which this helps to ensure that employees make the 'correct' decision.

Heroes develop with the corporate mythology and become the people who personify the culture. Perhaps the founder may be dead but he still breathes life via the culture he created. At Marriott Corporation the CEO logs 200,000 miles a year visiting his hotels and resorts. As one of his managers said in the *Wall Street Journal* 'when you start trying to anticipate what he'll find you get better as a manager'.

Other basic components are the rules and mode of operation – the formal written rules and equally important informal structures. Does the company have an open door policy, do people call Mr Smith A. Smith or Andy Smith, write memos or make telephone calls? Is every manager encouraged to hold staff meetings or does he keep his staff ignorant on the basis that information is power? Informal structure is about networks and alliances, cliques and coalitions, where people ascertain 'what's really going on'. Staff may find circumventing the rules is the best way to bring certain projects to fruition. Stories are the way a culture is perpetuated. Stories told to new staff are indoctrinated and thus internalized.

These stories, shared values, heroes and structure all create a dynamic mix we now call corporate culture.

It is a pity that the word has become prostituted. It is important that the linguistics of a company's communication are clearly defined. The over-use of the word culture is an example of this type of loose woolly thinking that has crept into so much inter-company communication during the last decade.

Words have clear meanings, and the more precise these meanings are the more accurate will be the message they convey to staff and external audiences alike.

By grouping a whole range of abstract concepts under one blanket term like culture, we destroy our ability to discuss the subtleties that make up the idea. We don't simplify our attitudes to management, we obfuscate them and ensure that others only partially understand their meanings.

George Orwell made the point in his book *1984*, when he described how 'countless words such as honour, justice, morality, inter-nationalism, density and religion have simply ceased to exist' in his world, because a few blanket words covered them and in covering them, obliterated them.

A tight, clearly defined use of words is crucial to the effective running of a company. The transmission of new words within a company's life that sound like one thing but may mean something else are as dangerous to the ultimate corporate mission as any piece of wasted expenditure or a new product failure.

Take the following example. One U.S. owned company operating in the U.K. started to use the word 'seamless' to describe what the U.S. headquarters called 'a consistent level of standards'. The word was intended to mean there would be an internationally accepted internal standard and systems. It would mean, they said in the New York HQ, that any client would receive a constant quality whether they bought the services the company offered in London, Paris, New York or Kuala Lumpur.

In fact, it soon became obvious to the worldwide staff and senior management at national level that what the word really meant was that the common standards and phraseology being talked about would all be set in the U.S. and it was a case of do everything the American way. We were back to the old era of corporate imperialism. The effect on the bottomline of this type of attitude would be slow and imperceptible. But what happens under such central control is that the more creative and dynamic staff soon leave because their freedom of thought is eroded. Only customers and clients who are attracted to, and want to, 'buy American' remain with the company. What happens ultimately is that soon more and more top manager positions overseas have to be filled by Americans because they were the only ones that would – or could – perpetuate the U.S. gospel as propounded from the centre.

In some companies this may be effective if the parent office label is a sales plus, but for many operations it is the first stage of a rigidity of attitude that prevents subsidiaries around the world responding flexibly to local demand.

A neat example of how communications and culture can be interwoven is Sperry, a company that some years ago had a blurred image and was perceived to have a rudderless direction. It was much in need of a symbolic rallying point. The CEO decided to find something 'unmistakenly Sperry'. Research showed that respondent customers said about their marketing division that 'you guys listen better'. The now famous 'listening theme' was developed and it was made to permeate all its communications and eventually evolve into something that was a part of the culture.

A mundane car parts manufacturer, Dana Corporation, breathed excitement into its operations with the slogan 'the productivity people', capitalizing on its mission by reducing everything to that theme. If all the external and internal imperatives that bear down on a company are brought together and made to work positively then the culture can be harnessed and the dilemmas of change, indifferent morale, retraining needs, and poor productivity can be redirected.

Sometimes the word image is used to mean a company's culture. Although it may be a direct manifestation of the culture it is not the same thing. It may be a perception of something internal or it may be something more complex. It may be the direct manifestation of say, the chief executive. Sir Terence Conran personifies Conran and he embodies the corporate culture within his own values and attitudes. All cultures need heroes like Tom Watson at IBM or David Packard at Hewlett-Packard.

Older and larger organizations accumulate over time a body of culture which flows naturally from its history. This can be a valuable asset as in the case of Marks & Spencer or it can be a sign of rigidity and a monolithic lack of response to new customer demands – a problem some of the U.K. clearing banks faced in the early seventies. The key to organizational culture is not to throw the baby out with the bathwater. With the new financial service 'supermarkets' for example, it is important to know whether to change one culture or decide which aspects are so far apart as to be treated separately, i.e. which parts can absorb a common denominator of acceptability. Corporate culture can mean stability or it can mean uncertainty and difficulties especially if in a merger the dissimilarities are too great to be integrated.

Corporate image, although an external perception, is also a reflection of internal attitudes about the concept of what we now call organizational culture. Because it is often implicit and almost impossible to state, it doesn't mean it is unidentifiable. Staff are part of it and are usually aware of it. To fully understand a particular company's culture requires an analysis of demographics, age, ethnic groupings, educational variations of staff, the management's stated mission and other factors specific to that company. It is necessary to know whether it is predisposed to change or whether the degree of rigidity that exists can be quantified. Here a linear scale must be used, otherwise it is too easy to succumb to black and white statements. An organization creates behaviour patterns, ways of perceiving and thinking, ways of reacting emotionally and ways of conceptualising itself. It can even affect the environment within which it operates by accepting or rejecting certain types of business or customer.

At its most simple, a company's culture can be said to be that set of assumptions about the life of the corporation which have worked well enough in the past to be considered valid and are taught to new members as a requirement of membership within the life of the company.

A corporation's culture can be seen in its visible aspects through physical layout – which will reflect the culture, as perceived by senior management – through the accepted dress codes, the individual office landscapes, the slogans and pronouncements bandied about, and the values and principles upon which the staff base their daily behaviour. They are values which are accepted. If rejected, the staff members will leave and be replaced by executives who will accept those norms.

Culture inside an organization is the source of a whole family of concepts that make one company different from another. This is apparent even if companies that are being compared are similar in size and trading category. The concepts we refer to include the symbols used, language and jargon phrases employed, corporate ideology, management beliefs, staff rituals, and the myths perpetuated in speeches and newsletters to staff or even through personal one-to-one conversations. They are important because they represent the reality of daily working life to individuals working within that organization. They are the factors that allow people to function and know their place within a given setting.

Let us look at this family of concepts. It is a family whose members when meeting together are extending an influence on each other. This inter-action provides the synergy that we call the company's culture. Any view of this family of ideas when analyzed will only constitute a snapshot because it is changing not from year-to-year but often week-to-week, depending on the dynamics of the company.

Members of families are born, have a gestation or growing-up period and then when their rightness – or maturity – is accepted they go on to grow and die. A corporation is the same. Its culture is enmeshed within the concepts that live on in the employees. A command to terminate them by management does not remove the original cause.

What then are these concepts? The symbols listed above are objects, facts, relationships and linguistic formulations that stand ambiguously for a multiplicity of meanings. They evoke emotions and impel employees to action. They include the structure of the work environment, the beliefs about the use and distribution of power and privilege, the rituals and myths which make these distributions acceptable.

By acquiring a corporate language, the staff adopt the social norms of their group and along with that the language, jargon, phraseology and values implicit in those notions.

We should look now at what we mean by corporate ideologies or sets of beliefs about the company world and how they operate. This 'ideology' will contain statements about the rightness of certain internal social arrangements and the actions that need to be taken in the light of these statements. They provide the essential links between attitudes and responsive actions.

The potency of the company's ideology is *how* it is supported and kept alive. It is here that rituals and myths find their greatest relevance. The ideology maintains the balance between what is legitimate and what is seen as unacceptable in the organizational culture. It is sometimes possible that myths may have qualities that can reinforce the solidity and the stability of the system, or they may be used in the furtherance of particular sectional interests. For example, myths about the founders or current chairman of the company are important as a reinforcement of the overall culture. 'Old Sir Bill always maintained that if you want to know who is the best departmental manager, ask the mailroom clerk', or 'Over at HQ John Smith will fire anyone with an untidy office. Says it shows a disorganized mind'. So the myths are perpetuated and used to reinforce decisions by managers. Slowly they become built into the departmental value systems of what is or is not done. They are so much a part of life in that company that they cannot be articulated. They are just accepted. But if, as in the case of British Airways, the attitude was a case of immunity from the outside world, and the airline was for the benefit of the staff as opposed to the customer, then stringent action had to be taken to turn it into the world's 'favourite airline'. A new CEO was appointed. He had a clear mission to put the customer first. Executives were switched to new roles, people with new ways of thinking were relocated, thus inserting new culture, new information and reward systems. In short, there took place the manufacture of a culture that would grow and feed upon itself.

If, of course, a corporate culture becomes too strong it can dominate the life of the institution to the extent that it becomes almost isolated from the outside world. This is unimportant if the institution is a monastery. Sometimes however a sense of exclusiveness and internal commitment can be created through the development of a distinct vocabulary, set of linguistics or a form of dress. This may be no bad thing. It can represent the outward signs of elitism. It will drive the staff and managers to higher and higher standards and become a force for achievement in itself. Certainly a company can reinforce this sense of exclusiveness by the way it selects staff and by making it known that only a very high academic standard will be accepted in anyone joining the company.

Many Japanese companies, and some in the U.S., have taken this totality of culture in other directions by creating a sense that all of life's needs can be satisfied within the bounds of the corporation – a cradle-to grave mentality. Indeed, 'Japan Inc.' is merely a corporate culture extended onto the national scale. The danger of these particular directions is that it not only reduces flexibility in terms of staff movement, but it takes away the freedom of movement a manager needs if he is to relieve people of their posts and respond to changing conditions. It is axiomatic that an organization being itself a component of its general environment, must be able to adapt to that environment if it is to survive. While corporate culture may provide identity, structure and unity of purpose it may also run the risk of isolating the organization from the market it seeks to woo, foster and sell into.

We must move towards the value systems that people accept and which support the overall culture. There are three values which tend to shape and change individual attitudes within an organization. These are the ones set by external influences, those set by influences which relate to the nature of the business, and those generated by the corporate culture itself.

External influences are composed of the values of society outside the corporation. National culture for example can influence employee motivation, management style and organizational structure. For organized groups, one example would be the view taken by members of professional bodies in respect to their professional role. In high-tech companies, operators often look to their own profession first, their company second.

This, together with their ethical implications, may not be in accord with the managerial view on how they can be best used as a resource within a company. As a result there are immediate clashes of influence. These may be resolved by discussion but more likely they will become an unspoken acceptance of a *modus vivendi* that totters on a knife-edge between what is and what is not acceptable to each side of the debate. Make no bones about it in the modern company, dealing with specialized professionally qualified staff, it is not a case of giving orders. It is a debate from which the outcome is mutual accountability. We're moving to the 'no boss business', where access to the boardroom will not be by the proverbial ladder but by true influence, example and respect.

When, however, we consider the influence relating to the nature of the business, we are referring to items such as market situation, the changing nature of technology or even those economic factors that impinge on the business. For example the recession of the early 1980s strongly influenced the values of people within organizations. Equally, technology and how it is handled by each company, impinges on employee values in a range of different ways. Secretaries for instance who place great store on traditional English values, and enjoy a life-style vested in the norms of British life, will often find great difficulty in coming to terms with high technology office equipment. This is not because they are incapable of handling it but because it seems to be repugnant to the values and ideals they hold dear.

The same attitudes can exist in craft workers who are expected to re-train for new equipment. In such cases the resistance is more to do with what they would call the importance of craft skills and 'the old standards' than any basic resistance to change.

An additional factor in analysing a company's culture is the effect that technology can have on the mix, and numbers of, people a company requires. If a company has developed for a long time with little outside influence its thinking and values become introspective. Changes in technology may necessitate the company buying in outside help. As a result this introduces new values to the company which can have a profound influence on the way the company views its future policy. Change is never absorbed and lost. It is a dynamic process of each side accepting a little piece of the other's ideas and values. This bonding of culture will be even more vital in the flexi-company or atomized hybrid of the future.

Finally let us examine the additional pressures on a company culture that can result from the feedback of individuals who, having been impacted, respond later in different ways to the pressure. These people imperceptibly alter the culture by their responses and thus force it to change very slightly step-by-step. For this reason we tend nowadays to see a corporation's culture as a growing, changing organism, one that is seldom static. Always it is responding to external pressure from new staff, from changing attitudes by existing staff. It contracts and expands like an enormous amoeba. Unlike the amoeba, however, which is controlled by a central nucleus, modern companies can exert powerful influences for change from the periphery inwards. The central management then have to respond to that change causing further change on the boundaries of their influence.

The big problem about a culture is that managements in their desperation to fit the culture to the new strategy forget that some aspects of the culture are worth retaining.

The other problem with culture is that once values are embodied in tablets of stone and the narrower mission statement on which it is based develops, it still has to be internalized, mostly unconsciously, by the relevant people in the organization. As Harold Leavitt of Stanford put it 'the test of whether or not a mission is truly a mission lies in members' beliefs, and ultimately in their behaviour vis-à-vis those beliefs'. A mission only becomes organizationally useful if it also generates a sense of urgency and commitment, which involves heart as well as head.

You can try to find a mission in this month's best seller on management, or at the local PR Consultancy. You can set staff analysts to work on the problem. But you won't succeed unless you fantasize, introspect and dream. Nor can it be a manipulative game. The missionary must believe in his mission. Many boardroom directors only pass lip-service to the mission statement, agreeing with it as an abstraction but breaking its rules in day-to-day decision-making. Symbols must be reinforced by action.

The mission-finding question is one we do not understand well in the West. Some scientists and artists and founders of religions have an overriding sense of purpose which is a critical component of charisma. It can at the other extreme be a pain in the neck manifested by stubbornness. Maslow ascribed this characteristic of overriding concern with one or more larger issues to his rare 'self actualizing' person discussed earlier. One way then to find a good mission is to bring in a good missionary like Sir Michael Edwardes or Colin Marshall or John Harvey-Jones. Another way is to ask ourselves who and what we are as a corporation?

A prerequisite for finding a mission is to have a thorough diagnosis of the culture, counter culture and sub cultures of the organization. These assumptions should then accord with the final mission statement.

Secondly it is important to understand that emotional processes are central. People do not become believers unless the messages are simple and respond to human needs. They must be allowed to participate in the process and find rewards for behaviour consistent with the objectives and symbols accompanying the mission such as the corporate identity. This is vital. The Hewlett-Packard version is 'Management by walking around', i.e. the CEO must be visible. Any plan for inculcating a new mission has to think long not short. The difficulty in most budget-driven corporations is to avoid cloning other senior managers in the same mould.

Returning to an earlier theme of the 1970s in the U.S., it appeared that the protestant work ethic of productivity, efficiency, achievement and thrift, had been eroded in favour of a more laid-back approach. The cold wind of recession may have dealt this a body blow, but it cannot be assumed in Europe or the U.S. that employees have returned to the old values. If managers want to inculcate a new mission into a large organization, it is vital to undertake a thorough analysis of the internal demographics of the organization – age, ethnic and educational.

Missions are not, of course, objectives because they communicate more via the heart than the head and are in large part a leap of faith. In politics there have been a few revolutionary leaders with a clear sense of mission, but very few in corporations. Ren McPherson of Dana Corporation is one such. Is it possible that Hewlett-Packard with its strong culture will begin to be perceived as a cult or as a model of cloying over-conformity? Management must be careful not to allow their zeal to cross the line that violates such values as individual freedom. To be effective the mission has to be both salient and achievable.

Even if something as unarticulated and implied as a culture can be diagnosed it is still hard to change. According to some consultants it is easier to change the people. But at least it should be attempted if the strategy has to be changed, so long as expectations are not too high. But beware, most CEOs lack the requisite theatrical skills to tackle symbolic and ritualistic behaviour. Dick Giordano again: 'I think a CEO spends 90 per cent of his time out there proselytizing. Most of the time he's teaching, nagging, telling people what business they're in, we want to be the best.'

Many firms for example ask for dedication and loyalty yet they also want the flexibility to let people go in bad times. Even IBM with its strong 'our kind of people' concept of loyalty accepts that loyalty is something that must be won. In Japan, where corporate loyalty borders on the mystical, it is said 'man, not the bottom line, is the measure of all things'. But as if to indicate the pace of change, while American executives jet to Tokyo to study their management systems, Japanese executives are flocking to New York to learn how to give the golden handshake. Is nothing sacred any more?

Of course corporate culture is not a panacea for poor products and service. Communicating good culture is not a substitute for doing the right things in production and marketing. The point of departure should be the preparation of a formal statement summarizing what the organization stands for – a cultural agenda if you will. In one company we visited all the employees are given a plaque signed by the CEO. It states the founding principles of the firm, the outward and visible sign of its internalized values. People want to feel involved in their organizations. Organizations are people at work and this implies improved internal communication about different departments and the people working within them. At People's Express, a company cited for its exemplary cultural traits, the CEO spends half a day a month on the orientation of new employees. Now that's management by wandering around. Change must be communicated at every stage, otherwise people resist it. The aim should be that in times of change employees are told what is being planned as soon as possible. They also need constant reminders of the key values and this can be done via external as much as internal communications. Employees need to be shown that excellence and creativity will be recognized. One CEO we know gives out pens and the employees keep a running total of who has most. The monetary value means little, it is the recognition that counts.

Culture must adapt not just to external strategic imperatives but to the changing nature of the employees as discussed. Participative management and more enriched job functions have to be built into the culture.

Quite clearly there is a conflict between the need for large organizations and the need for individuals to have more time and space. Maybe this is ultimately antipathetical to a strong corporate culture. Corporations today look and think more alike and to some employees are simply interchangeable. Culture is now thinner than it used to be. Organizational mores will have to meet changing attitudes to work. These in turn must be consistent with market needs. The risk of mergers and acquisition doesn't help this process. Of all the organization men, the true executive is the one who remains most suspicious of the organization's grip!

Of course it is always easier to talk about change than to bring it about, to write than to manage. However a corporation without a strategy is like an aeroplane running out of fuel at the mercy of the elements. Without a vision of its own future form – a more responsive and flexible type of organization – the corporation faces disaster in the coming era of turbulence.

The rapidly changing business environment, the new workforce, and advances in technology are therefore forging a breakdown of the large, traditional hierarchical organization of the past and in many instances of the present – highly decentralized organizations in which work will be handled in small autonomous units linked to the mega corporation by information technology. This will turn everyone into entrepreneurs and transform the middle management corporate ladder. It will be replaced by social influence in a no-boss business. Deal and Kennedy in *Corporate Cultures* called it the 'atomized organization'. But it requires strong cultural ties and a new kind of symbolic management. The small, task-focussed work units, each with management control over their destiny interconnected with large entities by benign communication links, will be grouped into these larger entities through strong cultural bonds. But in the atomized organization some glue is essential, the culture's role therefore will be crucial. The winner in the business world of tomorrow will be the hero who can forge the values and beliefs, the rituals and ceremonies and create a cultural network of story tellers and priests. Like the Roman Catholic Church, IBM, Disney and McDonalds, he must capture many of the expressive aspects of living that have been seen as soft by modern management, the heart, spirit, mystique or soul of the corporation.

Strong cultures will be able to adapt to external conditions and create more flexible organizations if managements are willing to take on board these changes.

The appropriate culture, flexible and adaptable, is more likely to exist in organizations where every employee feels he is dealt with 'justly'. This implies a fair and equitable payment and reward system, a fair and open promotion policy, a clear understanding of its boundaries of power, authority and responsibility, an individual appeals procedure, and a right to participate in the control of change. This is not a political programme. It is a programme which follows from the nature of man. Ultimately if the system protects risk takers and gives rewards for independence of perspective, the company will not die from over management and lethargy.

A shared strategic vision is fundamental to an organization aligned with itself and its market place. It is the ideas, the visions and the hopes of the company's leader, not just its product, its market strategies, which drive organizations.

Management needs therefore to inform people, involve them, share success, create pride, instil trust, offer accountability, assert authority, show dedication and display competence. That's all, not an easy task.

What therefore are the elements that stand out in this Hampton Court maze through which the modern chief executive must lead his flock? First there is the uncertainty, then there is the complexity, and finally there is the need to monitor something that changes week in, week out. Changes that are of such small degree that few managers even recognize them as they happen. Within this magic, corporate soul or spirit, there will have to be certain strands captured by a company that is concerned about its changing infrastructure, the motivation of its employees, and how it intends to maintain its competitive advantage. It cannot be done without the insight of the CEO, the man in the centre.

4

Strategic serendipity

'Success often comes from taking a miss-step in the right direction.'

Anon.

Today's giant corporations dominate the business world. Indeed some like General Motors are larger than the Gross Domestic Products of some smaller nations like Luxembourg. There are even a few examples, such as AT & T in Chile, where a corporation has helped overturn a government. Their productive marketing and financial strengths are such as to make their position as the locomotives of the world economy appear wholly impregnable. But with all the external and internal pressures that we have discussed in previous chapters exploding and imploding upon them, corporations and their managements (despite a renewed realism since the recession) are finding that a flexing of muscles is now a futile gesture. Just as the might of the U.S. military machine was unsuccessful in taming the new Iranian regime, which merely threw sand in the President's face, corporations cannot hope to huff and puff their way to success any more. As the political centre of gravity disperses, so too is the power of corporations. They are having to adapt in size, shape, system and above all, in style. The old production focus needs to shift to a more marketing-led focus if companies are to survive, let alone succeed.

Future professors of science and society will conclude that the final quarter of the twentieth century saw the extinction of the giant company, the dinosaurs of the corporate world, replaced later by small, entrepreneurially run operations. In *Dinosaur and Co* Tom Lloyd tested this thesis in the context of what he calls the 'Era of Rapid Technological Advance (ERTA)'.

What will herald the end are the twin threats – one being economic and the other psychological. The economic threat to corporate giants results from a dramatic contraction in product life cycles which transpired during an ERTA, the resultant economies of scale, and the 'L'-shaped cost curve. This depicts a continuous decline in unit costs as production volume rises. With a compression of the time frame this assumption becomes invalid once product life cycles contract beyond a certain point. In a typical case a company will find that by the time it has geared up production volume sufficiently to be price competitive the product has become obsolete. The strength of the small company, providing venture-capital and entrepreneurs are available, is its ability to counter unplanned obsolescence, and show greater agility. It can bob and weave betwixt and between the usual market segments, picking up temporary monopolies and nudging product development paths away from the direction favoured by large organizations. During an ERTA, 'corporate fission' follows 'critical mass' a hazard for the larger organizations already above critical mass when the ERTA began.

This is where the human element comes into play. There is evidence, particularly in the U.S.A., in the fields of electronics and biotechnology, reinforced by Lloyd's case studies, to suggest that these 'scientist-entrepreneurs' are not only rare creatures but they are moving out of the universities and R & D establishments of large companies to set up their own companies as entrepreneurs.

The founder of Atari, Nolan Bushnell, explained the proliferation of small, high-tech companies in California in terms of young entrepreneurs, who know 'at least two millionaires they think are stupid'.

The fact that Atari and other high-tech companies have had their problems on both sides of the Atlantic is a testament partly to the ability of the large companies to survive against all the odds, providing they can develop the 'intrapreneurial' spirit discussed earlier. Another reason is that there is an institutional bias in their favour.

The way in which the capital markets evolved suits large companies. Big unions like dealing with big employers. The lack, too, of an appropriately diversified venture-capital market, and above all the political influence of large companies, are all examples of the way they can affect the business environment in their own favour. Yet they will still fail unless they learn how to adapt more quickly.

There is a built-in resistance to the changes going on around them, changes which could be summed up in the phrase 'the disintegrated economy'. Shareholders have nothing to gain, employees en masse have nothing to gain, and top management have a lot to lose. One possible scenario is for senior executives to encourage demerging in the form of management buy-outs where they turn themselves into specialist investment trusts.

Central banking is often retained along with staff roles such as personnel and PR/public affairs, while the running of the satellite businesses is left in the hands of entrepreneurs. Such federal systems are beginning to emerge even in certain parts of British industry. Few senior managers recognize these and other changes as a means of changing course quickly to avoid collisions like tankers in the English Channel. They need not lose everything if they stop rationalizing. Such hypotheses are of course predicated on having the right mix of technology, people and capital while still ensuring the strategy chosen is workable in the market place. As James Lawrence of PA Strategy Partners said, 'strategy is not what is planned to happen but what actually happens'. Indeed Michael Porter of Harvard goes further in saying there is no point having a strategy at all unless it provides a competitive advantage.

In their headlong rush for diversification and growth in the 1960s and 1970s, particularly internationally, corporations missed this very point. Strategies are useless unless they actually work, i.e. unless they find the niche – the difference that makes the difference. Companies are often too narrowly product defined. They underestimate the cost of being different, as Jaguar found, until quality control was improved along with its marketing. The trick is to keep the edge sharp. Texas Instruments found what happens when you don't to their cost, with their watches competing against the Swiss then Japanese.

Many conglomerates could benefit from cross links with other businesses if only they could shift the balance from a production to a market focus. For many British export earners, the failure rate against the Americans, Germans and Japanese is a function not of technological or financial inferiority (although this may be the case in some instances), but poor feedback from the market.

Marketing has never been a strong point in European, particularly British companies. A recent study by Bradford University of forty

U.K. and Japanese companies concluded that while Japanese companies instil a need to win in their U.K. employees, British marketing men remain largely defensive. This is borne out by the attitude of British firms to doing business in Japan and even studying Japanese methods. This attitude sadly permeates right to the top and reflects the production and financial backgrounds of too many managers. Many U.K. companies show a marked ignorance about customer needs and their competition. A Japanese would be hurt if you underestimated his market share, say, of the Australian automobile market. The British tend not to be very international, relying on a Buy British mentality. They are poor at branding their products or finding a differentiating personality. Poor marketing, weak design and insufficient attention to changing consumer patterns is in danger of leaving British firms at the low commodity end of the market, the Bradford survey notes.

What is the reason for this weakness? Is it our old friend the traditional organization structure? The structure spreads out authority so that there is no 'product champion'. Budgets and computer back-up are often insufficient for planning a specific strategy. The obvious conclusion is that European, particularly British, companies should break down their top-heavy functional structures into smaller business units around a product and a market. British companies above all should develop more of a 'marketing culture', ridding themselves of purely short-term profit considerations and an over-emphasis on traditional production skills. As we shall see later, the CEO needs to take the lead in demonstrating a commitment to market leadership. There is a need for closer links between the universities and business, not only in R & D, but also in marketing. Many CEOs and managers are not only narrow, they are downright uneducated in the 'soft' skills of handling people and in marketing skills.

Professor Theodore Levitt's famous doctrine states that corporate survival depends on doing everything necessary to satisfy the customer. That everything is ultimately reducible to what is better known as marketing. For too many, marketing is just selling with a college education.

There are twelve main areas that senior management in Europe should correct if they want to rise to the challenge of Levitt's concept of marketing:

1. *Organizational barriers*
   Marketing strategies so often run foul of vertical barriers between the corporate centre and line management and horizontal ones between different functional specialists. The Japanese have found ways of crossing disciplines. Such a group culture is alien to many Western companies, even some in the U.S. This is why 'team briefings' and 'task forces' are potentially potent forces for market success in the future. Even marketing itself has become specialist, rather than a process which should permeate the entire company. (We are happy for the same reason that public relations people for instance are being drawn from different disciplines such as finance and the law, marketing and government.)

2. *Structural failings*
   The problem of poor communications and inadequate cohesion is compounded by a failure to break up the organization into smaller business units, without which it is difficult to get and keep 'close to the customer'.

3. *Hostile cultures*
   Apart from packaged goods industries, most companies are dogged by technical, financial and possibly short-term sales cultures, with the executives having a 'trained incapacity' to think longer term, and in discrete market segments. If marketing people are seen as fast talking upstarts you can imagine why PR people with their even more elusive communication skills are seen as 'flannel soaked in gin'.

4 *Myopic marketeers*
   This means they are good with research data, less good with human behaviour, motivation, communication and strategic vision. To some extent they are the Trojan horses of the other traditional thinkers.

5. *Confusion with sales*
   This is a classic example of the Peter Principle where most marketing men have been trained as salesmen and then become promoted beyond the level of their own incompetence. Semantics plays a role here. Marketing, like public affairs, is a grander title than sales and public relations.

6. *Confusion with customer service*
   Many service organizations, especially airlines, confuse marketing with customer relations – the 'have a nice day' syndrome.

7. *Confusion with market research*
   Many managers use it as a prop for decisions or a decision substitute. The more innovative the product, the less valid is the market research as it has limited predictive properties.

8. *The strategic planning barrier*
   As can be seen in strategy boutiques, the emphasis is on financial and portfolio analysis rather than marketing, let alone communication skills, viewing them as operational tools. In fairness, this is now changing.

9. *Short-term horizons*
   Rules of thumb return on investment are useless unless accompanied by an assessment of competitive advantages. The one-year horizon is a constraint.

10. *The 'Theory gap'*
    Corporate marketing should be the interface between the corporation and the outside world, a motivating force which challenges the established ways of doing things. In short it has frequently ignored the organizational and human aspects of how strategies can be made to work. The teaching of this subject has reconfirmed this feeling, and trivialized marketing in the process.

11. *The 'competitive gap'*
    'Know thy competition' is as important as satisfying customer needs.

12. *Degeneration*
    Successful past practitioners of marketing have become hidebound, inflexible in approach, slow to respond to changes in competition, market structures and distribution channels, not to mention the human factor. Few company chairmen view marketing, like Proctor & Gamble, as everyone's responsibility. (We're chiefly talking here of European experience in comparison with the U.S. and Japan.) But the Japanese are beginning to show some chinks in the armour. Changing expectations,

> despite their tremendous resilience, are creating new pressures. The Americans tend to be short-term, unsubtle, and overly aggressive in their salesmanship. This is not good marketing, it is salesmanship off course.

Hewlett-Packard is often acclaimed as one of America's best-managed companies. It recently sent shock waves through its engineering-dominated ranks by establishing a centralized marketing division and then making other structural changes aimed at improving its marketing. It realized it could not compete on technology alone. So began a painful transformation in corporate culture. In Europe, Philips took inordinately long to learn from the marketing-led strategies of the Japanese. Only in packaged goods has there been anything like a marketing focus in the Western world. It is only since telecommunications and banking have become deregulated that they too have realized the need for real marketing. According to Jean-Claude Larreché, one of Europe's top marketing academics, some managements on both sides of the Atlantic *still* confuse marketing with market research, or with promotion or more normally with sales. The slow response to change is amazing. Even those companies which have changed tend to confuse the tools with the concept.

Despite Japan's success in penetrating one Western market after another, U.S. and European companies are still insufficiently aware of the sophistication and flexibility of the Japanese in using a multiplicity of competitive weapons with varied degrees of emphasis: price, promotion, quality, product-range, service and of course, distribution. More worryingly in a recent book *The New Competition*, Professor Kotter & Co. warn Western companies that not only must they think more long-term and develop a marketing culture instead of a preoccupation with accounting profits, but be prepared to fight the new 'Gang of Four' – South Korea, Taiwan, Singapore and Hong Kong.

Professor Levitt of Harvard wrote the article *Marketing Myopia* in 1968, promoting the dogma 'Know Thy Customer'. The question 'What business are we in?' which he promulgated as the prerequisite of marketing-led strategy, is constantly being asked by newly appointed marketing managers and managing directors. But the

West still persists with a production/sales mentality, with some notable exceptions.

Companies tend to sell what production makes rather than what the customer wants. Increasingly the customer will want bespoke service, so how Western companies will cope, only God and the Japanese know. Concepts such as market segmentation and product differentiation are too new to the vocabulary to have been inculcated into the corporate culture. Most European companies according to McKinsey & Co. have not even defined what markets they are in or who the competitors are. The problem of course is how to broaden marketing from its narrow, functional role in many companies. Managements fail to realize that most of marketing's impact is felt before the product is produced, not after.

The U.S. car industry is a classic example of myopia. It tends to research preferences between the kinds of items it has already decided to offer the customer, rather than what the customer might want. It thus lost share to foreign 'compact' cars.

To change gear from production to customer orientation requires a profound understanding of human organization and leadership. Management must begin to think of itself as providing customer-creating satisfactions rather than producing products. This means a complete cultural revolution.

So far most managements have flunked the challenge to make marketing an all-embracing philosophy, where flexibility is the keynote to any response to competitive and consumer changes. Constant change is anathema to most corporations, so a once successful strategy becomes quickly ossified into rigid attitudes and procedures, from which even Proctor & Gamble sometimes fail to adapt in the face of shortened product life cycles and the massive increase in European retail buying power. Ultimately it is all about identifying, selecting and interpreting the right information, which in this electronic era tends to result in 'information overload'. Would the Japanese have succeeded in destroying Pearl Harbor if the signals had not been misread?

Clark Olsen of PA Management Consultants in the U.S. has conducted research programmes for Johnson & Johnson and AT & T, correlating culture and marketing. He postulates that the culture of an organization profoundly affects individual behaviour and performance. Secondly, changes in culture will become most effective as a byproduct of management's concern for key bottom-line results. These are not purely financial but can relate to concepts such as pride, caring, and client needs as well as profits. If true, what we are discussing is not pie in the sky. Values he says must be shared by management at all levels. They must not be arbitrarily imposed. They must be seen as part of the subtlety and vision of that elusive creature called leadership.

Christopher Lorenz often argues passionately in his well-read *Financial Times* management column, for the vast majority of European companies, particularly in France and Britain, to concentrate on the soft elements of McKinsey's 'seven S's' of style, skills, staff and shared values rather than the hard areas of strategy, structure and systems. It is no good however moving in this direction if the basic systems of budgeting and reporting analysis do not exist. 'Excellence was intended to restore the balance, not revive the flat-earthers' says Lorenz.

But even the 'strategy boutiques' are jumping on the 'excellence' bandwagon, preaching corporate culture in addition to scientific analysis as the key to strategic success. Obviously it is all a matter of balance. Yet it is equally obvious that not all of today's issues are reducible to rational, quantifiable analysis.

With the pace and complexity of environmental change, consultancies need to be able to assist with far greater organizational and strategic adjustments of firms constrained by intransigent corporate cultures. Some consultants are developing packages that meet the dual market need linking culture management with market-analysis. The bridge here is communications and should be uppermost on the CEO's change agenda.

Hewlett-Packard was recently forced to abandon decentralization and technical innovation in favour of gradual centralization and market culture. This was the weakness of the excellence bandwagon. It begged more questions than it answered about marketing communications and how this aspect could be integrated with, rather than be peripheral to, decision making. Consultants in their obsession with systems and structures tend not to cope with softer elements and fail to be susceptible to its analysis and quantification.

While we agree that it is vital to get the loose-tight balance right and hands on, value-driven productivity through people, etc. as

Dan Carroll pointed out in the *Harvard Business Review*, such an approach still ignores the important aspects of national culture and economic trends, such as government policy towards unemployment. The point here is that managements do not succeed by sticking rigidly to rules. If management is not a science, then leadership is an art form.

The interaction of the now famous 'seven S's' with each other and the environment is the key. The problem is that so many CEOs are still locked in to the recessionary siege mentality, failing to think up interdependent strategies for cooperation, joint ventures and partnership. Exceptions are Italy's Olivetti which now has links with over twenty U.S. companies, and France's Thompson-Brandt which went into partnership with a Japanese VCR company. It is healthy to see some CEOs moving strategic planning into their executive offices, away from the finance director. Personnel policies are also being rethought so that employees are more in control of their own careers. In that way round holes can be made to fit into square pegs.

Philippe de Woot, from Belgium's Louvain University, in a study of nine French and Belgian firms, including Empain Schneider and Pechiney-Ugine Kuhlman, warns that because many European firms have barely emerged from a state of managerial 'feudalism' (not possessing the professional resources, information systems, expertise and outlook) they have several stages to pass through before they could absorb some of the 'excellence' criteria. For instance 'tightness' based solely on financial controls is inadequate since HQ must also give strategic direction. His report *Le Management Strategique des Groupes Industrielles*, showed that some senior managers did not believe in defining objectives or giving a strong lead. Not surprisingly in a vacuum of internal values, employees were slaves to external values.

Given Europe's late start one wonders if it is even possible to leapfrog from the feudal system, through decentralization, straight to corporate strategic management without even the requisite professional infrastructure? In that context it is interesting to watch the financial institutions getting to grips in quick time with globalization and the changing boundary conditions of their businesses. We hope the big bang won't paralyze them.

As Lorenz again has argued, CEOs need to be more papal with real power, less like impotent Shakespearean barons, full of intrigue and instability. Will the real European leaders come forth and act out the massive change that is needed to create the managerial revolution? What is important is that companies cannot just copy others or try harder. They must create their individual success factor. Just as a USP can make a product marketable, the success factor is the crucial component of the organization's competitive advantage. Strategies that follow fashion gravitate towards conformity instead of moving towards uniqueness. If identified, every organization possesses one or more attributes that causes a decisive advantage. Excellence, quality, commitment, can only lead to success when linked to specific properties. Today's success factor can become tomorrow's failure factor if the strategy is static and fails to take account of a dynamic environment. This is where early warning radar and the need to manage the issue enters in.

Individuals should be analyzed separately from the organization, which has a life of its own, as we have seen in a previous chapter. There are four potential success factors – *initiative* (routines and rituals constrain action), *independence* (resisting conformity), being *rational* (instead of emotional), and finally *creativity* (lateral thinking; a powerful ally to rationality). Creativity enables people to think the unthinkable, do the undoable. Logic however is easily contaminated by wishful thinking. To understand the dynamics of the organization, and the external environment, takes flair. When departmentalized and regimented the strategic process loses touch with reality. (The long-range planning approach suffers from information overload and inflexibility.)

To identify and create new success factors and abandon the shackles of established routines and beliefs puts people and systems under stress. Winning strategies represent effort and activities beyond the normal day-to-day business, demanding a correspondingly high degree of management. A success factor is transitory. Management must therefore use the contribution created by the current success factor to create conditions to find future success factors. This is what building and maintaining competitive advantage is all about.

Strategy is therefore about doing as well as planning. Reconciling the need for flexibility, when longer-term commitments in people and technology are having to be made, is perhaps the greatest paradox. We are certainly not suggesing it is easy. The entrepreneurial, flexible company can only operate well with clear objectives, assiduous use of information and a willingness to take risks. All these aspects affect the shape, size and structure of the company. 'Market pull' and 'technology push' can only be reconciled in an informal hierarchy and via an interdisciplinary approach. Ultimately only performance counts. This must be reflected in incentive systems which should reward strategic as well as short-term action, improved internal and external communications.

Europe's ability to obtain competitive advantage from the U.S., and East Asia countries in particular, will depend on a more adventurous source of venture capital, the reduction of supply-side constraints, and a greater commitment by government to R & D, so as to add value to technology based products. Also the willingness of European firms to cooperate with each other can become crucial as investment costs rise. It will depend also on attitudes by the educational system towards industry and wealth creation, on less risk aversion and a culture that stresses solutions not problems, on more action and less talk and above all, on charismatic leadership. The preoccupation with finance and law has led to a missing ingredient in people motivation. Excellent Companies (EC) respond to complexity with fluidity while the rationalist model discounts informality and values.

The EC system reinforces degrees of winning rather than losing. What is needed is positive reinforcement which can only come from the top down. There needs to be a balance between stability and entrepreneurship. Managers should change from being analysts looking for specific data to the monitor looking for unusual signals. It is often the communication expert receiving feedback from various stakeholders and from targeted research who could more frequently be the monitor if only someone would listen.

Unless strategy is to have a sense, serendipity and decisions are to continue being made by default, CEOs and their senior managers must learn how to sail their ship by positioning it exactly right. To maximize its strengths and culture to give competitive advantage in the marketplace is not easy.

5

The three Martini Luddite – shaken but not stirred

> *'Luddite (Member) of band of mechanics (1811–16) who raised riots for destruction of machinery. Leader was called Captain Ludd.'*
>
> *Concise Oxford Dictionary.*

In the 1950s and 1960s the executive suite was tranquil. Piled carpets and a bevy of secretaries shielded and sheltered the CEO who spent his time pouring over production runs, financial statements and possibly market statistics. He felt less need for long-term planning and such abstractions as accountability to anything other than shareholders. The 1970s proved that burying heads in the sand of business not only hampers development but offsets the company's success, indeed its very survival. It was in this period that C. Northcote Parkinson coined the now famous aphorism: 'The vacuum created by an absence of communication will soon be filled with rumour-drivel and poison'. Senior management failed to realize that all organizations have an image whether they like it or not, or whether they want a low profile or not. Then, as now, a major priority must be communication – informing, consulting, persuading, convincing.

Yet with some notable exceptions there is a gap between the middle manager's concern for immediate issues of profit, productivity and facts, and the more conceptual, visionary thinking and behaviour where top managers need to make their strategies, if they have one, work. Few senior managers, this chapter contends, while technically and professionally qualified, are prepared for the quality of change inherent in today's turbulent business environment. Nor are they trained to interpret the new signals because previous experience and learning has led them to misinterpret the signals. The implication being that new learning and development need to take place and possibly even unlearning. How many CEOs are even prepared to admit that this may be the case, let alone do anything about it. They get trapped in the past, particularly the older ones. Twenty years' experience may actually be one year's experience twenty times over.

There are many blockages which can prevent top managers climbing up the learning cycle – the macho maxim that 'management is about doing, not thinking or planning', and the rise of experts which has effectively de-skilled top managers who become overly dependent on them.

Yet many senior managers, particularly in Europe, actually scorn hiring academically qualified people, let alone going on courses to update them, to unlearn, rebalance learning habits, sensitize themselves to new situations, and above all train for the new interpersonal skills now required. (The educational implications of this are discussed in the next chapter.) The Courtaulds courses at the London Business School are a good example of linking relearning with immediate business problems.

Sir Alex Jarratt, ex-chairman of Reed International poses the question: 'Are you a helmsman or a navigator?' A helmsman is a hands-on manager-leader, whereas a navigator develops the strategy from a position of detachment. It is our contention that the CEO must be both, as well as being captain. But he should not be more, which means staying out of the engine room.

A helmsman is only a tactician or an operator, finding and holding that thin line along which the elements join in driving the boat forward. (The very word 'leader' derives from 'laed', which in old Norse meant the course of a ship at sea.) But a CEO has to be a strategist too. So the leader must have navigational skills. As Henry Kissinger once said, 'The task of a leader is to get his people from where they are to where they have not been'. But as the Duke of Edinburgh has said, there are too many one ulcer men in two ulcer jobs.

The first responsibility of leadership, says John Adair, Professor of Leadership at Surrey University, is 'to achieve the common task'. In order to do this the CEO must have the ability to 'think deeply', which is different from meddling. Second he must have the ability to communicate. All negotiators tend to bow down to the God of routine. The message should be to look ahead and make pre-emptive changes. Lastly there is a need to be able to make things happen –

toughness but fairness. He believes the critieria are ambition, ability and track record, a determination plus ambition to make the business grow, but above all creative motivation leading to satisfaction that the structure is growing and flourishing. Why are some CEOs so vain they make no succession provision and merely find someone who fits their mould? Nothing succeeds like one's own successor.

Olivier Lecerf of the French firm Lefarge Coffee even believes CEOs should take a year's sabbatical at an appropriate time, as he did in 1983, not only to satisfy intellectual curiosity but to chart the company's future. He typifies the perennial student requirement for CEOs and senior managers. Although he doesn't advocate it for all CEOs in all situations, (there are obvious practical constraints and risks). In a world of change, it helped him reorientate, rethink, reposition. He learns from the Japanese that the priorities of the CEO are to maintain group harmony and loyalty, set strategy goals and make the key appointments.

The in-search of excellence concept of 'managing by wandering around' is an idea which encapsulates many aspects of leadership such as listening, teaching, facilitating, just being in touch. In the same way the new significance of corporate culture referred to earlier is placing great store on the importance of management by symbolic behaviour. Not every CEO is an influential founder or charismatic leader who individually personifies a firm's vision and values. But the lament of the extraordinary many doesn't cut much ice when we live in extraordinary times. You have to put the business into your heart and wear it on your sleeve. Legendary leaders aren't uniquely omnipotent, just savvy. But this does involve an element of showmanship and most CEOs lack the requisite theatrical skills. If you're a masochist a visit to most AGMs attests to that. The real constraint, although many would not admit it, is not lack of skill but the reality that their group norm is not of the outside world nor the company at large, but a few senior colleagues with the same attitudes as their peers at the golf club. This exerts tremendous pressure on the hired gun or public affairs director who must play drama coach to help the CEO trumpet values internally and corporate marketing messages externally, preferably without tinkering with their personal style, if they have one. There's no set formula.

It is true that more and more CEOs are out in the community 'doing things' as well as in their firm 'troubleshooting', especially in the U.S. But they need to balance their time between internal/ external priorities, and still change their attitudes from dictator to coach. If they're introvert, as they so often tend to be, accountants or engineers, then the company has problems. More and more issues should be PR driven, more horizontal, less vertical, requiring a more holistic, less functional, approach. The media prefer the broad underlying issues rather than the minutiae of day-to-day accountancy. The pressure is coming from the bottom up and outside in. Without a spearhead a corporation cannot be mobilized for competitive advantage. Yet if only he will grasp it the CEO can seize the initiative.

Somehow few have the requisite liberal arts background or high tech skills. A few even still retain Luddite qualities that would shock some trade unionists.

Technology is the lifeblood of Cie Generale D'Electricité, France's new multinational corporation in the electronics sector. But the CEO, Jean-Pierre Brunet, has no computer terminal in his office because (as he says in jest?) it 'wouldn't go with the eighteenth century furniture.'

Before reviewing the job spec for the new managerial head it's as well to remind ourselves of the nature of the 'gigantic mutation' which is no longer limited to purely economic and financial factors but to basic questioning of values.

Demographic figures, the contraction of manufacturing, the microprocessor revolution, the relative fall in product innovation and stiffening competition from the newly industrialized countries (NICs), and long-term unemployment have rightly concentrated the mind of CEOs; as have the 'flexilife' concept leading to part-time jobs, longer vacations, shorter working hours and multicareers discussed earlier. If economic change moves, swiftly followed by political response, then social change lags further behind. Ironically it is here where people, including CEOs, internalize their values and attitudes. Personal self-discovery, can work as a means not an end. It will soon preoccupy more and more employees. The demand for flexibility and participation in decision-making will be linked by many with a search for a new sense of meaning and stability. Woe betide CEOs if they fail to fill the vacuum left by the politicians and their pundits in setting the new agenda.

In dealing with all his constituencies the CEO has had to search for common ground and gain that increasingly elusive share of mind. Many, not all, still remain defensive or oblivious to the need for an understanding of wider horizons, preferring to leave the stage to politicians, trade unionists, academics and journalists. The Confederation of British Industry still complains that it cannot get sufficient competent businessmen to appear on television or take part in public debate. Some CEOs have been goaded into responding to the growing acceptance by the public that businessmen are criminals and that profit is a dirty word. To protest that without wealth creation where would pressure groups be, is not enough. Incidents such as Bhopal and Three Mile Island don't help, but progress is being made. It's more than putting the case on a targeted basis. Equally important is the need to apply the same formula as they would for marketing their products. Patient explanation of the corporation's role in society helps to reconcile conflicting interests.

The failure of business to speak up for itself and tell the truth clearly has led public opinion (whoever that is) to assume the defendant guilty. The modern CEO must articulate awareness of, and hold views on, the changing social, economic and political system while simultaneously explaining how companies are changing from large bureaucracies to federations of small enterprises. They must show how they are concentrating on core activities, and lean and hungry how they are operated more and more by a flatter management pyramid on a task-force basis.

Over the next twenty years therefore the changing corporation will have to recruit new categories of talent to help redefine their role in society.

It's not easy for managers to chart the future when paradigm paralysis sets in at age thirty, and few predictable landmarks and safe havens remain. The ability to comprehend this phenomenon and confront it is a major management opportunity if seized quickly. They just can't make judgements based on their own prejudices any more.

The changing needs of top managers, the CEO in particular, is low on the management agenda in most corporations and likely to remain so unless they can turn outside in.

What type and characteristic manager is needed for the next decade? How is a man or woman chosen to lead a company into the nineties? What normally happens is that job specifications and staff qualifications are carefully analyzed and assessed by professional personnel advisers for middle management recruitment and below. Nobody thinks of doing it for the top echelon. His job is filled by a strange, almost haphazard, collection of subjective assessments, outside testimonials, believed social graces and, finally, an historic ability to handle companies as they have been rather than as they are or will be. The merry-go-round in the boardrooms of some European companies is merely recycling the same faults.

How are senior jobs specified? A typical job specification for the situations vacant column – seldom actually used for really senior posts – might run:

Personal Characteristics Required
Polished and socially confident
good communicator with winning personality
articulate and literate
open-minded, innovative
good listener
doer as well as strategic thinker
strong belief in collaboration not confrontation
ability to motivate people
intuitive as well as rational
ability to balance complex issues.

Experience/qualifications
The successful applicant will have held a number of appointments at senior level in different corporations and will preferably have experience in consultancy and possibly even in government or academea. He or she must show a track record in achieving financial and competitive advantage as well as demonstrating an ability to integrate the key ingredients of style and shared values into the strategic process. Should have made a major contribution to management thinking and social action. He or she must be issues driven, able to demonstrate a deep understanding of the forces at work within and between corporations in society and internationally. A good diplomat, able to build bridges with a wide variety of stakeholders, will be an essential prerequisite. In addition to a strong academic background straddling science and arts, the candidate will have attended a variety of training

courses and management workshops in recent years. Above all the post requires the ability to learn and act fast.

Do these bland, undefined phrases ring a bell? An inability or unwillingness to closely define and analyze what these characteristics really mean is going to be a fundamental problem for the future. Somehow we need to find, then train, the new species of multidisciplinary 'polymath' if we are to ring the changes within the new top management team. However, something fresh is now required. New styles must impact and change emerging CEOs, who now need to be a whizz with the balance sheet, comprehend the application of technology, but must also hold a broad overview. He will be able to forge new frontiers and move easily and comfortably between the past, present and future of an organization understanding what that means.

The ideal type may not always exist in any one form but be spread among the management team. Increasingly, but sometimes unsuccessfully, the role is divided too simply between Chairman and M.D. or President. This worked once, but today the lines should be drawn more precisely within the context of a wider 'executive committee' team.

The multiple executive office or OP (Office of the President), of which there are about 150 in the U.S., is a way of sharing CEO responsibility among a group of managers. Back in the 1890s the Michelin brothers – 'If I am the champagne, he is the bubbles' – set up an 'Office of the Entrepreneur' to combine their respective entrepreneurial and marketing talents. In the 1960s, because of a decentralized operational structure, and a need for strategic business planning as the company grew in size and complexity, General Electric put in place an OP, which was aped by many. The rationale for this was the greater sensitivity needed to tackle social, political and environmental issues, the accelerated pace of decision making, increased demand for contingency planning and a requirement for rapid response. Despite detractors the GE experience created flexibility and balance, a collegiate atmosphere of shared responsibility each challenging the other's assumptions. The most popular number is five, thus distinguishing it from the executive committee concept. But the key is that the CEO's style governs its composition.

As top management has moved away from the shop floor and

become more involved in staff utilization, service orientation and public accountability, the complexity of the top jobs has risen, hence the need for a multiple structure. This is also the best way to manifest less authority in an era of participation.

What brought the need for the OP? Two reasons dominate the literature and quotations of CEOs up to 1970 – the growing complexity of organizations and the pressures of time. Thereafter two more compelling reasons emerged – government regulations and again the pressures of time. Obviously as we have indicated, the pace of change in technology, market dynamics and financial acumen have resulted in megacorporate structures that are beyond the ability of any one person to manage and control. Too many top executives are forced into short-term thinking. It is preferable therefore if the chairman at least can concentrate on the long term. Information is instantaneous, widely shared and interpreted in different ways by different people and different publics. Response must be pruned to the timing of these new publics that corporations must now address. Government and pressure group issues are constantly changing and in need of response. These are good reasons for shared responsibility. Above all theoreticians point to extensive research on leadership that indicates separate functional demands to achieve the goals of the organization while still motivating employees.

This style will not work for all CEOs or for all companies. Without using the OP as a panacea against the ultimate responsibility of the CEO for policy and positioning, a team can still be useful for decision making and for external projection.

One way of maintaining the effectiveness of the CEO and his management team is for the Board to minimize adversarial relationships between them. This can be done by helping the CEO develop board agendas, schedule one-on-one sessions and tap the expertise of outside directors and consultants. Of particular interest are the views of Peter Scotease, Executive Committee Chairman of Springs Industries Inc. who believes there is too great an emphasis on short-term financial goals. He says there is a tendancy to forget that corporations usually have a longer life than the CEO and that matters of recruitment, training and development are increasingly important matters for the CEO as well as their respective department heads as they have a long-term implication.

Some companies are likely to have the communicators function at the helm, or at least on the board. The reaction of other businessmen is that they should have gone into showbiz, politics or the Church if they'd sought the limelight. What a stultifying attitude for someone with responsibility for employing and working for profit in an age of the mass media, pressure groups and massive social change.

The other hat the CEO should try is that of the champion of innovation. Constant innovation is essential to survival. It is axiomatic that the level necessary to become and remain competitive is only sustained by a genuine and visible commitment by top management and the CEO. Very few CEOs can be expected to keep abreast of the galloping technology impinging on their company. But at least they can ensure that the R & D Director, like the Personnel and Public Affairs Director enjoys the same status in corporate decisions as other departmental chiefs and that the CEO himself takes over their leadership. Recent research by PA Technology showed that most companies are complacent on this issue. It remains low on the management agenda.

Office automation cannot be uncoupled from human resources, from corporate funding or from product marketing. The company whose CEO isn't interested could go out of business. Decisions on automation and innovation must reside with the CEO.

Fortunately, according to a Booz Allen survey, more and more chief executives appear acutely aware of the information problem and the need to avoid drowning in a rising tide of data. It doesn't matter if the top manager does not have a personal computer on his desk so long as his office has immediate access. Productivity improvements are no longer just a question of saving money or cutting costs but of getting and using the best information possible. But how many realize this? Judging from their failure to develop secretaries and provide them with training and new hardware, very few.

Above all the CEO must be the strategist-in-chief. A truism perhaps but scarcely practised in many corporations. This is due to a lack of feeling for the broad brush approach to business often caused by a background of experiences that has been blinkered within vertical over specialized skills.

This role is increasingly one of management of change, leaving time to evaluate new business areas and new organizational concepts that will allow greater flexibility in the market place and in the work environment. Few managers practise what they preach on speaking platforms because they immerse themselves in short-term, tactical day-to-day situations. In the mad dash to the year-end financial altar, many company managers have failed to grasp that seven out of ten new companies are not high-tech or even low-tech, they are service-oriented small businesses using simplified elements of the high-tech revolution. The future is services, education and information, as well as the need to throw CAD/CAM at smokestack industries. The common denominator however is this new type of management. There is an increasing need to integrate divisional strategies into a unified corporate plan. In doing so we must ensure that the overall plan reaches out to the customer and then back to the functions of design, manufacturing, service, finance management development and public affairs. A completion of the circle.

The key, however, is to know which tasks, whether strategic or operative,should absorb what proportion of the senior executives' time. In an age of modest GNP growth, the primary need is often said to be one of fostering innovation. There is the need to identify those few key issues which will create the competitive advantage – show creativity and find the 'difference that makes the difference'.

Strategy and values have to be communicated internally and externally and its contribution to the wider society continuously examined.

One age is ending, a new one beginning. Old ways will not work on the macro-scale. Quite obviously there will always be small businesses specializing in crafts or discreet personnel services. These will succeed. This is an age where material reward is inadequate. The successful manager will respond to the needs of the productive spirit, and to the achievement of some ego-directed element in his self-esteem. The task of management now is to cause people to think creatively, to learn and to share. This concept is best fostered in a spirit of excellence via participation. Individuals now have broader options so management by fear and intimidation is dead. The actual number of senior managers may decline but the most critical determinant of international corporate success will still be senior managerial competence.

Mobilizing all this will require a new set of beliefs about the nature of work, of needed skills and of tasks for management. The adaptation required is not only in the systems and structures but in the spirit of those involved.

One way of analyzing the new criteria was put forcibly by Alfred Latham-Koenig, a retired McKinsey consultant.

He broke it down into five categories:

(1) 'the politician-statesman' who will probably find his way to the chairmanship of large companies because of his ability to be a shaper of policy and a credible participant in public as well as private decision making. Lord Weinstock of GEC recognizes this only too well in his appointments of successive chairmen.
(2) the trustee/non-executive director who has responsibility for giving outside perspective and skills to the boardroom will more and more be needed.
(3) the scenario planner. A new breed of cat will be needed who takes future uncertainty for granted and builds that into the planning process and tries to identify what information is relevant for adaptation and flexibility.

Other talents in demand will be:

(4) a manager of conservation and contraction, for example on energy costs, as Marks and Spencer have shown particularly in the personnel area, helping employees find other work, formal/informal, full/part-time and retraining as well as reforming the trade unions.
(5) the entrepreneur, the skills for whom are innovation and action learning. Managers will quite simply have to re-invent their tasks, responsibilities and functions, re-define their parameters and goals (possibly with the help of employees and outside stakeholders) within the new technology and its political perspectives.

For example, if authority is replaced by consensus, and hierarchy by task forces, the manager will have to combine social with material knowledge. Learning political and consultative skills will be crucial. Shared values and better communications will result in greater operational effectiveness. 'Leadership is a priceless gift that you earn from the people who work for you – and have to earn the right to that gift and continuously re-earn that right', said Sir John Harvey-Jones, Chairman of ICI.

The chief executive's commitments, workstyles, rewards, personality, even ideologies, as well as the experience/education mix, will alter dramatically. It isn't for us to prescribe what this will be but some points are apparent. Chief executives are likely to spend more time in person-to-person interaction. They will become more comfortable with multivalue, uncertain social situations, as well as paying more attention to international affairs and political/social issues. We should not forget in all this that economic performance remains. Discipline and selectivity is needed in setting goals, and the creation of efficiency in the marshalling of resources. Quick response to the signals of the marketplace are important. Another conceptual cut at the qualities required of senior managers is McKinsey's 7–S model, mentioned in an earlier chapter, which has the added advantage of distinguishing between leaders and managers.

Worked in harmony, McKinsey says the 7–S's are the point where leaders, not managers, manipulate to effect organizational change and superior performance.

The implications of these are manifold. Some managers cannot ever achieve 7–S performance. Society produces far fewer leaders than managers and the socialization process which cultivates the latter reinforces tradition, the opposite of what is required. The art of Japanese management of course utilizes the hard and soft levers in harmony. The British educational system is slow to change, and marketing and communications are new subjects, unlikely to help for some time. In the U.S. too the predominantly short-term orientation of management could preclude its total adoption.

According to Abraham Zaleznisk, the leader has a broad focus on multiple elements of the 7 keys while the manager's attention is limited to the small set of organizational factors. At no time are leaders more necessary than today, yet we've evolved a rare breed called the manager and a cult of collective leadership. It may ensure competence, control and balance of power, but not necessarily imagination, spirit and creativity.

Without this imaginative capacity and the ability to communicate, managers, driven by their narrow designs, perpetuate group conflicts instead of reforming them into broader goals. Maybe what it takes to ensure the supply of great leaders inhibits the development of great leaders. Ironically our technologically orientated and economically rich society has tended to deprecate the need for great leaders on the grounds that rationality is god.

Managers tend to be rational and impersonal while leaders are more likely to be artists, shaping ideas and projecting them into images that excite people.

In *The Varieties of Religious Experience* William Jones describes the 'once born' and 'twice born' personality type (not to be confused with born again). The former group have had an easy time adjusting to life, the latter are marked by a continual struggle, a profound separateness. Leaders are of the second type, attempting always to bring about change. It is said that for gifted individuals to flourish they need an intuitive mentor who can cultivate latent talent. This has obvious implications for organizational structures in the development of leaders. The myth is that people learn best from their peers, which leads to cliques and rivalry. The mentor relationship acquaints the junior with power and the vital antidote to the power disease called hubris – performance and integrity. We are constantly surprised at the frequency with which CEOs feel threatened by open challenges to their ideas, comparing it to an open challenge to their authority.

To confront is to tolerate aggressive interchange. It also has the effect of sweeping away the veils of ambiguity and signalling the characteristics of managerial cultures. It also encourages the emotional relationship leaders need to survive. With the changing business structure and systems of corporations, leaders are likely to be more at home than managers. Leaders work in, but never belong to, organizations. The choice is there – mediocre performance, bureaucratic structures and ponderous decision-making systems, or motivation and high performance. There is evidence that some managers could acquire the requisite skills, developed consciously and applied systematically. Conversely leaders can focus more on the hard elements, thus achieving balance. This, as we have seen in Japan, leads to excellent performance.

What is needed is a management-leadership plan to parallel the corporate plan. The way to create a mould is quite obviously to bring in strong leaders such as Sir Michael Edwardes at British Leyland, Lee Iacocca at Chrysler ('Have a strong ego, never a large one'), and John Harvey-Jones at ICI. This is easier said than done however. Leadership can only be assessed in the context of each stage in a company's evolution.

As the seed of a new corporate venture germinates, it needs a champion to fight for and defend the seedling business. The champion must obviously have a wide range of management skills. 3M has an excellent innovation record based on a policy of appointing champions.

In the growth phase the task commander is needed to drive people and sense market opportunities. Such a manager needs a strong supporting team. A mature firm, however, needs the skills of the housekeeper to maintain order and manage the business economically. Who can impose discipline on a large structured organization with flair and adaptability. A business in decline needs a lemon-squeezer who is tough and innovative. Finding and fitting the manager-leader best suited to each situation is delicate. Most managers are of one type or another. It is important to recognize that appropriate management is a part of the strategic process like appropriate technology. This may mean an engineering dominated firm hiring less engineers and more English majors. The future will mean less prominence for accountants, as every executive will need to be fluent in the language of finance as I.T. transforms the situation.

In *The Awakening Giant, Continuity and Change in ICI*, a book by Andrew Pettigrew, published in the 1970s Millbank House was described as Millstone House.

Until John Harvey-Jones became Chairman, raising the pain level and concentrating minds on the need for change, there was decision by default, natural cloning, gamesmanship and endless paper-chasing. The company culture valued stability and continuity but Harvey-Jones recognized that in the harsher trading environment of the early 1980s it had not just sprung a leak it might sink. The reasons were the over-technical bias, too few people with entrepreneurial flair, and above all an inward-looking mentality that seemed to be impervious to outside advice.

The executive team now comprises a small team of directors united in their concern for strategic decision making rather than divided by functional, territorial and product loyalties.

As a recent U.K. Department of Employment survey of boards of directors points out, most board meetings are like a dinner party where real consensus is unlikely because of peer group insecurities, misinformation and lack of clear facts. The board, like the organization and practices of the company, may even prevent the Montgomery principles or ten Pillars of Leadership (as Robert Heller calls them in his *The Business of Success*) from working through to the point of true effectiveness. Since boards are supposed to set the strategic direction of the company, it's amazing that, according to the survey, the incidence of meetings is so variable. In practice too, members spend far more time discussing cash flow, trading position and profits than future planning, R & D, major external issues and the cohesion of the company. The defect is glaring. In the U.S. attaining the board is a rare prize, but it is often a disappointment when you get there.

Analogies between the conduct of war and that of business should be handled with care, but Montgomery's famous speech of only a few hundred words to his officers/executives struck every note of effective arrangement, every chord for turning group potential into successful achievement. It is too well known for us to quote here.

Robert Heller cites his ten principles the 'Superboss' must apply as:

- i Trust is a two-way process
- ii Team work
- iii Atmosphere
- iv The chances of effective collaboration depend on the climate – the culture
- v Objectives of the organization must be sharply defined
- vi The aim must be communicated to everyone . . .
- vii . . . With the self-confidence of the speaker
- viii Total emphasis is on performance
- ix It is vital to tender discipline with humanity – the touch and attitude which communicate caring
- x Aggression of the controlled type focussed on the competitor.

The fact that in war generals have clearer objectives than peacetime management is no pretext for those who have pursued mergers into all manner of unrelated activities, rather than (as the Japanese did) consolidating and improving their positions in their base business. In the 1980s the mergers are still coming thick and fast despite the overwhelming historical evidence that so many acquisitions made little sense and too frequently didn't work. While this was getting under way in Europe, American companies now in the thick of a new merger boom themselves, were selling off divisions at the rate of 12 billion dollars a year – literally demerging.

The sad tale of British Leyland tells a lot, not just about mergers but managing. So does the success of BL (and BTR) where for instance there is a basic principle of conducting all labour negotiations at plant level. Centralizing what doesn't need to be centralized is an error.

A second principle is that if a business is bad, bought or not, you move the bad managers. Citroen did this successfully after the takeover by Peugeot. Extreme care, however, must be taken not to disturb or undermine the existing cultures of the good parts. The man at the centre must at all times show as much concern for the internal cohesion and success of the division as for the group. What is good for the subordinate activity will more often than not be good for the whole, but the reverse may well be bad for everybody.

There is some positive evidence cited by Daniel Goldberg of Harvard, that instead of having precise goals, successful senior executives have general overriding concerns. In addition to depending on their ability to analyze, they also rely heavily on a mix of intuition and disciplined analysis in the decision making process and incorporate their action into their diagnoses of it. The higher you go in a company the more important it is to combine intuition and rationality, all the while thinking and seeing problems as interrelated. It's significant that so few of the senior executives we talked to saw it that way. As Descartes once said, 'It is not enough to have a good mind. The main thing is to use it well'.

The difference between the simple manager and the real leader is that leaders create energy by instilling purpose in others. Western business has insufficient leaders and if there were more we could do with less managers. Our civilization, like our corporations, were built on leadership. Today it is not the norm for individuals to perceive higher purpose in their work. More people would like to be motivated but they're not. The ultimate need of our business society is to exact exceptional performance from average people. The 'success revolution' must be predicated on the creation of real leadership if it is to succeed.

The leadership of the institutions of free enterprise have a sacred responsibility to make a correlation between the effectiveness of their organizations and the demands of the human soul. The word capitalism evokes in the mind pictures of imperialism, selfishness, inequality and exploitation. At best it evokes the ultimate in materialism. The problem is that for so long business has appealed so little to the human spirit. Making money is superficially rewarding but it doesn't touch the emotions. It is business achievement alone that transcends national boundaries, pays for and demands mass education, helps to eradicate poverty. Perhaps the first priority of business leadership is to raise the morale of business by mediating on its role in helping to achieve society's collective purpose.

In an age of change this would be difficult enough even if the man in the centre had all the requisite skills. Executive search consultants are hopping in and out of jets in a global search for top managerial talent that can fulfil these demands. Getting the best available man or woman is critical to corporate survival. Few can be found from within companies for reasons already outlined. Recession has put paid to the names of many aspirants to the executive suite. Failure can destroy able managers or make them wrecks of their former selves. Leaders need a certain type of motivation, a driven evangelism. If destroyed by an economy-based failure, it may not survive. Companies are no longer willing to gamble on potential. They are wary of bright young MBAs. The demand now is for performance in a larger number of areas – the areas discussed in this chapter.

In the past a favoured candidate would be someone home grown, with good financial skills, capable of maintaining tight controls over costs. Now they're looking for generalists, who know the industry as well as the company, and who have shown turnround skills in other sectors. Yet still there is a trend, certainly within the U.S., to appoint uncharismatic financial officers. This compounds the loyalty and motivation problems, particularly in the absence of a strong culture of the type found in say IBM (they are also lucky in having had strong leaders). There are a number of buttons the CEO (chief elevator operator) needs to push to make it work – guessability, quick internal communications, listening ability and a channel for expressing dissent. Without them the boss's expectations may get stuck between floors.

A keyword is change. The market for refrigerators took thirty years to mature. For the newer appliances such as microwave ovens and dishwashers about ten years is the norm. Most electronic products are less than five years old and the majority of high-tech products will be old in the next five haven't even been invented. The product life-cycle of a piece of normal office software is now 9–10 months. Cut-throat price competition in mature industries has reached down to the younger newer ones. Price cutting now starts on a product line when it is only one or two years old. The man in the centre must take rapid decisions or be sunk without trace.

Fortune surveyed a number of chief executives who have helped their companies return good profits in turbulent times. The executives themselves believe new skills must include:

- An ability to plan new products and be ready to bring them to market quickly
- close contact with customers
- staying close to the competition
- an ability to move fast
- and that means learn fast

There is a risk that generational stasis will set in with senior management passing down the same stagnant pond of knowledge within a self-perpetuating oligarchy.

There are, however, some grounds for optimism. In the same way that external pressures are forcing management to rethink its roles and parameters, so too are the changing values of junior managers soon to exert even more pressure for a total reconceptualization.

The generation gap is nothing new in families and society, it grows wider as each set of siblings matures earlier and gazes more strongly away from the home for its entertainment and its opinions on the world. What is emerging in an unusual form now is the fact that it has become an issue in the classrooms of business schools, and through them is creating a pent-up potential for disruption in the corporation.

There is an age group of managers now joining the ranks of senior executives whose liberal outlook puts them philosophically at odds with their superiors and subordinates. Older managers find these colleagues hard to understand and communicate with. They are apparently softer in their approach to profits, more socially orientated and less concerned by hard economic facts of life. They are less motivated by normal company goals. More significantly these new middle managers find the 'old guard narrow, cramped in outlook and enemies of change'.

There is no doubt that there is a progression to a people- and society-orientated style of management, but it is slow to come about.

This is chiefly because of the resistance of senior managers to let go of the reins and release their power over the educational system, through their seats on boards of governors and access to levers of power, and do something about an institutional system that divides the development of our youth into either the culture of science or of the arts. We are building obsolescence into careers in the new environment. More CEOs and senior managers should probably retire at fifty or fifty-five to pursue a less demanding activity like running a gourmet restaurant in the South of France, or less demanding still, secondment to government. 'Repotting' should be the order of the day. Oddly at AT & T, the new blood appears not to want to be led, nor do they want to lead either, compared with the same intake in the 1950s. They just aren't interested in advancing up the corporate ladder. They are less motivated and less optimistic.

As we have said earlier, there is a third generation arising. The graduates of the oil crisis, the recession and the age of electronic hardware. They are in their twenties and moving into middle management. They are technology- and task-orientated, tough, aggressive and goal driven. As we asked in an earlier chapter, will the soft, people-orientated group be sandwiched between the 'old guard' and the 'new conservatives'? Will the traditional, stern, father–rebellious son balance be upset? Oversimplified or not, more research needs to be undertaken. Maybe the result will be a blend. The question is will it be the right blend for the next decade or will they, like their current 'elders and betters' be equally out of date as they assume more power?

A special *Business Week* poll in July 1984 showed how the 'baby-boomers' are pushing for power, at least in North America. It is undermining traditional corporate structures and reshaping the marketplace. These 25–35-year-olds' values are a mixture of liberal and conservatives. They are right wing on economic policy and single mindedness, left wing on social and military issues – hence the ambiguity in attitudes by the young towards Reagan and Thatcher.

This new power is already hitting the labour markets and the corporations. The huge number of well-educated people in their twenties and thirties scrambling for a limited number of jobs is igniting fiery competition within the 'boom generation'. It is intensified by the dramatic flight of women from kitchen to office.

Nearly 70% of women from age 25–35 now work, double the rate of a quarter of a century ago.

Corporate managers in their fifties and beyond are coming face to face with demanding, upwardly mobile staff in their twenties and thirties. In some instances the young turks are taking control and introducing change. In others, senior management are questioning how far they should go in accommodating these alien demands.

The emerging conflict is not merely about numbers but new values, values which are reshaping corporate cultures and what many see as a 'greening' of management. But squeezed from both sides and bumping up against the top, many élite boomers are opting out of mainstream corporate America and heading for high-tech and more personal human interests. Many are setting up in competition within the groundswell of the small business movement. This new generation is more committed to its profession or personal skill than to a particular company, and to them hierarchy is the enemy. The shortfall expectation is nowhere more apparent than in industries undergoing technological or regulatory change and where the need for new skills is highest. Their ability to use computers is giving them significant advantage over older managers. The challenge the survey asserts is to create islands within the organization where the creative spirit can flourish or even create new hybrid organizations.

But because most of the current generation of senior managers are white and male, tend to run away from computers and are less entrepreneurial, a clash is inevitable. Unless of course they rise to the challenge and change they will go under, but in doing so can bring down the company with them. Many CEOs are rationalizing this situation by blaming the MBA ethos that nurtures expectations of power, mobility and cash that can't be met. Many CEOs interviewed in the survey thought they were spoiled as a group, having swallowed all the media hype about themselves.

There is now doubt, however, that business schools have much to answer for, and much of corporate America and Europe is questioning their relevance. Harold Leavitt, the conscience and scourge of these schools blames the professors and the MBA mania for the current malaise. Sixty per cent of top British companies still deliberately choose not to recruit business graduates and almost never to sponsor their studies (this is probably equally wrong). In Europe a recent Harbridge House Survey showed MBA graduates were perceived to be financially greedy, misfits, constantly on the move, too Americanized, over theoretical and altogether not too masterly. In the U.S. the catalogue of woe extends to overreliance on quantitative analysis, obsession with short-term corporate performance to the detriment of long-term strategy, neglect of the practical techniques needed to implement decisions, and inability to think entrepreneurially, ignorance of technologies, the international business environment, and above all an almost complete absence of 'leadership-skills'. This is because both they and the professors who develop the programmes do not reflect many of the attitudes and standards of the world around them. They rarely talk to each other about these external needs and fail to grasp the emerging realities. The paradigm revolution is growing and transforming society, not like a hurricane, but through deep cracks in the earth's foundation yet it may be paving the business schools by.

A new debate is emerging, probably too late for the current crop of senior management. It is a debate as to whether it is actually possible to teach the practical processes of management as distinct from the intellectual concepts of business analysis and decision taking. The *Harvard Business Review* has suggested that business school research should be made more practical. Stanford, one of the overly quantitative schools, has belatedly introduced courses in several aspects of implementation, as well as on such qualitative and soft themes as 'power aspects of management', 'excellence' and 'creativity'. Wharton School at least now insists that the Professor of English tests all MBA graduates for literacy before they pass. Good for them.

Having led the way with courses in the management of production, Harvard has also appointed professors in leadership, entrepreneurship, government relations, ethos and social responsibility. Manchester is embracing many of the attributes of non-academic 'action learning'. The Ashridge and Sundridge Park management centres are also advocating 'life long' learning programmes in place of the one-shot MBA approach. The business demands of the 1980s go far beyond changes in curricula, they include changes in attitude.

Having said all this we cannot blame business education for all the ills of our economic society. The Henley School of Management argues vociferously that industrial weakness in U.S. and British business must not be correlated with the existence of business schools. After all Japan and West Germany have none. Henley and

London Business School say the problem resides deep in recesses within the whole educational system. In Germany and Japan an enormous effort is made to prepare people for entry into business. They leave the postgraduate level to in-house company training programmes. Undergraduate level courses need to be far wider to accommodate the more horizontal skills now required of the man in the centre. Instead of settling on one set of skills which will be obsolete in a few years, children should be taught how to think and to rationalize. Certainly in Britain a recurring theme is the long anti-intellectual tradition which devalues education and training, particularly in the commercial sector – hence the 'gentlemen versus players' snigger.

Quite obviously there are exceptions to this, such as the Masters course in business at the Polytechnic of Central London and at Cranfield which lay enormous emphasis on management change. To conclude, however, the growing number of business studies courses all point to a much needed innovative blending of knowledge and skill designed as components that can be injected into managers mid-career. Generalistic pre-career programmes are needed to prepare the ground for a vastly different type of business environment over the next decade. The forces of social change demand a shift in the managerial agenda. This is reflected in the new products being developed by management consultants – the 'Excellence' programme – being the most widespread. Social change and corporate strategy are interlinked. This is the prime responsibility of the new generation of senior management. Whether academe chooses to ignore or provide guidance is up to them. The signs are that it is, but is management sufficiently ready to provide the leadership to develop strategies that integrate 'corporate culture' and 'environmental' questions? It can of course be argued that a company's success is determined more by the organization than by the personality of the CEO, although the smaller the operations and the more family dominated, the less likely this is to be so. But failure to take into account the personality of the individual who has the power to develop and implement strategies will leave the horse at the starting post. Indeed the human motivation factors must be built into this strategy for change.

In Search of Excellence and all the programmes it has spawned, and the new European version – *The Winning Streak* – state the stunningly obvious. But it needed stating – that leaders must be visible, articulate act and be seen to act (sometimes by the simple expedient of walking around the office and plant), stay close to the customers, create an environment of entrepreneurial and perpetual motion, provide a clear mission and act it out in word and deed, making sure by commitment to staff that *they* do too. Leadership is about belief and an obsession with corporate mission.

If corporate managers are to lead our economies to a new high ground by regaining lost markets and re-establishing the competitive edge, they are going to have to face a tough obstacle course – they need to undertake for themselves a crash course in effective communication. Research shows that what employees think of top management in their organizations has a more powerful influence on productivity and profit than any other factor.

'Renaissance man' calls to mind a person of broad intellectual interests encompassing a full spectrum of available knowledge and wisdom. True, the Renaissance represented a time of renewal for the human spirit, till now unique in history. Industry and commerce, indeed society is yearning for this new dawn. Such a renaissance of corporate leadership must be solidly based on a high plain of principles of modern communication. The corporate leaders we seek to develop today are a tiny minority, less than 1 per cent of the workforce. What then are the artisan, intellectual and emotional qualities that make up this leader? Communication is the thread. It is one pathway out of the crisis. Top management is the focal point for the effort. There is a sixth sense not learned in business school, or majors in linguistics, sociology or even divinity that some corporate management possess, a combination of good instincts and a keen sensitivity as to what works. Good communications per se cannot solve every problem. But in a changing world the most brilliantly effective communication if it is about some outdated shibboleth will still avail nothing. What is more vital than how (although the how becoming more complex) is what.

However it's the why that in many instances still has not been learned. Business schools don't teach enough on motivation and people skills, and senior management tends to put minimum value on intuition and the feel of the business, this aggravates an already alien stakeholder, the employees, and also pressure groups, such as the Church, the politicians and particularly the media. Business has fallen prey to the same stultifying force of bureaucratization that makes government ponderous, unresponsive and – you've guessed it – paralyzed. True it's the so-called soft subjects that are the toughest to teach and to learn. When push comes to shove, soft subjects are often interdisciplinary, requiring interfaculty co-operation and links between academea and outside institutions. They require visionary leadership. The myth that a study of history and literature is the idle acquisition of social polish rather than a necessary means of increasing mutual understanding unfortunately pervades the whole business culture. We need to break the circle of the quantitative, elitist insistence on 'relevance' via a working partnership of enlightened educators, visionary business leaders, scientists, artists and politicians.

Carl Sagan in his *Dragon of Eden* wrote of the remarkably gifted multidisciplinary scientists and scholars, and the contribution they made. These polymaths are more than ever needed today to develop broad and powerful thinking. Business education should have as its goal the nurturing of the polymath. Business and higher education will have to work together as a single team if this is to succeed. Yet how can they do this when governments which control education are locked into an agenda that finds little time to concentrate on the training and education of products for the life-blood of our economy, i.e. industry and commerce.

Part of the price business leaders, whose style is secretive and close-fisted, must pay if they are to unleash their potential power is the psychological pain inherent on changing their behaviour. There are no short cuts, and 'we are already doing this' is no retort. It is usually a lie or a half truth based on indifference or nationalization.

The renaissance does not begin within the giant multinational corporation alone. It begins with the individual in the community, moves towards new frontiers, and forges new linkages. The CEO has to make the necessary connections.

The complication is that there will be great changes in the commitments and work styles of senior managers, the rewards they seek, the personalities they develop, and the ideologies to which they subscribe. They will be much more comfortable with uncertainty and multivalue situations. They will spend more time on person-to-person interaction. They will also spend more time on trends in national and international affairs and they will need a highly specialized staff to help them.

It's partly about new skills, it's partly perspective and emphasis. A cautioning note however: there is no single prototype to train but rather a diverse family of leaders and supporters. Forecasting is a seductive business and it is easy to overestimate the transformations and to underestimate the ability of management to deal with them.

Being CEO is still one of the toughest assignments. The greatest challenge to executive ingenuity is for the CEO to become a catalyst of an intellectual revolution which breaks out of the current paradigm paralysis. Above all, the corporation will survive or die depending on the ability of management to be polymaths with so-called 'high-touch' skills. A more multifaceted, interdisciplinary, approach by CEOs and senior management could make corporations innovative and flexible enough to emerge, if not unscathed, then intact. To achieve the paradigm shift will require on the part of the man in the centre not just an understanding of these trends but an ability to build them into the individual corporation's approach to the apparent contradictions between business self-interest, wealth creation and community well being. 'Our worst enemies are not bad men, but ill-informed ideas about the framework in which conflicting goals can be reconciled' (Anon).

The CEO still needs to keep a close eye on the basic function of perpetuating the organization, making profits and building for the future. But his perspective must be broadened and he must be more creative, more marketing- and people-orientated. He must be entrepreneur and intrapreneur. The CEO and the senior managers are the residents in the chair of leadership. Changing a corporation's direction is predicated on leadership. Recognition of the need to communicate ought to be written into the job specification of every senior manager.

We are now entering the post industrial society. Whatever name we use it will require a new set of management priorities and practices. The relationship between employees, organizations and their managers will be remade. It will require a new ethos, unifying wealth creation and the interests of the individual with the institution. Material and spiritual will be integrated. It is a noble contribution. It rests on the CEO's shoulders whether the living organism called the corporation moves from adolescence to maturity.

6

Corporate de-schooling

'Essentially we feel that success and making money are vulgar. We don't encourage the education or development of managers who are somehow regarded as a lesser breed.'

David Puttnam, British Film Producer

When Disraeli said in the nineteenth century that 'on the education of the people depends the fate of the people' he was voicing less of a truism than if he were saying the same thing today. At that time, as we have commented earlier, there were many other factors upon which Britain's economic strength and the wealth of its people depended. The rigid class structure and the 'old boys' network' ensured success rather than merit or individual capability ever could. There were exceptions of course, and Disraeli was one of them. A society could not be that ossified if it allowed the son of a poor Jewish man of letters to become the most senior representative of a snobbish and rigidly structured society.

Today, as we move into the new technological revolution which parallels Disraeli's industrial expansion, the need for sound intellectual strength at every level of society is all too obvious, not only in Britain, but in Europe generally. Leadership is important as we have shown in Chapter 5, but leaders need to have people to lead. Leaders may be at the very apex of the corporate system, yet their power is not dependent solely on platoons of well-skilled management technicians who will put their ideas into action. The concept of Aldous Huxley's *Brave New World* which divided us into leaders and led went out almost as fast as Marx's own out-dated diagnosis.

Some companies can and do grow under the power-house leadership of a Dick Giordano or Pier Gyllenhammer, Lord Hanson, Tony O'Reilly or Owen Green. They are few far between, and for every successful company that has risen to overpowering strength and influence there are thousands which have been strewn over the entrance to the bankruptcy court. More likely they peaked at an optimum size which satisfied the Peter Principle of performing at least one rung below the maximum level of incompetence.

It would be fair to say that 99% of successful companies have arrived at their position in the marketplace by a process of continuing dialogue between leaders, board and management committees, department heads, unit heads, middle management, junior management and trainees. This interactive element of corporate culture requires a level of intellectual excellence at every level, not just the facility to absorb vast numbers of facts. The observation that an effective company marches on its secretarial feet is not quite such an exaggeration as may at first seem. Secretarial excellence nowadays should embrace administrative skills of the highest order together with an ability to bridge the gap between high technology needs and high technology implementation – office automation is now in the hands of secretaries. Transforming a management concept into reality can frequently be impeded at secretarial level. Intellectual and knowledge-based skills should permeate every part of the corporate structure.

But, have we yet come to terms with the importance of the educational element in producing these necessary skills? The Japanese certainly have with their educational conveyor-belt which takes the child from pre-nursery through to post-university education. America produces a higher proportion of well-rounded graduates than any European country because the system isn't fraught with class bias and degrees of specialization which make the European system very rigid and out of kilter with the needs of business. At this point teachers and university lecturers will be nodding their heads in agreement as they mouth 'I told you so', thinking no doubt of the last time their particular union tried to persuade a government of limited resources or will to put more money into a particular part of the education system.

Yet why should European governments put more money into a system that will merely perpetuate an unsatisfactory status quo? Europe has a secondary school system that has not yet come to terms with the need to raise standards, teach pupils basic skills, and use modern communications technology to extend pupils to their individual limits. In France and Britain the education system is riddled with political disease. A large number of further education teachers in the U.K. do not even believe we need to produce standards of excellence. They consider the capitalist system should be brought to its knees in favour of an idealistic dream of society. A society in which the poor no longer have to fight for a living but can sit around enjoying poetry, art, music and a little gentle philosophy.

The reality of the situation is worse than this. In what is laughingly called a 'child-centred' philosophy of education, this school of British educational thought is still adamantly opposed to shaping children for the real world outside. It considers a child should grow into a 'whole personality', 'happy within himself' and 'able to come to terms with life'. It may be argued that this is a blueprint for the creation of a population that will be unable to pay for the artistic endeavour that such a rational hope would inspire. This would be even more true when the standard of living has fallen, because of economic incompetence, to that of a third-world country. Competitive endeavour is not an element we can afford to dispense with in a tough marketplace where the rest of the world is dedicated to a philosophy of commercial competition.

In the business environment we are faced with a situation that we ought to tackle at its roots. Too frequently, businessmen and the professional organizations representing them consider it is not right, or acceptable, to become involved in or attempt to influence the business and technical training which are relevant to their operations. The contact between academea and business is poor in Europe. Discussion is often between the argument of manpower requirements against scholarly pursuit. This is a false contrast. The skills of business are the skills of life. There is hardly a subject taught in the classroom that does not in some way help shape the views and decisions that ultimately the manager will be forced to take.

Unfortunately, classrooms do not teach an ability to cross-reference, to connect one subject to another in any imaginative and useful way. Understanding history, especially recent history, means understanding the purchasing influences – many passed on from parents to children – that for example, make the Newcastle housewife respond to an advertisement in a different way to that of a housewife from a similar socio-economic background living in

London's East End. A businessman in the Paris office of a multinational company will behave in a different way from his counterpart in Lyons, even though he must conform to a world-wide consistency in conducting his corporate affairs. History, geography, literature and language all influence facets of the manager's personality.

A degree course must start from what the entering student can be assumed to know already. There is a two-way interaction that is often forgotten. In England and Wales, for instance, education between 16 and 18 has been influenced by the wishes of universities to an extent quite unparalleled elsewhere; and the wishes of the universities have been that they want as much specialization as possible. It is questionable whether such courses are the right ones even for the brightest students. As we move down from the top universities through the range of higher education, such courses become less and less suited to the needs of the student. There are two reasons why this is bound to change. First, the British Government is pressing for a broadening of sixth form education and has made proposals to achieve this. They do not go very far, but none of their predecessors has had the courage to attack the problem at all.

Moreover, reforming sixth form education may prove to be like ski-jumping: the first step requires a considerable effort of will but subsequent progress is almost inevitable. In the long run, we hope to see all schoolchildren continue to study both some science and some of the humanities until they leave school; and to ensure that they take these seriously. Entry conditions to higher education should require a respectable performance across a wide range of subjects, as they do in most other advanced countries. Degree courses need to become less specialized, because the second influence for change will be pressure from potential employers and therefore from students. Outside pressures will be for more general degree courses, establishing a wider intellectual base on which graduates can build in a greater variety of ways.

What becomes then of the demands of the technology industries for more and more specialization? We submit that responding to this demand is not the role of degree courses. Skills that are needed now in, say, the electronics industry will need more people who can continue to acquire advanced technological skills as and when they are needed. Many such skills have not yet been invented. The old theory that education ceases when one enters the world of work is crumbling. The increasing importance of continuing education is becoming accepted, but not, we suspect, being acted upon except in the largest and most advanced corporations. There are a number of Foundations poorly funded, which aim to become international networks of academics and business people, designing a curricula for the training of professional generalists to counter the increasing diversiveness brought about by specialization and lack of communication between different groups in society.

There is no doubt that the confluence of social pressures which have led to new corporate strategies and changing corporate values has left most of the educational system totally out of touch with the educational and training needs of management. Chief Executive Officers need to develop a dialogue with university professors on curriculae to find the optimum balance between practice and theory. So far it's a dialogue of the deaf. Bradford has developed a course in Business and Society, which is a start. Philosophy, literature, the arts and social sciences in particular are relevant to the quest for survival that is usually couched in economic and technical terms. Peter Drucker has argued for a humanistic perspective that can integrate advanced professional and technical know-how into a broader awareness of experience and learning. The disciplines of accounting, engineering and traditional management do not provide a liberal arts foundation, and face the prospect of becoming irrelevant in the new environment of the 1980s. Business schools tend to have a built-in bias against change and fail to develop personal decision-making skills, nor do they teach a broader perspective on the corporate world and its environment. We need to challenge the sacred cows, avoid fractionalization and develop a more holistic approach. Inter-faculty rivalries must be obliterated.

Realization is dawning slowly within relevant opinion-forming groups that the whole education system is awry, not in terms of its organization, but in terms of content. Even the *Financial Times*, a newspaper not normally seen as the champion of educational reform, said in its leader of March 27, 1985: 'The protest by teachers who feel discouraged and underpaid is only a sympton of numerous deep-seated ills. What the 450,000 school staff have been trained to teach is in large measure out of line with the needs of children growing up to live in a society dependent on exploiting advanced technology. Curriculae concentrate on imparting knowledge about academic subjects to the neglect of developing pupils' practical understanding and skills. The minority of children with aptitude for, and interest in, subject learning are mostly led by the dominance of public examinations from an early age, usually in either numerate or literary studies but not both . . . often the main effect is evidently to give them a distaste for formal study which lasts for the rest of their lives'. The leader goes on to make the point that this is not some new flash of revelation on the road to a tougher market-oriented Damascus.

Back in 1976, British minister James Callaghan opened what he called his great debate on education, yet today, three education secretaries later, the same debate continues, and the same battle of the pay offer, strike and counter-strike obscures the real problems. A new generation of young people are ushered into new dead-end jobs. Untrained brilliant pupils clutching first-class degrees from Oxbridge colleges in subjects totally unrelated to business requirements are taken into graduate training schemes in the hope that they can be made fit enough intellectually to hold their own against the Harvard Business School products of U.S. companies or their equivalent from Japan.

This is no idle cry of wolf. The National Institute's *Economic Review* (No. 112, May 1985) took a look at German schools and tried to find out why they appeared to give a better foundation for work skills training than British schools. The main difference between the two countries was that there were far more vocationally trained people in Germany, not more graduates. By this they meant that whereas the British were quite good at educating the brighter end of the spectrum (we would dispute this as far as education for business was concerned) the Germans had come to terms with the need to raise standards of the middle to lower band of pupils, those whose abilities lay in directions which were not necessarily academic.

In Britain the comprehensive system was constructed according to a sort of sub-grammar school academic system. The Germans, however, have accepted that there are differences of aptitude among pupils and adhere to a selection system similar to that which began to be abolished in this country in the sixties. Only a minority of pupils in Germany attend academic schools. The rest pursue more practically-oriented courses in 'Realschulen', similar to Britain's old Technical Schools, or 'Hauptschulen', the German equivalent of Secondary Modern. What a turn of the circle from the late fifties to the early seventies.

The authors carried out a series of tests and saw that pupils at the end of their Hauptschule career were well ahead, in mathematics particularly, of a similar group of British pupils tested. In one amazing mathematical test, 66% of the German pupils, all taken from the bottom half of the academic-aptitude range, came up with the right answer, against only 4% of British children taken from a similar sample.

Their final point is that 'in the present day, when the scope for unskilled labour is so patently reduced by advances in automation, the need to raise the level of competence of those of average and of below-average academic ability has acquired an even greater urgency'. There is no wonder that we have the paradox of a massive unemployment problem at the same time as a Confederation of British Industry (CBI) survey in 1984 found that 12% of the firms surveyed expected skill shortages to limit their output in the months ahead. This applied particularly to the machine tool, textile and electronics industries. In a nutshell, we have a huge oversupply of unskilled labour – or labour with redundant skills – on one hand, and a major skill shortage on the other. When we move up the remuneration scale we find that the job market for management, professional and technical staff continues to be significantly more dynamic than the market as a whole.

This problem is deeply ingrained in the British class and social system, and was heavily argued over in the fifties and again in the early seventies. It needs the concentrated effort of government and the educational establishment to crack it. The *Financial Times*, in a leader in 1983, discussed the problem with great prescience.

> 'The development of practical skills and attitudes in the U.K. has long been hampered by the public image of technical and other work-directed training as suited only to young people not clever enough to succeed in academic education.
>
> The £950m which the Government is to spend on expanding its Youth Training Scheme in the coming year will do little to get rid of this unhelpful image. For it is taken as almost self-evident

throughout the country that entrants to the scheme will overwhelmingly be people who have ended formal education with few if any pass grades in the essentially academic school-leaving examinations.

It is beyond question that academic education of the rigorous kind which develops truly critical intellects is of great value to a society. But it is questionable whether it is wise for a society's future leadership and even middle-rank managers to spend the formative years between 5 and 21 concentrating on academic study to the virtual exclusion of tutoring in technical and other working abilities.

There is a strong case for the introduction in schools of a significant element of practical learning as part of the central curriculum to be pursued by all pupils from an early age.

Since pass grades in only five academic subjects at Ordinary level are required for university entrance, whereas pupils commonly study seven or eight to the age of 16, there seems no intrinsic reason why the substitution of a couple of practical studies should inhibit the intellectual development of children whose interests run in academic directions. Amongst those inclined in other ways, the possibility of gaining recognized success and developing their abilities by an alternative route of practical education could often stimulate them to pursue academic achievement as well.

A start towards the development of practical studies in schools is now being made by the British Government. The Manpower Services Commission is offering £7m in 1983–84 to local education authorities wishing to experiment with technical and vocational studies for children aged 14–18, with the last two years including experience in working organizations. The Government has found another £2m for projects of a similar kind. The combined sum of £9m represents only about 0.06 per cent of the U.K.'s total educational spending of nearly £14billion. But it is 100 per cent more than any of the Government's recent predecessors has done to promote the alternative route of study in schools.

The trouble is that the initiative is unlikely to bring about improved practical attitudes and skills in the children destined for senior positions in society. While the new courses promise some interest at school for the practically minded 14-year-old, otherwise consigned to at least two more years of watered-down scholarly study, the technical and vocational path will probably be largely ignored by pupils who are academically inclined.

The reason is that although the alternative route will lead to the qualifications of the City and Guilds of London Institute, the Royal Society of Arts and the like, those qualifications are not accepted by university admissions tutors. It is therefore clearly wiser for any child whose prime ambition is a university degree to continue concentrating on passing the academic Ordinary and Advanced level examinations.

If the Government wants to prevent its new practical courses from languishing along with their predecessors in the image of being a catch-all for dullards, it is not enough simply to find money. Ministers also need to press for the qualifications available through those courses to be accepted as the equivalent of Advanced level passes at least by the universities and polytechnics which were set up to emphasize the development of technical and other practical skills.'

However, there are other factors to be considered. *The Economist*, as always a great compromiser, said in an article on September 8, 1984: 'It is probably true that systematic vocational education and training programmes contribute to economic success. Only probably, because nobody has yet proved that cause and effect are as simple as some boasters claim. There are no doubt better training programmes for the banking and distribution industries in West Germany than in Britain, to little obvious effect. Britain needs many more programmes. Its work should be more skilled and adaptable. But these goals are not achieved by making training a fetish.' The trouble is, they say, 'the more the firms step into the breach . . . the more the state steps out, and vice versa . . . Britain needs a workforce prepared to change jobs and update skills as new technologies evolve. It must be self-confident enough to learn. The real objective is a well-educated labour force that *then* wants to be trained . . . this means more general education, earlier, not more technical training which they have not been educated to want or absorb. Stressing the virtues of general education over training is unpopular in metropolitan Britain, so low has the reputation of teachers fallen. Choosing education as the essence of a training policy would mean shaking Britain's education system to its roots. That is the only choice that will provide a demand for the quantity and quality of training that Britain needs.'

A practical example of this widening gulf between Britain's industrial needs and the supply of staff at all levels by its out-dated education system was highlighted in an article in the *Financial Times* on September 5, 1985 by David Fishlock, the FT's Science Editor. Discussing the reluctance of Britain's universities even to help meet the technical challenges from overseas companies, he quoted Professor Sir Peter Hirsch, an Oxford don who spent two years as Chairman of the U.K. Atomic Energy Authority. Sir Peter said that there was a great difference in attitudes. Dons, pressed for cash for research, paid lip-service to the promotions of science parks, which were in many cases cosmetic. Professor John Ashworth, a former chief scientist with the Cabinet office 'think-tank' and now Vice-chancellor of Salford University, said that there was too often little contact, 'never mind fruitful interaction', between companies which base themselves in university science parks and the associated universities and their lecturers. 'If the universities are going to build a better relationship . . . then they must expect to have to devote a significant amount of time and expensive staff effort to it.'

Salford, a small technological university, has been closer to industry than Oxbridge, yet we wonder which attracts the brightest pupils from schools, and in those black days after finals when everyone is hunting for the big jobs, which gets the more interviews. Thus, the brightest of our young people are accepted to ancient pillars of learning to study subjects which, although possibly making them civilized, leave them quite ignorant of the knowledge they really need to earn enough money to afford the type of civilized lifestyle their education has trained them to expect. Many do quite well by entering the City of London and working in merchant (or investment) banks, and by British standards they do appear to be well-off. By the standards of their American, Japanese or German counterparts they are almost paupers.

How can Britain hope to create the leadership described in the previous chapter when a university system exists that is proving so highly resistant to change? Fortunately, some institutions are recognizing that change must be initiated. Sir Henry Chilver, Vice-chancellor of Cranfield College of Technology, claims to have the highest contract research income of any university in the U.K., at around £10m–£12m. Cranfield, under his leadership, has been ruthless in closing flagging departments. 'Most universities', says Sir Henry, 'are not interested in closer ties. They pick failed academics as liaison officers'. There is another side to this, as David Fishlock points out in his article. One of the senior scientists at ICI's research centre in Runcorn is quoted as saying that he has no wish to see universities 'as a poor, cheap extension of ICI research'. However, he is almost alone in this view, and we must remember that, and he does, after all, have an axe to grind. Dr Ron Coleman, the government chemist in charge of Britain's national programme of investment in biotechnology, says he is disappointed with university response generally as far as this leading-edge sector of technology is concerned. Yet apparently the universities led the call for more government-backed research in this branch of science. When Dr Coleman managed to obtain substantial funds from the Government for research the universities failed to come up with ideas worth backing.

David Fishlock puts his finger on the root cause of this 'dialogue of the deaf' as he calls it, and it is a cause that we espouse in this book. There is a fundamental difference between the needs perceived by the academic world and the demands of business and industry, and it must somehow be bridged. Fishlock says: 'Academic scientists (or academics generally, perhaps) are narrowly, even selfishly, concerned with their own chosen problem . . . but industry's problems are multi-disciplinary – industrial research means projects and programmes pooling many different scientific skills in an effort to see that the problems are resolved systematically on the way to a well-defined objective. British universities, with their highly autonomous faculties, are simply not geared to undertake projects'. Neither, we suspect, are they able to merge and re-structure the disciplines they teach so that the students have the breadth of training they need to succeed in the outside world.

Having attacked the traditional universities for failing to break the mould in order to meet new challenges, it is only fair that we close this section by mentioning Oxford University's joint project, whereby the Clarendon Laboratory, engineering sciences and metallurgy departments are discussing the possible combination of their forces to facilitate the study of future generations of semi-conductor chips. This follows another major interdisciplinary project put together by Professor George Radda of the biochemistry department, whereby a team of 35 with funding of £2m, work in new laboratories to explore new techniques for diagnosing obscure illnesses.

Nor should we assume that all the faults are on one side. The consistent indifference, bordering on antagonism, of senior British managers towards the whole concept of business training, management degrees and MBAs would be amusing if it were not so dangerously misguided. What is it that makes businessmen think their trade is the only one you cannot study for? How can anyone assume that unlike lawyers, scientists, accountants and no doubt bankers, the one great employer of more than 50% of white collar workers, i.e. the line managers of manufacturing and service industries are the only profession who need no training? Worse than this is the belief that narrow on-the-job training is better for a line manager working in a department where immediate needs must be fulfilled than studying the general principles of business, testing them against case-studies, visiting a wide range of different companies and then being tested in these skills.

For some reason the post-graduate masters degree or MBA has come in for even more criticism. It may not be perfect; we would certainly like to see the majority of MBA courses in Britain linked more closely to commercial concerns (as technologists and scientists find so important in their particular fields of interest), but we also feel that the usual criticism voiced by businessmen about MBAs is misguided.

Businessmen have told us that MBA courses teach students strategy, and even then in theory only. The comment is made that MBAs become arrogant and that they think they can walk into any company and reorganize it from top to bottom. A young person with any guts at all would not think otherwise. Those who do not think like that should go into local government administration or become meticulous civil servants, but for the future of British industry we need such conceptual thinkers. It is up to the employer to hold the reins, to know that this is a lively filly who mustn't be given his head until his judgement has been tested. Somehow we must overcome the opposition of those who are scared of their own inability to think analytically or know they are faced with pressures for changes they cannot understand. Certainly there is a healthy demand for the shorter courses for experienced managers but generally European businesses are far more reluctant to recruit graduates from the longer post-gratuate courses than are businesses in the United States, whose MBA courses have been flourishing for the best part of a century.

The first U.S. Management School was founded, after all, over 104 years ago by Joseph Wharton at the University of Pennsylvania, and in 1911 it was followed by Harvard, Stanford and the Massachusetts Institute of Technology's Sloan School. Today, with more than 60,000 MBAs being turned out every year in the U.S., they are recruited as a matter of course by industry, and as a result the standards of analytical and systematized management are rising at great speed. Too many British and European businessmen try to laugh at U.S. management with its jargon, its emotional clarion cries, and mission-statements, but beneath all this top dressing, often donned by the second-raters to give an appearance of underlying intelligence, is a standard of management skill at middle-management level that makes most European managers look like amateurs.

There will not be an underlying change of attitude to business training in Europe until the top layer of seat-of-pants managers move over. The total output of around 3,000 MBAs a year in Europe will not be enough to shift opinions for some while yet. Recruitment agencies do not help matters, because they too are frequently staffed by the untrained and the failed manager. Thus they fail to lead, and normally respond to the prejudices of their clients. As one head-hunter, who shall be nameless, said to us: 'An MBA is wonderful if he comes from Harvard'. Even if the quality of the output from British and European schools is not as high as that from the leading U.S. schools, the difference does not justify this 'Harvard or nothing' attitude. Although Claude Rameau of INSEAD rightly stressed the need for greater emphasis on an international outlook in Europe.

Sometimes Germany is pinpointed as a country which is both economically successful and leans away from formalized management training as a part of discrete, structured degree courses. That view misses the point of German education. Financial analysis, personnel function and marketing is included in many conventional academic courses in specialized subjects like engineering. German students may well continue with their academic studies until they are 26 or 27, thus allowing them to build many extra subjects into the core curriculum. This merging of business studies into, for example, a technology degree, is interesting because it thus prevents precisely the production-led atmosphere permeating so many companies held up by an engineer or technically trained manager.

Dr Kees Krombeen, Philips' corporate director of management development at Eindhoven, says that 'it is not only MBA courses that produce arrogant graduates. I came from university with a doctorate degree in economics thinking I knew everything in the world. It took a couple of years in industry to teach me I knew very little'. Sir Christopher Hogg, chairman of Courtaulds and an MBA from Harvard, says that even there the leading staff go to great lengths to discourage arrogance. 'They tried to tell us that we'd come out jacks of all trades and master of none, that it would probably be years and years before we worked ourselves up to a job senior enough to look on business from the high perspective from which we'd been regarding it at the school. But that is a warning young people find difficult to take.'

There is a danger that by arguing the case for more business management training we can be accused of believing an MBA is a cure for all our ills. This is not the case. An MBA is only the basic foundation upon which we then have to build further skills, such as judgement and leadership. Dr Krombeen endorses this view when he says that 'to be a successful manager and not just a backroom specialist, one needs many qualities which are not intellectual but personal, such as leadership'. However, as Jean-Louis Masurel of Moet-Hennessy in Paris says, good managers can come from sources other than specialist business schools but 'the necessary commitment, competence and leadership is only sometimes found in MBAs . . . they usually have great ambition, which, although a disadvantage if it's excessive, is often beneficial'. M. Masurel also points out an extra dimension that often comes from business school and which fits into the general thesis of this book: 'Another advantage, especially, though not only to international companies like ours, is that if they have been to management school which teaches from a perspective different than the one of their own native country, they have generally acquired at least a second culture. To do that, they need not go outside their own land. At schools like

INSEAD, French students are exposed to other national cultures'.

Having argued the case for more attention to business training and a need for us to find ways to get the brightest and the best away from soft-option subjects like English literature, politics and philosophy at Oxbridge, perhaps now we should say 'so far, so good'. But how can we improve training and ensure a supply of managers capable of meeting the criteria we set out in the previous chapter?

Harold J. Leavitt, the in-house scourge of the U.S. business school system, is particularly critical. He argues that the Japanese are now running rings round the U.S. in terms of management and this must therefore be the fault of the great business school institutions. He is a professor of organizational behaviour and psychology at Stanford. According to Christopher Lorenz, writing in the Management page of the *Financial Times* (6–2–84), the catalogue of woe in the U.S. includes: 'over-reliance on quantitative analysis; obsession with short-term corporate performance to the detriment of long-term strategy; neglect of the practical skills needed to implement decisions especially in line management; bureaucratic mindedness and inability to think or act entrepreneurially; the almost complete absence of leadership skills; ignorance of technology, the international business environment, and many other factors'.

Apart from that, you might as well ask: 'How did you enjoy the course?' Obviously it is easy to draw up these lists which seem to dispute every argument we've put forward in this book. We consider that such lists probably justify our own view because their criticisms have been formulated by managers who have usually reached their current high office through exactly the type of anti-intellectualism with which they see any move towards rigorous academic training for management. It is their tendency to measure younger managers against their own experiences and prejudices which signifies the problems we are pinpointing. In the U.K. this view is seen as more pronounced than in the U.S.A. If the training of future managers and staff can be lined up with the next, as opposed to the past, ten years then we will be moving towards the conditions needed for the U.K. to meet its international competition. At least the competition in the U.S. still have some of these problems themselves.

However, it is in the nature of that country for change to occur quickly, and already we are seeing U.S. colleges taking on board these criticizms and meeting them head-on. Several institutions, says Christopher Lorenz, have already responded by introducing courses in various aspects of implementation as well as such qualitative themes as 'power aspects of management and creativity'. Lorenz says: 'Having led the way with the re-establishment of courses in the management of production, Harvard has also appointed Professors in several softer aspects of management, notably leadership, entrepreneurship, government relations, and ethics and social responsibility'. In the U.K. too, 'several schools are moving well away from U.S. practice; Manchester is embracing many of the attributes of non-academic "action learning", while Philip Sadler, principal of Ashridge, is advocating "life-long learning" programmes in place of the one-shot MBA approach'.

Christopher Lorenz's short report on Harold Leavitt's views is worth quoting in full because the debate on this subject must be seen in shades of grey, rather than in black and white. In this chapter we have tried to postulate the basic importance of a re-structuring and re-analysis of the total education system at curriculum level, and have argued for business management training as the *sine qua non* of entry into the business world. Having laid down these positions we can now consider what needs to be done in re-thinking business school training itself. For this reason we should examine Leavitt's own concerns, since he in many ways is taking forward the underlying tenets of this book. Leavitt, according to Christopher Lorenz, is softening the business school pre-occupation with hard sciences of quantification when he says:

> ' "Pathfinding", "problem-solving" and "implementation" are the three essential elements of management. Companies and business schools have been obsessed with problem-solving – the most analytical piece of the jigsaw – for most of this century, though they have at last begun to pay attention to the third.
>
> But pathfinding, which is one of the keys to Japan's industrial success, remains "the orphan of Western management and management education".
>
> This, in essence, is Professor Harold Leavitt's challenging critique of Anglo-Saxon management, and of American and British business schools. "We profess to be schools of management", he complains, "but what we actually are is just schools of

financial analysis and analytical problem-solving. We need to do much more".

Problem-solving ("analysis, thought and reason") still represents almost the entire effort of many business schools, according to Leavitt. He estimates that about four-fifths of the MBA curriculum in top American schools is concerned with it in one way or another.

Implementation ("acting, changing, doing") has attracted growing attention since the late 1970s in response to the clamour for business education to be made more relevant to practical issues in fields like production.

But pathfinding ("mission, innovation and vision") has been not only entirely neglected, he says, but actively fought by the problem-solvers and implementers.

Leavitt's trenchant view of Americans' shortcomings goes much further than most of the recent attacks on U.S. managers and business education. It not only focusses on the difficulties of linking the middle and last elements of his management "model", analysis and implementation, but also gets to grips with the widespread absence of pathfinding (in Leavitt's terminology this overlaps with part, though not all, of what others call "leadership").

Describing the role as "pro-active" rather than "reactive" (the nature of problem-solving), he likens it to the function of an architect in the construction process. Such people "don't try to forecast the future, they try to create it", he argues.

Leavitt distinguishes pathfinding from leadership. One form of leadership – often called "transactional" – is concerned with getting people to implement things. It is, he says, dealt with by social psychologists as a set of functions and processes, rather than as traits and attitudes. But another form of leadership – "transactional" – is one of the pathfinding skills.

But can this imprecise concept be taught, at a business school or anywhere else?

At a public presentation of his views in one of the London Business School's series of Stockton Lectures, Leavitt largely ducked the question. He has subsequently pointed to various developments in cognitive psychology as pointing the way forward, and is himself trying to teach it as part of his course at

> Stanford on "implementing change" – one of the most fashionable subjects in the U.S. at present, but which is usually taught in terms of processes rather than vision. Leavitt crystallizes the distinction by saying "I'm teaching people to listen to their guts – treat the subjectives as relevant data".'

In the same issue of the *Financial Times* (6–2–84) Lorenz puts a more temperate view based on views expressed in the Henley *Journal of General Management* (Winter 1983–84, No.2 Vol.9):

> Tom Kempner has had quite enough of the popular wisecrack that the industrial weakness of the U.S. and Britain is the fault of their business schools, whereas the strength of Japan and (until recently) West Germany results from the fortunate absence of these iniquitous institutions in the two countries.
>
> "British managers are not having the hell knocked out of them by amateurs, but by professionals", snaps Professor Kempner. This professionalism consists not just of a host of practical skills which have been learned on the job, but all the benefits of a business education – notably the ability to think rigorously about all the complexities of doing business today.
>
> The principal of Henley has not only ceased to be amused by the joke about Anglo-Saxon business schools, he also contests its basis is in fact. He agrees with Professor James Ball, his counterpart at the London Business School (LBS), that Germany and Japan "make an enormous educational effort in preparing people for entry into business". It's not just at undergraduate level, but is then followed up directly with internal company training programmes.
>
> In other words, the prime reason why business schools are so necessary in the U.S. and U.K. is that undergraduate education in business studies is so rare. One might well add a secondary fact, that in-company training also falls short.
>
> Professor Kempner argues that "given the length and thoroughness of German undergraduate degrees, it is not surprising that MBAs have not been needed". One of the most popular courses, Betriebswirtschaft (business economics) can last up to six years. Many engineering students also spend the final two years of their long six-year course studying business administration, stresses Professor John Stopford of LBS, who frequently teaches in Germany.

Countering widespread complaints that Anglo-Saxon business schools are too theoretical, Kempner points out that German undergraduate business education is internationally strong on theory.

It's a similar story in Japan, not only does a remarkably high proportion of the population go to university, but the management or "skill content" of the many in-company programmes attended by budding and rising Japanese managers "is similar to business courses in the West".

In Britain, by contrast, just a tiny proportion of school-leavers go on to further education, so "the solid foundations of substantial numbers of undergraduates and postgraduates is missing". Not only does Britain award only about 3,000 undergraduate business degrees a year at universities, polytechnics, technical colleges and elsewhere, but unlike the U.S. it then compounds the problem by sending only a few people to postgraduate business schools.

The current annual output of barely 1,000 full-time MBAs has hardly changed since the early days of British business education in 1970, the British total having actually fallen, with well over a third of the graduates now coming from abroad. The recent launch of part-time masters courses has restored the total, but Kempner fears that the quality of some of them may fall short; on the other hand, critics of business schools argue that they may prove more relevant to practising managers.

Faced with similar problems in undergraduate education, why have the U.S. and the U.K. gone such different ways in the postgraduate sector? Kempner attributes much of Britain's inertia towards full-time business education to its "long anti-intellectual tradition, which devalues education and training, particularly of a vocational kind" – hence his crack about amateurs and professionals.

Growth in the number of business school post-experience courses might have been expected to compensate, but they are too short, he complains.

Whatever the perceived shortcomings of the over-sold and technique-based MBA in America, Professor Kempner's article constitutes a strong case for more business education in Britain.'

This dire problem is being further aggravated by a new debate in Britain about whether the state should continue to give grants to 'B' schools. The significant point, however, is that this has not come from industry, always critical of the 'overly academic' approach to teaching but from the Trojan Horse of Professors Brian Griffith and Hugh Murray of City University Business School in London.

They assert that the state financed university system has proved 'fortunately ill-suited' to providing the high-level management education wanted by industry and commerce. In the increasingly competitive, de-regulated world economy they are failing to supply the sort of management education needed by companies.

By contrast Professor Peter Forrestor (Economic and Social Research Council), former head of Cranfield Business School in the U.K., says that state funding would help lead to a situation where an MBA becomes a necessary qualification for middle as well as senior management jobs. To achieve that aim the schools would need to produce far more British business graduates than the present 1,200 a year, of whom some 300 come from part-time courses. An annual output of about 10,000 would be needed merely to replace the less educated managers who retire each year, he claims. He suggests, we believe rightly, that the so far modest demand for MBAs by many British companies is that many of them do not have 'company cultures that are dynamic and challenge oriented'.

Another view put by some members of industry is that the 'B' schools for whatever reason – lack of contact with industry, interfaculty rivalry or excessive specialization – are not the total answer. Industry will increasingly have to grow their own. Some businessmen believe that the hype surrounding 'B' schools has led not only to arrogance and overly high expectation on the part of the students, but to a presumption that they are not decision makers, but intellectual civil servant types. These misconceptions can only be overcome if academics, politicians, civil servants and managers co-operate on shared solutions to the issues facing society.

There is no doubt, also, that the wave of the future may be for individual companies to sponsor colleges, as in the case of the International Management Institute in Geneva, which is supported by sixty 'associate' companies. A combination of government funding and private funding is probably the optimum. Either way we cannot do without these schools in the future if senior managers as well as aspirant senior managers are to keep up-to-date with their perennial student cards. They can't produce soul and intuition. They can produce motivation and rigorous conceptual thinking.

The need to crack this problem has been emphasized even more strongly than we have done here by the economist, Sir Charles Carter, who told the British Association in his Presidential address back in September 1982, that 'there was no doubt of the capacity of science to produce further marvels but there was doubt about the capacity of human beings to use wisely and well all the opportunities promised'. 'Britain', he said, 'has too few managers of breadth and toughness capable of managing progressive companies. What I mean is a readiness to face the facts of a firm's position, to analyze them in a careful and rigorous way, to hold on to a problem with tenacity until it is solved, to delay only when there is good reason for delay, to take the calculated risk of timely action on partial information rather than wait for the unattainable certainty'. Sir Charles listed four reasons for the problems of British industry:

- Too many teachers who had only taught all their lives.
- Industry which discriminates against those with breadth and toughness in favour of the company man who can be relied on not to subject his colleagues to the inconvenience of a new idea.
- Too high a ratio of large to small businesses.
- Poorly trained managers and an education system that instills the belief that we can 'muddle through'.

We have tried to argue in this chapter for a massive re-examination of the Western educational approach – particularly in Europe, drawing on all our U.K. experience – not necessarily with the object of driving the whole system towards one great commercial end. Indeed, we suspect that the wealth such a change would create would satisfy even the most hardened believer in the tenet of 'every pupil reaching his own fulfilment, not the needs of society'. But until we blow away outmoded attitudes, knock down our compartmentalization and learn to communicate across the specialization, we shall never succeed. We must first start at source, which is the education system.

The need could well mean a new Education Act in the U.K., more revolutionary than the 1944 version, so that with one massive stroke we could start to gear our children for the world they will move into rather than the one they came from. Perhaps we should finish with the words from the Bow Group (a Tory pressure group) memorandum 'Learning for change' published in 1984. 'Education should be a lifelong experience for all, as and when the opportunity arises, not a joy for the few and a trial for the young. Retraining at reasonable cost, social cost as well as economic cost, needs to be available at any stage of life, independent of the desires and needs of the current employer. A major shift in resources away from the 14–21 examination treadmill and from non-vocational education is required. Most of the basic skills needed over the next hundred years can be predicted with reasonable certainty, but many of the trades and professions cannot. Fundamental changes to the education system are necessary. Information technology makes these possible at economic cost. Encouragement and favourable publicity are more effective weapons of persuasion than coercion, but many actions at all levels are needed, if the inability of our education system to cope with changes is not to deny us the benefits which the new technology is bringing to other societies.'

The arguments then are laid out. A new type of leadership will be needed if corporations are to be prepared for the business environment of the next two decades. These new managers, however, will only appear if we re-structure our education systems to help produce them. Although we speak mainly of the British model there are implications in British experience for many other systems too. Commercial success can only go hand in hand with educational success. What is success in education? We would submit that it is a system which turns out products who are sufficiently well trained and developed to be able to reach fulfilment on their own terms within an environment that is able to provide it. One will not come without the other.

As Mark Twain said: 'Training is everything. The pearl was once a bitter almond. A cauliflower is nothing but a cabbage with a college education'.

7

The new boardroom constituency

> *'What matters is not merely that business maintains good relations with society, but that it understands others and is well understood in return. This responsibility is so vital that often only the CEO himself can carry it out.'*
>
> G. Wagner,
> Chairman, Royal Dutch Petroleum

In dealing with all his constituencies, the Chief Executive has had to search for common ground and gain a share of mind. Many senior managers still remain defensive or oblivious to the need for an understanding of wider horizons, preferring to leave the stage to politicians, trade unionists and newspaper proprietors. At least some CEOs have been goaded into responding to the growing acceptance by the public that businessmen are criminals, and profit is a dirty word. Management are learning to put their case more forcefully than they have and to apply the same targeting they would use for the marketing of their products. Patient explanation of the company's role in society does help to reconcile conflicting interests.

The failure of business to speak up for itself and tell the truth clearly has led the public to presume the prisoner guilty. The modern CEO therefore must articulate awareness of the key social issues and business must respond to them. This requires a shift to more 'open-cast' communication and an enlarging of what we now call the 'response repertoire', a menu of different methods for responding to situations as they affect the corporation.

Twenty years ago the CEO spent 60 per cent of his time running the business, 30 per cent on the golf course, and 10 per cent communicating. Communications often meant informing staff after the event rather than involving them before. Externally it meant saying 'no comment but don't quote me' to any journalist who called. Of course *they* never called them. Now the proportions have radically altered. With the experience of the 1970s when CEOs hid defensively behind the executive suite's barricades, some at least have now discovered that society has set a new agenda over which it has control, and that control is not always in the interests of business. At its most superficial level, society is now able to force businessmen to spend more time explaining their actions and finding solutions to wider problems than their own bottom line. All this at a time when profits are needed more than ever before.

In the current decade we have begun to see the full dimension of the quiet revolution unfolding in the executive suite. There does seem to be a growing perception that management, in addition to acting on behalf of shareholders and customers, is alive to the interests of employees and other stakeholders. As large corporations in particular become more persuasive in society this trend will intensify. The conventional balancing of corporate and societal interests through 'labour-management' confrontations and restrictive government regulations will be seen as wasteful and counter-productive.

Top management has generally become more proactive in articulating its message, although it has not become sufficiently widespread in its range of targets. Yet what is the message? At the heart of the understanding gap is a lack of understanding by the public and many company employees of the process of wealth creation. It is here that the CEO must put the record straight. It is the fault of the education system that managers are not skilled in the art of communication and that the rest of society has failed to comprehend the role of business. It thus frequently bites the hand that feeds it. In the early days of the industrial revolution, managers at best concentrated on defending business's traditional values. Now the stakes are higher. The debate in the media, in the conference hall and the universities is about our way of life. This is a challenge to management to change minds – to explain that life is not risk free and that it's about contribution as well as 'rights'. To expertise in finance, law, engineering and marketing must now be added psychology and politics. A new armoury of weapons and skills is needed by the CEO. He needs to be activist, outspoken, to lead, to motivate and to persuade, to set a high moral tone in fact. With increasing specialization too, it is important for the CEO to converse across disciplines, across technology and marketing, as well as across cultures. The biggest concern is not the doctrinaire enemy but the silent majority who lack clear and credible information and understanding. If information is power, to lack it is to be deprived. In the knowledge society where material standards are rising, information deprivation can be as dangerous as income shortage.

The CEO must even up the odds by supplying not just more information but more relevant information, targeted to key constituencies. If he doesn't adapt his company will die of starvation – shortage of relevant staff leads to a failure to win and hold business.

But changing gear from defensiveness to proactivity is not enough. Companies must move into an interactive mode. Executives need not just put their view and have their say, but must become involved in economic/social action. Using their resources of knowledge, people and capital they can inject ideas, help and experience into co-operative ventures working with other institutions – academea, government, financial institutions, self-help groups etc. to enrich their total society and the environment within which they operate. This could be a powerful aid not only to competitiveness but as a building block in a socially responsible business system. This is not do-goodism pie in the sky. It is a protection against damaging legislation and also could attempt a permanent repositioning of those political parties likely to hold power and use it against business. The so-called European technology gap exists because Europe is slow to change, has inflexible institutions, is not motivated for results, and above all has insufficient links and dialogues between business and government.

The private sector in America and in Japan has shown what can be done. Greater involvement on the part of managers can ensure that the various constituencies accept business as a valued partner. No longer can the manager hide behind the clichés of the Annual Report – 'This has been a difficult year due to circumstances beyond our control'. Were they really beyond control or was it really a failure to foresee problems because of unwillingness to get involved in the public arena and force changes on government or social pressure groups. Or maybe it was closer to home in the marketing area, revealing a lack of understanding of consumer needs, or just sheer neglect.

Roger B. Smith, CEO of General Motors, summed it up neatly when he said 'The modern top business executive is a quasi public figure, representing his or her company not only in the traditional marketplace where goods and services are sold, but also in a new marketplace of ideas where the forces that shape society are determined'. But he doesn't believe it is unrelated to the corporation's primary role. Strengthening GM's high-tech base and broadening business opportunities via joint ventures are long-term security indicators for employees. Smith sees a close connection between corporate social responsibility activities and the marketing of products, recognizing the positive contribution to sales a good corporate image can make. Effective two-way communications between management and employees is also essential to productivity and business expansion. GM is also committed to 'betterment of the community', hence their support for local community programmes. 'We believe that business activities must make social sense, just as social activities must make business sense,' he adds.

Sensitivity to external issues is a critical part of what Goldsmith and Clutterbuck call the winning streak in their book of that name. It is a significant component of leadership, integrity and market orientation. But, as they point out, this pre-supposes the company has a clear concept of its role in society, which in turn is predicated on knowing who and what it is – its corporate integrity – as Prof. Keith Macmillan from Henley Management College describes it. This means that external relations or public affairs cannot be delegated. It must have the commitment and involvement of the CEO. Without this understanding, reaction to external events is likely to be ad hoc and poorly controlled. Public affairs practice, in our view, is inescapably linked with the need to rethink the philosophical basis of the business function in the 1980s.

When a business's actions are challenged, managers have to reflect on the basic rationale for the corporation's existence, what it stands for, its values, its very identity and the stakeholders it serves (stakeholders implying a relationship of gain and loss, rights as well as duties).

Professor MacMillan in his inaugural lecture to his college – 'Contradictions – a re-examination of relationships between business self-interest, wealth creation and community well being', said 'When a business is accused of some anti-social behaviour who exactly is being accused? Who is the business? Is it the shareholders however defined, is it the employees however defined?' He believes corporate integrity requires that the CEO is selected inter alia on the basis of personal integrity and that the company communicates corporate values to the key stakeholders in a credible manner. If conditions apply it is then easier for there to be an absence of deceit and coercion in dealings with stakeholders. Few companies have ever stopped to think what their business ideology is, let alone sensitize themselves to the external environment. In many companies the response to governmental and pressure group pressures or unfriendly take-over bids is ad hoc. Worse still it usually means fighting a bush fire that is already raging. More often than not a company has failed to anticipate, and reaches for advice when it is in deep trouble. Its previous behaviour is less than publicly defensible and it hopes someone will know someone who can 'fix it'.

Recent American Management Association reports highlight a trend that shows how directors see themselves as not only responsible to shareholders but to employees and a wider constituency.

Peter Drucker, long-time student of the executive suite, wrote that in addition to allocating capital, appointing people to key positions, ensuring innovation and the adequacy of strategic plans, there is a fifth obligation: 'Finally, the board is responsible for making sure that a company has adequate policies for its key outside relationships . . . and then the board has to demand there are adequate performance standards in these areas against which a company's results can be measured.'

All business people are at fault for not portraying business as a social phenomenon as important to society as law, medicine or art. We should never accept the notion that businessmen are only concerned with their own interests. The connection between profit and society's well-being has to be made clearer. Wealth creation is the most socially responsible action a company takes, but it must be demonstrated.

A new management tool is 'social reporting', which attempts to quantify the firm's achievements beyond meeting consumer demands, to the maintenance and creation of jobs, wealth creation, and the creation of the material basis for social security and enhanced life style. Areas of focus could be wider opportunities for employees to participate in decision making, what to do about long-term unemployment, codes of conduct of transnational corporations in the developing countries (LDCs), changing aspirations of minority groups, regenerating communities like Detroit and Liverpool, or the role of business in South Africa.

With a few notable exceptions in the U.S., European companies are leading the world in the publication of social reports. Germany leads the way with 35. Obviously as with all disclosures there are risks attached, as corporate opponents use the information only to counter it. But it does serve as a stabilizer to management, and educates employees.

Obviously not all relations between a corporation and outside constituencies need be conflicting. Supportive rather than competitive relations could become the order of the day as government, labour, finance and the universities co-operate on specific projects with industry. This could aid European competitiveness. Business could take a lead here. After all, businessmen tend to last longer than politicians, although trade unionists, clerics and academics it is true, last longer than all of us. All the constituencies need to accept business as a valued partner for the health of society as a whole. But industry must take a lead in explaining itself and the discontinuities which sum up our age. As Sir David Nicolson, founder chairman of The American European Community Association puts it 'By the year 2000 we shall see a new structure evolve, a link between a European Business Round Table and the European Parliament.' The international Round Table of some twenty top European industrialists, whose expert pressure could halt Europe's declining competitiveness, has already set a good example.

It does not just mean ivory-tower philosophizing but practical common sense. For example when sponsoring a conference of security analysts it is better not to withhold information which will send the stock plummeting, or like Nestlé, during the U.S. church boycott of its products, underestimate the impact of its marketing practices in Africa; or like Union Carbide appearing to have no prior contingency public affairs plan for the CEO at the scene of the tragedy, with aggravating effects. Making ill-prepared speeches under cover of a crisis and expecting employees to believe you is a not so uncommon an event. Making a song out of a string of good orders could boomerang badly if workers get into the habit of threatening blackmailing restrictive practices whenever they see their company over-committed on its workload. The key to providing information is relevance, credibility, and consistency.

Some CEOs are coming to realize that the success or failure of crucial corporate strategies can depend on how their companies are perceived by the outside world. All too many see keeping the press at bay as the major preoccupation of their job. Now as Opel's PR Director and board member Hans Wilhelm Grall said 'The interaction between government, industry, the environment and the public has become extremely complex. PR can make or break a company'. Enlightened managers today consider image an important basic resource, in the way they have previously viewed finance or people. Professor Per Olof Berg of Sweden's Lund University put it well when he said 'They find out what they are and what they stand for. They find out what they want to do. And they try to communicate this to the outside world.'

As one of the world's leading public relations practitioners, Harold Burson, put it 'To what do I say, has been added – what do I do?' He argues that companies must have a decent respect for the opinion of mankind. Favourable public opinion is the foundation for legitimacy. Without suggesting companies should be expected to reshape society, they should nevertheless have accommodated social goals. The leverage of business is to execute its strategies with the consent of the constituencies whose goals they understand. The former chairman of British Rail, Sir Peter Parker, summed it up thus 'PR is at the flashpoint. Value needs articulating. It is the art of the credible. It is about leading at all levels in all functions'.

It is not just hostility to oil, chemical, tobacco and pharmaceutical companies to which we are referring. Even Japanese companies, which have never suffered the wrath of public opinion, are now turning to corporate communications in their fight to stave off competition. It is one of the major issues of this era when not only the goalposts are changing but the ground from under our feet is cracking. People like Carolo de Benedetti of Olivetti and Dick Giordano of BOC give their companies a go-ahead image by believing with total conviction that PR is part of the way of doing things. At SAS Chief Executive Carlzon returned the airline to profitability using high visibility as a weapon. The SAS dictum is that an employee without information cannot take responsibility, but an employee with information cannot avoid taking responsibility. It is a high risk strategy, but with a leap of faith it can be made to work. In fact ICI is disturbed if board members read something in the media they do not expect. That is how in control they hope to be of their situation. It is all a question of taking the offensive and setting up early warning systems. The European car manufacturers squabbling over EEC restrictions on lead in petrol prove they have not learned the lessons of history, namely the carbon-copy wrangles in the U.S. during the 1970s.

The social contract is being rewritten. Whether this will clarify the contradictions and transform them into collaboration is largely up to the CEO and his public affairs advisers. The issue here is the perceived legitimacy of the corporation which is reciprocal and accountable. It is the relationship between business self interest, wealth creation and community well-being that has to be re-examined by all of us in the eighties and nineties.

At the heart of all these conflicts lies the debate between ethnocentric nationalism and geocentric technology, over how far the multinational corporation (MNC) has broken the political monopoly of the nation state and the extent to which corporations can help or hinder the optimum creation and allocation of the earth's resources. That balance sheet has not been documented.

It's as if we're still living in the Second World War and Bretton Woods, in a 'time warp', having not caught up with the changing realities begun with OPEC's formation. 'Positive sum' co-operation (where all parties gain) rather than 'zero-sum' conflict is the new name of the game. That this macro issue, which is the backdrop to a range of micro issues differing from firm to firm is a continuum of constantly changing regulations, attitudes and technical or market factors. Some multinational companies lack the right kind of information mechanism to deal with the underlying trends. This is illustrated by the volume of information published by pressure groups in the field of food and health and the dearth of information supplied by most companies. By the joining of forces among various groups against apartheid with little response from international companies active in South Africa.

This is not to judge the fairness or otherwise of the arguments themselves (Nestlé has changed attitudes on both sides). There is a need for more 'shared values' among the international institutions – the ultimate challenge being for the MNC to justify itself by deed and word in a critical and vociferous world.

With all these conflicting issues the debate should become more concentrated on a limited range of issues agreed among the various international players, with a formative role played by the MNC. Currently there is no 'ideology free' forum where these debates can take place. The UN is scarcely neutral.

Nestlé was obviously a watershed as AT & T is now appearing to be for different reasons. There is a failure among some MNCs, not so much ethical as practical, to anticipate external pressures, then analyze and above all act upon them. Conflict can be resolved before it spreads beyond the original issue. For instance the drug companies will have to become more sensitive to media onslaughts and the stability of the local social fabric if Health Action International, a coalition of 27 country concerned groups isn't to get the better of them. The Interfaith Centre on Corporate Responsibility in the U.S. has a combined investment portfolio of $10 million, and with that leverage it coordinates shareholder resolutions and other pressure. The U.S. Church lobbies group is particularly vociferous, exerting pressure where it hurts most, via shareholder resolutions. More research is needed to track those public interest groups and the life-cycles of public related issues. This is even more important with the impact of 'narrowcasting' discussed in another chapter. Stanford Research Institute, by developing a values and lifestyles technique (called 'VALS') which helps identify and reach nine different types of American target audience, pinpoint inter alia particular 'societally conscious' people who are more active on issues, join pressure groups, vote more often, write more letters etc. The OECD code of conduct is a start but even it lacks the precise information for weighing rights and obligations. The chemical industry is certainly ahead in this area. In the absence of international law with sanctions, codes are a second best to reduce ambiguity and uncertainty. Disclosure requirements must be stepped up, but as we've seen with Vredeling, industry must become involved earlier in the debate.

According to Gladwyn & Walters' *Multinationals under Fire*, 'International pressure tends to push firms to accommodation rather than avoidance techniques. Even so more contingency conflict management systems should be adopted.' Just as MNCs must avoid the trap of believing host governments present the views of the people (Grenada?) so MNCs must be wary of transmitting home-grown values abroad, a diet of Reuters and Sesame Street!

The lesson for public affairs is that we have not yet come up with a suitable international political mandate that corresponds to the operational scope of the firm.

With more joint-ventures, more joint funding with international agencies, minority shareholdings, management contracts, hybrids and public affairs has a role as the corporate conscience and monitor. As Brandt put it 'When a corporation operates in many countries, its task of being responsive is complex. Efforts to articulate clearly the claims of corporate constituents will bring about more socially responsible relations.'

Just as consumerism and environmentalism were the revolutionary issues of the 1970s – affluence and technology led to socially accountable pressures not only for goods and services but for basic air and water. Now it's more about North/South, working for mutual benefit and new life-styles. Professor James Halloran of Leicester University, a specialist in mass communications, observed that the overlap between home and work, leisure and work, the development of an expressive work ethic, new forms of association, the changing man-machine relationship, and above all whether the new media technology can be put to socially constructive purposes are all scenery to a play now being enacted. As Andrew Knight, ex-editor of *The Economist*, said 'It's necessary to see the tides as well as the waves'.

Ironically the information revolution is being greeted with open arms by the pressure groups, more so than by the rest of the community, including industry. Companies should co-operate in using available information technology, network more and make more connections. Interestingly Des Wilson (formerly head of Friends of the Earth) and the scourge of British industry during the 1970s, like Nader in the U.S., has written a book *Pressure – the A to Z of Campaigning in Britain*. This could just as well be a manual for industrial activism. Interestingly, as though holding out an olive branch, he argues quite vociferously that industry and citizens could in many areas reconcile their differences with changes in perception brought about by positive communications and more positive action. He recommends not polarization but finding the common ground. It makes pragmatic sense to care about the environment because consumers and politicians do and because in the long run it will be cheaper. Dow Chemical once had a slogan, 'Making pollution control pay'. Companies need to show they are not just a positive economic force but also a socially and environmentally positive one. A recent MORI survey in Britain found that only 25% of the general public believe they can trust business leaders.

Perceptions are the reality of the world today. Indeed they are facts because people believe them. Endorsement of large companies remains high but there is widespread concern about the power vested in them. There is a volatility in the correlation between profit and consumer benefit. The understanding gap remains great, but as Robert Worcester of MORI constantly argues, while there are many layers of perception, belief and feeling which contribute to the reputation of a company, there is a high correlation between familiarity and favourability.

Of course the media do not help, partly because of constraints on space and time, the bad news bias and the educational background found among some editors and journalists who cover business. Accordingly a number of surveys, attitudes to industry via the press are worse than they used to be, and CEOs themselves think so too. Business will have to take a role in changing the anti-business ethic that permeates the educational system. CEOs believe journalists display a total misunderstanding of how industry operates and therefore get the balance wrong. There exists no consensus on the most promising path out of the mire. The official mouthpieces of industry do not command sufficient confidence in their ability to present industry's case. What is more, industry has failed to grasp that for the most part the role of the media is to present news as they see it, not analyze long-term trends. Inevitably they go to the politician or the trade unionist for quotable quotes rather than the business leader because they are usually more approachable. The CEO is always too busy, or if prepared to talk, talks without any coherent message or corporate ideology. To leave the nature of the message to chance, means management is abdicating its normal function of 'influencing'. Sometimes industry can have the courage to speak out and be admired for doing so.

There are journalists, as Mobil found out, who whatever the arguments will take a political anti-business stance. The *Washington Post* and CBS TV have been much criticized for this. But most journalists are just trying to do a difficult job well. They are not all very good or very specialist and businessmen fail to realize it. Even specialist business writers complain about the difficulty in getting an interview with management at all.

The Arthur Scargills of this world would never have derived the coverage they commanded if the British Coal Board management had evened up the odds by handling their public relations more effectively. Even then it was left to the Secretary of State for Energy, Peter Walker, to do it for them. It is about setting the agenda. Companies only have themselves to blame if they are regarded as something mysteriously apart from the mainstream of life. If, in the vacuum provided by their silence, it is left to others to make the running. Then politicians, trade unionists, TV pundits and even clerics enter the fray. Much animosity towards the press stems from a misunderstanding of their role. A businessman judges a story by the effect on his company, a journalist whether it is interesting to his readers, colleagues and peers.

At more than sixty American campuses apartheid has replaced Vietnam and inflamed the 'ME generation' that was thought too materialist to care. This upheaval has led to the suspension of some new investments by U.S. corporations operating in South Africa. Divestment in South Africa is a major new issue, and so far the idea has been adopted by six states, twenty-six cities and thirty-nine universities. Yet how many companies in the U.S. tracked the development of this issue via the local media, through grass-roots feedback and used their links into academea? How many have a position on the issue and have assessed the options for them individually? Few companies are structured in a way which allows them to reach a position let alone organize a campaign as between, say, their South African subsidiary, their U.S. divisions and their corporate HQ in London.

Integrated strategic planning that takes account of the external political environment is vital. Every segment of the organization is profoundly affected by information availability. Issues which used to be operational have become strategic. These issues, thanks to the spread of mass communication, information technology and the growth of global business, acknowledge no geographical or organizational boundaries. The time is opportune to study the dynamics of international, national and local pressures so that they can be better understood.

It is vital for corporations to evaluate the life-cycle of pressure groups, (there are many more ad hoc ones these days), identify and weigh the issues and evaluate the focal points of power and influence. The friends, enemies and collaborators and the interrelationships and linkages between pressure groups, the media, government and inter-governmental organizations are important. Prior to developing strategy options to manage an issue all these factors must be balanced and assessed acurately. Society is more issues driven today. This requires targeted research and tracking mechanisms to analyze and influence these overlapping minorities.

Business is bombarded with too many issues and conflicting stakeholders. Just as social issues must be managed business-techniques, business issues must be managed in a socially responsible manner. Everyone wants to be included. This kind of participation will help adaptation, but as Andrew Gollner in his book *The New Managerial Revolution* advises: 'The Achilles heel of our system is the incapacity to manage the forces of inter-dependence.' Grass roots activism is on the increase, issues are bottom up, and fads top down.

Grass roots activism, the tendency for information technology to make representative democracy unnecessary, and the need to involve stakeholders, means the task of sending messages becomes even more complex as we see in the following chapter. But the CEO must commit resources to issues management which is essentially a strategic information and decision-making task.

To function in optimal fashion, according to IBM, a public affairs programme must balance both externally and internally focussed activities. There must be an understanding of host country needs and an attempt to meet them. There must also be an attempt to understand all the overlapping local constituencies. On the internal side, the programme helps establish and co-ordinate positions on external issues, educate executives on them, and train them in articulating company positions using a variety of techniques. It is all a question of quantifying the issues balance sheet (not purely the financial one). There may be pressures to build a manufacturing plant in a certain country, but this may not make practical business sense. So IBM uses other ways to ingratiate themselves, such as the lending of consultants to provide much needed resources, sabbaticals or secondments of its executives to universities, and business/government partnerships on particular projects. This is particularly beneficial in the LDCS. IBM also attempts to leverage its resources via coalitions with chambers of commerce and trade associations. But above all they define their base audiences, track the issues and are thus ready to deal with conflicting requests. When it comes to identifying emerging issues there are many little snowdrifts which could end up in an avalanche of controversy. Newspapers are not very good at persuading people what to think but they are successful in convincing people what to think about, i.e. setting the agenda. Unless you track the issues, you will be preoccupied with crisis management. Three Mile Islands and Bhopals may be unavoidable but there is such a thing as damage limitation.

Now that the trend is for governments in the West to give greater freedom to the business sector, companies should assume a larger share of responsibility for the wealth of the communities from which they draw their employees and customers. Sir Hector Laing, CEO of United Biscuits, believes that no sector of society can sensibly contract out of concern and involvement in the economic and social problems and opportunities affecting the climate of the community. 'The ultimate responsibility of business is to serve the needs of society', he asserts. This is not wholly left-wing idealism because if the fabric of society is allowed to degenerate, the prospect of making worthwhile profits recedes. In the U.S., some companies contribute (as cash or people) five per cent of pre-tax profits to community projects, but in Europe it is less than one per cent in most instances. In the U.K. the Business in the Community and Action Resource Centre have established nearly 200 enterprise trusts and business ventures, which help create new jobs, tackle social, educational and environmental problems and advise small businesses. They help to bring together groups of private sector firms in constructive partnership with local authorities, trade unions and voluntary bodies. Secondment can be a valuable form of management development as well as benefiting the community.

One of the greatest sins of omission by politicians and industrialists is the failure to explain the long-term trend in unemployment and to create new forms of work. Moral blight could lead to social blight if business and government fails to act. There is some recognition that business philanthropy is more than just charity and church bells. It is a co-operative effort to regenerate inner cities, create jobs and stabilize society. As Levi Strauss U.K. puts it 'We try to use what money we have as seed corn and in partnership with others.' IBM believes 'We are inter-dependent and must contribute to the quality of life'.

Obviously this is not entirely altruistic. BAT Industries concentrate their efforts on Liverpool because they have provoked hostility through factory closures there and IBM, via its community activities, counteracts criticism that it is a giant predator. Life is a trade-off. Social responsibility is being replaced by social action. In West Germany the universities and corporations are beginning to co-operate more in founding research centres which encourage product and process innovation and new enterprises, putting new life into local communities and cities. Increasingly business is becoming more 'politicized' and businessmen are having to put their 'case'.

Their structures are being changed to include representation by various groups. Businesses are becoming involved in social action. Business leaders need to think about this and act accordingly.

In a climate of complexity, where the profit motive is no longer the sole raison d'être, the growing power of individuals, and instant transmission of facts and opinions, the CEO and his senior directors have a choice. They can become unwilling victims or they can utilize the expertise and resources available to them to shape the society in which they play a part. If business fails to learn to adapt, it could well find itself replaced by other institutions or else increasingly controlled by government. As Peter Dunstan, of Unilever Australia, put it, 'A company by providing the information before it is asked for, indicates that it perceives the need to act responsibly . . . in identifying the issues which can develop and affect the future of the company, management is highlighting opportunities for development'.

Corporations should not forget that their first duty is to manage their own affairs properly and profitably, to compensate employees, reward investors, create favourable working conditions and produce goods and services that meet the highest standards of safety and reliability.

They should also not forget that public relations is not the substitution of imagery for substantive acts. The CEO, helped by his PR/PA department, should research social trends, formulate policies to adapt to them and communicate these policies internally and externally. The role of the PR/PA executive is to be a vigilante guarding against corporate introversion, and the self-conscious withdrawal from open dialogue. There is a need to introduce balance and realism into contemporary discussion lawyers and investment bankers tend to take a different view.

The problem is that the corporation is a conservative institution filled with pragmatic people unlikely ever to sit through endless local political committee meetings. Businessmen are not usually reformers otherwise they would not be in business. The real measure of a corporation should be its ability to think long-term and stabilize society, so long as they are already profitable and efficient.

We will not attempt to develop a list of 'Thou shalt nots', as all encompassing dictums can be damaging. There are companies with excellent pollution abatement programmes which have not yet begun to think about minority employment. Ultimately, individuals must accept full responsibility for what their institutions do, and that means the chairman and his board of directors. This means reconciling the individual with the corporation, particularly as most corporations function in a technological and urban environment.

Social pressures have always been there, it is just that time-frame compression has set in so that tomorrow becomes today. Future shock really is here. The critical question them becomes when should the corporation react to rising social pressures and start its own reforms. Those who anticipate are far less vulnerable. Timing is critical and the real burden for the multiple stakeholder's responsibilities rest on the shoulders of the Chairman, to see the inter-relationships, to distinguish trends from fads, reformers from revolutionaries. Wilson and Nader are in the former category. CEOs must be the corporate sensors and the conscience, the corporate monitors and ultimately the corporate communicators, aided of course by the PR executives and others at senior level.

There have been three eras in the twentieth century. The first era was dominated by invention, the second by management. The surge of new industry was left to multinational corporations. Professional management then arose. The next era will be dominated by the human climate. It is the attitudes of stakeholders – investors, workers, pressure groups, politicians, that determine what any institution can do. Even *In Search of Excellence* does not recognize the vital emergence of the restive human climate. This has led to forced changes in corporate cultures and provided a heaven-sent opportunity for CEOs to instil values and promote beliefs crucial to strategic success in the tough outside world. Indeed the environment on which business operates is arguably the most significant element of organizational culture. The public is becoming more segmented. In addition to shareholders, employees and customers, we now have legislative pressure groups, knowledge workers, the new media, church groups, public interest groups, even terrorist groups. Organizations have changed to meet new conditions but people have changed more. The global electronic village renders it impossible to cut people off from most aspects of life whether in Moscow or Malaga. Expectations are elevated into demands. The understanding, dealing with and directing of public attitudes will become the most vital skill during the remainder of this century, according to another leading PR practitioner Philip Lesley. The increase in diversity and splintering of viewpoints will only make the task tougher as specialization leads to a far greater need for communicating across boundaries. Combined with the decreasing readiness of people to read or understand, the importance of expertise in communicating to gain share of mind (and heart) is increased. These facts require that senior management be attuned to the paradox of first specialization, to the idea of segmentation versus broad vision. There must be a readiness to call in expert help in dealing with these problems.

Second, managers who are accustomed to determining events now have to cope with them. They want to impose their disciplined methods on the human climate.

Third, people have seen massive advances in areas where technology is the key. But these same people expect the same multiplication of capabilities where human capacities are still important, such as teaching, health care and corporate communications.

Fourth, the conflict between institutions and individuals is heightened by the electronic revolution of screen-based information based in the home which exudes instant emotion, and quick solutions. The electronic revolution in management information and systems stresses facts, organization and hard reality. Senior management must understand that the problems of the outside world and public attitudes are not susceptible to easy measurement and tangible ideas.

Fifth, the PR person and the CEO is or should be the outward and visible sign of this function pivoted between the company and the critics, a delicate balance – the flash-point of PR is the bridge between the completely practical and the conceptual. The key here is giving stakeholders a sense of involvement, communicating with people, not at them. In this age the chairman and managing director must be great *facilitators* not *dictators*.

In drawing to a close let us pull some of the strands together. Major institutions are locked in each other's grip. Management have become prisoners of an outdated system. There has been a crowding-in of issues, government intervention and more exposure of corporate profits. The Achilles heel of the system (no one institution, department or function is to blame here) is an incapacity to manage the forces of independence. The greatest challenge to executive ingenuity is for public affairs people, through their CEOs, to become catalysts of an intellectual revolution which breaks us out of the current 'paradigm paralysis'.

The corporation will survive or die depending on the ability of mangement to be 'polymaths' with soft, high-touch skills. It is up to senior management to build the bridge between the national, scientific, qualitative skills and the critical, pragmatic, co-operative skills of the holistic age.

A more multi-faceted, inter-disciplinary approach, could make corporations innovative and flexible enough to emerge, if not unscathed, then intact.

Only the CEO and the public affairs executives are all pervasive in terms of corporate functions. To achieve this paradigm shift will require not just an understanding of these trends but an ability to build them into the 'corporate integrity'. The individual firm's approach to these contradictions between business, self-interest, wealth creation and community well-being is all-important. Gap analysis helps us measure the distinction between perception and performance and between real substantive action and cosmetic response. The public affairs function is to anticipate, monitor and manage a corporation's relationship with the forces discussed in this chapter. If this function is ever to become legitimate, interactive, diffused, institutionalized and above all strategic, what the executives in this role say must be worth listening to. But it is up to CEOs to take it more seriously. If they don't then corporations will become fossilized. In our view, sales and profits in the 1980s will depend more on the successful explanation of community and social action than on many other parts of corporate activity.

Public approval is becoming so vital that socially aware companies are likely to be the only ones able to grow successfully in the remainder of the twentieth century.

8

Anarchy or Lego

'How can management have fooled itself for so long. Can it really believe in watertight communication departments – design, PR, advertising, packaging – when the consumer in his wisdom sees the company and everything marked with its name as one?'

David Bernstein.

How does all this affect the manager in his day-to-day work? Can we argue that the job of the company's external communications and its position in the marketplace, are the responsibility only of the chief executive? Is it a case of clearer job definitions, more division of labour, better horses for courses? This is the conventional wisdom of management theory. Four generations of businessmen, each learning more about management as the industrial revolution forced new skills on the ruling classes, became lodged in pigeon-hole management. The inherited skills of one layer of historic managers were passed on from one generation to another without any new thinking or value added.

Yet television business programmes will show you that today it is not possible to confine the control of a corporation's position in the outside world to one person. We may argue in this book for new leaders, new skills of leadership, but never let us think that modern business lays out some sort of divisionalization, with an officer's mess, a sergeant's mess, and a canteen for the other ranks.

Post-Second World War managers, coming hot foot from their service life in the navy, army or airforce, perpetuated the divisions that an historic class structure enforced. If we believe that the internal life of a company is governed by the norms and attitudes developed in the employee's home and his or her leisure life, then it is no wonder that a country untouched – well, almost – by the social levelling of wartime invasion and destruction should mould its people externally to accept the same hierarchy from its company managers. We talk a lot about the levelling effect of two world wars on the British people (for instance), but this is not altogether true. Service life perpetuated the divisions. The social structure – unlike in, for example, Germany or Japan – remained intact. How else can we explain the almost total resistance to women's equality during the last fifty years, given that they played key roles in all the armed forces?

The total change in social attitudes encouraged possibly by our Western open media which allows views to be expressed and absorbed by even the lowest socio-economic groups has forced a new, more potent type of democracy on Europe which has spilled onto its business life. The old corporation has died in tandem with the old social structure.

Given that this is so, any company which tries to prevent a journalist or investigator talking to any responsible member of staff causes itself a problem created by the very act of trying to impose such a rule. The phrase 'We've been told not to talk to the Press' can be quickly woven into a TV news story to create all the symptoms of a company in trouble. All the more important therefore for PR's best ambassadors, the employees, to know and believe in the corporate message.

There is a need therefore for any company to integrate its communication programme into its mission and its culture so that contact by staff with the outside world can perpetuate and modify the communications message. This is not necessarily a conscious process. It is a natural influence or shaping of views that takes place unconsciously. It is partly about use of language but partly about doing what you are saying.

Because a corporate culture is unconscious, it defines the starting point for any manager or member of the staff who is approached by the media about some external issue. It also creates the base upon which a company speaker constructs his speech to a local Rotary Club, national conference or international seminar. Yet so many managers approach this aspect of their job with inadequate preparation and rehearsal, something they would never do in other aspects of their work. It is hardly rational.

For all these reasons it is obvious that any corporate communications policy at either national, international or local level, cannot be designed in isolation. Every manager in the company has a right, and can demand to know, what the company's policies are towards the external environment. After all, his career and livelihood depend upon the company handling its affairs efficiently. An uncoordinated approach to government relations can mean that a company may well leave it too late to press for changes in legislation if no attempt has been maintained to establish continuous dialogue over the years when no specific developments are in the pipeline. A failure to respond or even identify major changes in social trends, leading to alterations in buyers' habits, can mean a steadily declining share of the market. This may not be something that is immediately noticeable, but for the middle manager it could mean a decline in the company's fortunes just at the moment when he is least able to find a new job if he is made redundant. Keeping close to the customer, a marketing approach is also vital. A British bus company accused of failing to pull up at bus stops to pick up passengers said it would never keep to the timetable if it did!

The need for the communications element of overall strategy to be 'integrated' – that word means more than just 'understand' – into all the key layers of strategy in a company is going to be the crucial element of success in the next decade.

The obvious publics for any external communications programme are customers and the trade, the financial community, government, the local community and pressure groups. Internally, of course, there must be an on-going process by which all staff are kept aware of what is being done to project messages externally. These are the traditional targets and have always formed the basis of any public affairs campaign. Even though they must be broken down on a segmented basis. There is always an 'opinion-forming' group of managers who can, if motivated, cascade information downwards, upwards and horizontally.

There is a wider outlook, however, and it is to this that we will turn our attention in this chapter. Macro-issues shape smaller ones, so to ignore the larger issues is to operate a PR programme in a condition of anarchy. If attention is paid only to smaller, peripheral issues, your communications programme will have the appearance of meteorites impacting a space-ship from some outer alien force. What is needed is a building-block system – a sort of corporate lego – that allows managers to be kept aware of this outer circle of forces which are shaping the narrow issues. Such a system will avoid the boiling up of a brew for the future which could create uncertainty and possible danger when it is too late to assemble an effective defence.

Despite these external pressures and the fact that they will intensify over the next decade, corporations do not appear to be seeing the warning signs. This may have something to do with the perpetuation of the 'old boy network' at the very top of European industry and the re-cycling of worn-out (with some notable exceptions) non-executive or outside directors in some of our most significant corporations. Dealing with journalists is not a game, yet so many businessmen still believe they should lay low in the bad times in the hope it will blow over. When they are exposed they believe they can 'wing it', rather than use the admittedly high-risk strategy of a planned communication programme as a management opportunity to make positive points, to establish credibility, correct distortion and fill in the wider perspective. Communications skills appear to be growing very slowly indeed. Certainly they are increasing at a slower rate than the abilities of external pressure groups to inflict hurt and pain from outside.

Back in the Spring of 1977, one of Britain's leading corporate affairs counsellors, Tim Traverse-Healy, joined with market research company Market & Opinion Research International (MORI), led by Robert Worcester, to review the discrepancies between different European corporations' external relations programmes.

They argued in an article in the *International Public Affairs Association (IPRA) Review* (September 1978) that in the sixties, companies undertaking regular programmes of public opinion research were few and far between – and those that did were almost exclusively American. In the seventies a steady change was observed. Major European multi-nationals such as Philips, BASF, ICI and Shell all conducted major pieces of research on public attitudes, and constantly made checks on users' and employees' views towards the companies and their products. A small number started to survey their relevant parliamentarians and civil servants and a few even dipped their toes tentatively into the explosive waters of trade union attitudes.

The authors of the article comment in passing that few pieces of research had been conducted on a trans-frontier basis to enable comparisons to be made between different national cultures.

Because of the undoubted authority of Tim Traverse-Healy and Robert Worcester, it is worth pausing for a moment to consider certain aspects of their methodology, because in this and the following chapter we are primarily concerned with some of the practical aspects and applications of the changes taking place in corporate affairs.

The writers in the *IPRA Review* maintained that there were four major categories of image influence they wanted to compare in European multinationals to judge their effectiveness in dealing with those areas. Because this is one of the benchmark articles against which we may wish to compare improvements over the next decade, we quote extensively from the results they cited.

The four categories of image that concerned them were product class image, brand image, brand user image and corporate image. The product class referred to the collection of attributes shared by all brands of a particular group, such as motor vehicles, cigarettes or a certain type of machine tool; thus every product class exists because it meets the needs of a group of people and plays a role in their lives. The brand image is self-explanatory. The brand user image is concerned with how well the brand fulfils factors which not only described the user, but possibly constrained or confined him. Such factors include the books and/or newspapers he would read and the social class he associates with that particular brand. Finally, the corporate image in this case was considered solely as an influence on the ultimate purchase. Thus the authors were concerned primarily with corporate image as an element of marketing. Robert Worcester therefore defines corporate image as 'the net result of the interaction of all experiences, impressions, beliefs, feelings and knowledge people have about the company.'

The authors of the article decided to measure sources of image which were quite extensive and included advertising, published information to shareholders and staff, brand packaging and the opinions, albeit very subjective, of users. They also included information emanating from the industry as a whole and from competing companies. This latter point is interesting because the authors mention the phenomenon that is often overlooked when a company measures up well against its competition, but when the relevant total industry group is falling rapidly in terms of esteem.

They see this type of image research as taking a certain chronology.

STAGE ONE:	Attitudes to, say, large company (companies) as a whole.
STAGE TWO:	Attitude to industries in which the company (companies) take part. Compare industry against industry.
STAGE THREE:	Attitudes to company against competitors.
STAGE FOUR:	How company rates as a product reputation, customer relations, employees, etc.

What is particularly important to us is that back in the seventies it was argued that to thrive in Europe – or the rest of the world for that matter – a company must get all the factors together to sing one song. There are still countless consumer studies going on week in and week out, but far too few studies were made or are being made of other target audiences that are shaping and affecting attitudes. In this group we would include employees, government, financial institutions and so on. The article quotes from a Thames Television MORI study in the U.S. which showed that although the British people were seen as friendly and worth a visit in tourist terms, their products were rated poorly against those from Japan or Germany.

Here was clearly a case of companies not getting the total act together. A six-country comparison carried out in Germany showed a similar pattern, with the U.S. this time scoring high marks on producing technically advanced products of good value and high quality, with Holland coming out top on strike record and quality and Britain lagging behind at the rear, only just ahead of Italy. Maybe if the research had included design as a feature on its own the Italians would have pulled ahead of Britain, leaving them in a very vulnerable position so far as future sales were concerned.

The conclusion to this in public relations terms is two-fold. If 48% of German respondents considered that the Italians could not meet delivery dates, it should not only be incumbent on Italian companies to improve their control methods but also for their public relations machinery to start highlighting to Germany those cases where Italian manufacturers did hit target and delivery dates. The role of the public relations director thus assumes a double function; first, he is the harbinger of doom by carrying out research in the first place, and arguing for improvements to meet the criticism, and second, he must forcibly project case-studies and examples of occasions when the Italian company did deliver on time.

A useful methodology employed by MORI is a scatter diagram that compares the Favourability against the Familiarity of industrial groups in a single country. The vertical axis demonstrates the favourability of the image of certain industries (remember the research was carried out in 1977, and there would doubtless be many changes since) as you move upwards, against familiarity which is shown to increase as you move across the scale from left to right. As MORI states once this type of survey has been carried out in one country, it can be repeated in others using one country as a base for comparison across other countries.

The traditional demographic description of age, income and class is not necessarily as penetrating as a more detailed segmentation being undertaken now in the U.S. in the area of lifecycle and psychographic groupings, for societally conscious people or achievers. In this way it is possible to identify and reach specific target audiences with the most appropriate messages on particular issues.

One point is important in using these techniques. The acceptance of the fact that good communications must not be used to cover up failings. If the failings actually exist, something *must* be done about them. If they do not on the whole exist, and it is really a matter of perception created by media slanting or competitor statements against the company, then it becomes a question of co-ordination of effort to project the true facts. No lasting effect will come from a single public statement or a letter in the correspondence columns of a trade journal. It may need a major investment in time and money to launch a position-countering campaign.

These views from the seventies have been used for two reasons. First they provide some interesting historical perspectives that readers may wish to use for their own company comparisons. In our experience, few companies have any benchmark studies and are only today setting them up for future use. Second, it is the methodology and attitudes taken by Worcester and Traverse-Healy are still of relevance.

Today we are seeing research budgets being included as a matter of course in the total corporate communications investment. In the seventies, this seldom happened. It is a sad reflection on the state of the art that few public relations consultancies even have a research capability in-house. Some do, or claim to, but on examination it is usually only a glorified librarian carrying out desk research primarily for new business development. What is needed today are fully fledged departments able to instigate and if necessary construct both attitudinal and quantitative research, write editorial media schedules, calculate penetration and frequency levels, and maintain a constant monitoring survey on the effectiveness of programmes. At one time the budget allocated to public relations was so small that any market research would have cost more than the activities it was employed to monitor. Today, as six and seven figure sums are being put behind corporate public affairs activity, it becomes a necessary element to measure whether or not it is effective.

Jim Dowling, President of Burson-Marsteller, the world's largest PR firm, says the future of this business lies in better research. 'PR people', he says 'must be able to adapt the management of their business to changing public perceptions and values, a percursor to which is research.'

Research is becoming particularly important to pinpoint targets and 'overlapping minorities' more precisely. Added to which in the electronic media maze – having moved from single source mass communication to multi-source directed at smaller, more tightly targeted audiences – known as 'narrowcasting', research becomes even more complex and specialist. Ethnic, local, and minority sport programmes are examples, as are the advent of teletext and interactive programming. The arrival of multi-channel cable and satellite programming has also changed the nature of the audience as well as the targeting of the message, and indeed the message itself, which needs to be finely-tuned. Regional radio stations, free-sheets, as well as the penetration of Benelux homes with British programmes via satellite and cable, has not only increased choice for the consumer but made it imperative to find new research and measurement criteria.

What few public corporations realize, in their intense preoccupation with the views of financial institutions, is that a wider communications programme aimed at other more specific audiences via a creative mix of the new media, whether government official, employee, local community, pressure group leader, or that often forgotten old lady who owns a few shares, may be small in terms of numbers, but may be able to exert influence out of all proportion, because they are opinion formers. Look at U.S. Financial, it grows at 25 per cent per year and has a multiple of 10. IBM grows at 15 per cent, yet its multiple is 40. That's corporate image and reputation.

There's bound to be media wastage, but the closer the targeting of the message using a variety of channels, the more that message is likely to be understood and supported, which may in turn have a positive influence back in these all-important financial institutions.

As the difficulties to gain a share of mind increase so the more vital it becomes to fine-tune a quality message based on sound research internally and externally. Niche marketing in relation to the competition takes on a new meaning as companies attempt a combination of 'who and what they are as they carve out a unique territory in the market.

This is why business leaders should become PR people, and PR people must become more business and marketing orientated. This has great implications for training and recruitment.

Before moving on, we would like to quote from the final section of the Worcester/Traverse-Healy paper. They state that the International Manager of Communications in a corporation 'needs to be in a position to demonstrate to his own colleagues and principals at the corporate headquarters (and in other countries) that in matters of public relations and public affairs, action has to be taken early at the frontier of thought. Unlike matters of development, marketing, production and finance, such corporate actions as are required are not necessarily or invariably, or exclusively, needed in those countries where the enterprise has major establishments or markets; or amongst those individuals or groups who normally experience the services or use the products of the concern. If thought knows no borders, it certainly does not recognize sales areas. The corporate flag need not always be accompanied by the sales drum. The jet set and the recorders of their antics cause fashion to leap-frog customs posts at an alarming rate. In the case of social thought, the established and developing trans-national links between special interest or elitist groups sometimes create a dynamism out of proportion to the importance of the originating source or the significance of the concept. In this respect it lends credence to the McLuhan catch-phrase 'The medium is the message'. The recent 'Live-Aid' pop concerts attest to that.

If we are concerned to develop a pro-active stance for companies that will ensure they are part of and interact with the issues that are relevant to them, it becomes necessary to analyze certain elements. Business does not normally manage ideas or trends – it usually reacts and by doing so changes the external perception of the issue. Corporations do not take over the work or the responsibility of governments, although they should assume responsibility in a wider context for any changes they produce in government thinking. Those changes are being made because they provide advantage to certain people – employees, shareholders, customers, subcontractors, specialist groups that run to many thousands of people. They are not the same people necessarily who elected the parliamentarians, although they may be. Equally, these people have a right to exert their own views or influences to their own advantage just as much as any other group within a state. The advantage then accrues to people outside the state or elected boundary of the parliament; in such cases, more complex factors often need to be considered. An element of differentiation is required here in terms of ultimate responsibility. The size of the corporation's constituency of interest can be quite enormous. An ICI or a Hoechst can argue that actions taken on behalf of their corporation will affect more people than the whole of a European parliamentary constituency electorate – certainly the sum of those actually voting. However, just as doing good for that corporate constituency may be excellent in itself in terms of size, it is not necessarily going to do good for another group, say, old-age pensioners, or residents living near a new factory, or holiday-makers about to be deprived of an amenity. The final decision which is usually one of priority and compromise, is the responsibility of the parliament concerned acting for the common good or the state as a whole. What is clear, however, is that just as the member of parliament for one area has the right to argue a case on behalf of his constituents, so too does a corporation have the right to argue for its constituency if it believes it will affect its life and well-being. The ultimate decision will be in the hands of the elected chamber.

There is a clear distinction between activities at the company level and at the national level. Although the corporation can only do the thing it is capable of, it can still have a view on the wider public issue. There is sometimes a belief that journalists can voice their opinions as part of a commerical product that is for sale, whereas corporations should not. In public places we will hear that the journalist or the non-elected pressure group representative is voicing views untinged by commercial influence. In the first place this assumes that commercial influence is *ipso facto* bad – as if wages and salaries paid to employees are not as important to the recipients as abstract and abstruse matters of ideas and ideology – and on the other hand we should cast doubts as David Hare has done so ably in his play 'Pravda' on the pure white milk of truth as purveyed by journalists and television presenters. Everyone has some ace to play or axe to grind, some external or even internal pressure that distorts objectivity. Corporations have the same rights as minorities and special interest groups. Of course it is difficult for the senior management when faced with the short-term perspectives of politicians, the stock market and a built-in bias against business. What methodology can we apply to deal with the interface of ideas and issues which can change the life of a company?

W. Howard Chase, writing in the April 1978 issue of *IPRA Review*, argued there were four major components of process management and they should take the following sequence:

1. Issue Identification
2. Issue Analysis
3. Issue Priority Setting or Issue Change Strategy Analysis
4. Issue Action Programme

If we assume that this is the correct order, then the first stage, that of issue identification, should be pre-organized through the creation of an adequate data base that maintains constant rapportage or records of events to be interpreted. The dangers are that such information collection systems are no more than that, a collection of undigested facts and data. It is therefore the continuous interpretation of this data which is important, and this has to see the light of day through more than a management digest sent to senior staff once a month – another pile of paper for weekend reading. That chore is usually sped through on a Saturday afternoon with one eye on the television sport, or the children's nagging insistence on some outside visit. Interpretation is a senior level function to be performed at corporate public affairs level and seen as a prime task in the sequence described by Howard Chase.

Almost as soon as such systems are in place it becomes an empire-building process, or it appears to be so to finance directors controlling budgets. The reason is the growing tendency to believe that the function of issue management or public affairs needs to be planted only in the home base, as if all that is important and which might affect the company will happen at headquarters. Even then, data bases and information are usually from home sources alone, relying on the media coverage of overseas events to monitor the great world outside. The reason why those particular events have been covered in the local or national press is because they are seen by editors who have a feel for their readers' interests as being likely to affect or be affected by events in the headquarters country. Public affairs functions by their very name are concerned with the public in those countries where the corporation has special interests. They must therefore be planted in those countries where the reporting is either by direct line (preferable) or by dotted line (not so effective) to the function at headquarters.

Quite obviously the collection of data is only the first step in the move towards an issue control system. A user/issue matrix, as John Hargreaves of Matrix Corporate Affairs Consultancy calls it, needs to be set up, which identifies those issues which are important, and at what level and to what function in the organization. It is necessary at that stage to identify the people within the company who are to be called upon to assist in the evaluation of the material as it comes in. Hargreaves makes the point that you cannot rely on line managers to do all the evaluation. There is a tendency for them to filter out disturbing issues. After all, who wants to work in a job with disaster looming each day? People who make whisky or gin do not want to be reminded each day they go to work some old lady was beaten up by teenagers given dutch courage by their product, or that an outbreak of soccer hooliganism may not have occurred if there had been no bar within sight of the ground. Managers tend to gaze steadfastly away from the unpleasant and for this reason it can be important to draw in the outside consultant or academic or provide an element of objectivity to the assessment.

Many public relations operatives in the past have tended to lump together all the various issues that can affect a company into a few categories, social, political, environmental, economic. By not taking an analytical approach and refining the issues into selective groups, and narrowing the focus wherever possible, there has been a tendency to cry wolf too often. Whole bundles of separate issues are identified in one major issue, and the process is made to appear over-generalized, resulting in a loss of credibility. The usual problem is that issues tend to be dealt with by different departments and board committees remaining uncoordinated let alone ranked.

Mechanisms have to be installed that will put the trends into priority order. The real issue behind the apparent one becomes all important, especially in areas such as employee participation. For example, sometimes it is not really a case of workers wanting to be involved in the decisions concerning the installation of new high-technology hardware. What is truly at stake is their fear of not being able to understand it as well as their work-mates and they thus appear foolish. The traditional hierarchy of respect can be demolished overnight and new young workers suddenly become the bright, apparently intelligent leaders because they are more readily able to cope with the hardware. The response should be to ensure that the older and more senior workers are given priority in training and familiarization so that they can become the primary group leaders in terms of group opinion-leading.

It goes without saying that any programme of issues activity must have a budget written in for measuring its effectiveness. Unfortunately, this is normally a lip-service payment. Everyone agrees it is a good thing, but somehow the actual setting-up of bench-mark studies gets put aside until the point has passed when it was of sufficient significance to take measurements. In the next chapter we discuss actual measurement techniques. All that is needed at this stage is to register the need. Measurement needs to be built into the system, a way of looking at communications problems that takes its raison d'être the need to know how much has been achieved. Perhaps if we called this function communications engineering its practitioners would think automatically in measurable or mathematical terms. After all, an engineer expects to measure every minute step of his work, otherwise there is no point in proceeding.

If we believe, as did Harold Burson, founder of the public relations consultancy Burson-Marsteller, that the PR practitioner is a mediator between the corporation and society, then some extra objective factor, such as survey and research, is needed to gauge the speed and pressure of the volume of the flow. Unlike Burson, however, we do not believe that public relations is 'more an art than science'. Burson says: 'The best people have an intuition, a talent that enables them to analyze a situation, propose a strategy and then communicate the solution.' This may be so, but you cannot be advocate, judge *and* jury. There must be some attempt by outside evaluators to judge how effective that communication process has been. The designing of the process may need that touch of magic, that element of the artist, but it is the scientific basis of the rationale and the design that ensures it is on target and the message has been correctly adopted.

We end this chapter by emphasizing the need to build the communications process like a structure, a 'lego approach' as we have called it, and quote again from Harold Burson when he spoke to the Columbia University Graduate School of Business in the United States 'Since the nature of corporations is to be pragmatic, any pressure for reform is going to come from the outside. As a result the corporation must have built-in sensing devices that can detect change in the social winds. The job of detecting those changes and charting a new course belongs to the public relations person. The real measure of a corporation is not whether it has organized itself to lead but whether it has organized itself to respond to social change.' Maybe a time is coming when corporations must do more than just respond to social change. Companies must communicate who they are and describe what they do. But in addition they must articulate what they stand for and get involved in the community, beyond their traditional function. Above all, the approach must be coherent, consistent and coordinated. Even quite different programmes at divisional or board level should reflect the basic philosophy of the group.

During his Columbia speech he summed up the responsibilities of a public relations officer working in a modern corporation as:

- To sense social change and help management focus its attention on that change.
- To serve as the corporate conscience.
- To be a communicator in the professional sense, i.e. understanding its technique.
- To monitor corporate policies and programmes to make sure they match public expectations.

He considers that too often 'the emphasis is placed on external communication. Although external communication is important, it is in many respects secondary to and dependent upon an effective internal communications programme . . . internal communications must do more than tell or inform. Its primary function is to bring about understanding . . . not only what is happening and what employees are expected to do about it, but why the new policies have been adopted. . . . We can't even think about communicating information outside the corporation until the policy has taken root and is working'.

In an earlier chapter we talked about the man in the centre, the type of leader modern corporations must nurture and develop to meet the new environment. Perhaps there is a need for the public relations function to be headed by a new type of animal capable of spanning the disciplines in his or her vision and experience. Sadly, as we've experienced in giving counsel, CEOs are increasingly recognizing the need for the function but are at a loss to define what it should comprise and the kind of animal to appoint; what John Hargreaves of Matrix calls 'Bachelors of Thinking'. People who have the presence to consort with leaders, the patience to work with the administrators and officials, and the humility to appreciate what the young or less articulate are saying. We doubt if many such paragons really exist. If they did, they would probably be insufferable, but they would be able to communicate. To communicate means listening as well as speaking. As Hargreaves says, 'These pioneers must possess imagination and have the ability to take thought, rather than time and money, into their work. There is no conventional wisdom on which to draw. They must be prepared to move into uncharted territory'.

9
A positive stance

'There's a well-known difference between improving one's looks by cosmetics and improving them by better health.'

Max Ways.

As the name implies, this chapter concerns itself with the mechanics of corporate communications once we have plugged this function into the decision-making process. How to structure the organization, its systems, and ultimately its methodologies, to set positive programmes into action. We see the required organizational structure as a staging post towards and from which a more flexible environment can be created. We are now half-way towards the mental attitude required for such a future restructuring. The acceptance of the communications function by the personnel, financial, marketing and corporate departments not to mention by the line managers will force an acceptance of dual, sometimes multi-leadership situations on the company. Dotted-line responsibility is not enough. Direct line control for communication cannot be divorced from the direct line control of any department's function. Once, we would have argued that communication was a support function to the prime purpose of each department. Personnel was there to recruit, train, and keep the employees happy. Marketing was there to sell products. The Financial division was concerned with matters as diverse as simple accounting and the long-term financial needs of the corporation. In order to help the directors in charge of these functions, a number of support activities were supplied to oil the specialists' wheels. The functional head decided on strategy and if that strategy entailed some activity that included communication with staff, customers or the City, the communications technicians were brought in to implement that need.

Today, communication is the function or an element of the function itself. It has not just moved up the priority scale. It is not a case of agreeing that more time should be given to its technical competence. The definitions have changed. It has taken two steps, one forward and one sideways. The forward step has been a change from a tactical to a strategic function, not because it is an additional element in the menu of techniques available for deciding on a personnel, financial or marketing action, but because it is now the function itself. Share prices are not based only upon the supply and demand in the market. The market can sometimes appear to be simple, but the demand element in the equation is governed by how the corporations are seen. That in turn depends upon the programme of communications, persuasion and availability of information available to the analysts and portfolio managers who make the decision to buy and sell the shares.

The ability of personnel departments to hold staff, or marketing departments to sell products, and the corporate suite to evolve and operate strategies, depends now on the extent to which the facts are transmitted to discrete target groups whose acceptance or rejection can mean action or indifference. We are faced, therefore, with the dangerous situation whereby four – possibly more – of the key functions in any corporation are being controlled by men and women who have received only scant training in a function that could occupy a third of their time. It would still be a dangerous position if that third of their time was discrete in itself, and the act of communication was a technique or system rather like discounted cash flow or market research. At least it would leave a clearly defined gap that could be filled by studying a management course or the employment of specialists. It would be less efficient, and would hinder the full economic and financial expansion of the company, but at least there would be a step down the road to understanding. To solve the problem in this way, however, would be to miss the point of our argument. If communication is a technique which acts like plaster on a cracked wall, hopefully to cover those cracks and even the decay beneath, we can then extend the metaphor to show that it is closely related yet again to the whitewashing function. The old chestnut voiced by public relations men at conference after conference is that they are brought in on a problem once it has happened, and only then as a technician to carry a message already decided upon, would still be true yet again. Communication should be integral today to every corporate action and must therefore be implicit in the thought process which is used to develop solutions to a management problem.

As we begin to consider an organizational structure for this area of corporate life, we should by all our logic say there is no need for a structure at all. If each executive is trained to see the communications element within each decision he makes, and that decision is altered as a response to the pressure exerted by the communications message, then all that is needed is a series of technicians. These technicians would be trained in writing, design, press and TV relations, and ultimately would have a co-ordinator to ensure that the tablets from Mount Sinai were correctly interpreted.

However, that situation has yet to come into existence, and such a black and white organizational interpretation of the concept may or may not apply to different companies in different industries. Until the training of managers includes the elements discussed earlier, and until this is combined with an altered climate of opinion, our immediate consideration must be the best organizational structures for use at this stage in the development of management thinking.

The concept of dual line control with overlays of dotted line responsibility has been nurtured by the service industries on the one hand and by the proponents of matrix structures on the other. The professionals, particularly accountants and lawyers, realized early on that although they were primarily individuals and had personal relationships with their clients, the concept of size soon reared its head. There was a necessity for an organizational structure. Structures need people to drive them and at once it became apparent that, whereas the system of clerks in chambers worked well for barristers, it did not fit the burgeoning and increasingly diverse world of the solicitor (as the U.K. distinguishes them). Someone had to be in charge when it came to deciding who did what, even if the final decision in terms of the professional work itself had to be in the hands of individuals.

Thus a twin set of rules developed. The accountants, faster on their feet than the lawyers when it came to finding new ways for expansion on the fringes of their business, were soon into management consultancy, high technology communication systems and, more recently, even investment banking. Soon, anything that moved in the financial world was coming within the aegis of the accountant. He had to evolve ways of running the show to allow management control to live side by side with individual clients' needs. He also had to find ways to enable clients to be moved from one specialist adviser to another within the same firm.

This system of twin responsibility to one's immediate professional boss and to the overall organization needed marketing in very careful terms. Job titles had to be formulated judiciously to retain the identity of a professional partnership. As the other service industries, from advertising and public relations to architecture and real estate grew in bulk and passed that psychological size barrier of 100 staff per organization, it became necessary to accept the duality of management structure as a norm. New skills, faster decision-making and a need to embrace new ideas all came together as an overwhelming force, pushing aside old-fashioned concepts of single-line responsibility. It may have worked in the traditional manufacturing industries, but even there the system was not only creaking itself, but may well have been one of the root causes of many companies sliding behind their competitors.

Tight lines of communication evolved from the military necessities of fighting wars and ensuring blind obedience. After all, you did not want any tremulous young soldier who is about to walk into the fire of an enemy machine-gun to believe that there is an alternative to the command: 'Move forward'. The belief that what seemed efficient in war-time must be equally effective in the management of a company was perpetuated by the dominating effect on the psyche of the Crimea, the Boer War, and then two world wars. Why else are ex-army officers frequently clasped to the corporate breast with such alacrity?

This is not to decry the training and education required by a modern military officer. In many ways the style of warfare in the last decade may have forced a new style thinking onto the chain of command. The fact does remain that if we are to approach any problems without the encumbrances of traditional thinking we are likely to find a solution more effective if we work as a group, interacting between disciplines and agreeing to differ on some issues but fighting over others. A form of *primus inter pares* leadership is required, rather than a rigid system of order and counter-order.

Research carried out by Philip Sadler of Britain's Ashridge

Management College some years ago showed under test conditions a higher level of efficiency and group response when this form of leadership was in play than the traditional autocratic, or non-leadership anarchy. The key to the 'first among equals' approach is its willingness to permit the existence of individual groupings, each perhaps with its own leader, but always to maintain the role of co-ordination at the centre, accepted and respected by those in the group. We might have said 'obeyed', but this would have been a typical response to the dated concepts we are trying to leave behind. In the post-hierarchical society, knowledge-based and driven by a new set of values, there has to be a different set of dynamics in even the most mundane of departmental operations.

Once there is an acceptance of the balance between leadership and co-ordination, it becomes easier to devise an organizational chart that allows disciplines to operate together and even to overlap. For example, tradition has set the finance department in a relatively tight jacket. This became looser in the fifties as financial strategy and longer-term economic planning extended the accountancy function and forced its manager into the boardroom. In some companies, corporate strategy even evolved into a completely new departmental function, but for the majority of operations there was a natural division occurring between 'doing the books' and planning cash-flow and forecasts for the future. Major restructuring of functions took place as even small business accounts departments became computerized. To a large extent however the discipline remained within tight boundaries, and it was a fortunate company indeed which found itself with a financial director who truly understood the wider problems of the business. Pressures of the media, the insistence of analysts and brokers on having a wealth of more detailed figures and a steady dialogue on information, forced many financial directors to edge into the realms of external relations. Often this was undertaken with a grudging acceptance that the financial and business plan might have some importance as to how the corporation was viewed by the stock market. Half-hearted presentations took place with insistent analysts and brokerage houses until today, the analyst presentation is seen as an important element in the overall financial relations programme.

As discussion on the 'Big bang' of de-regulation got under way, take-over bids became the battle-ground for skilful communicators. It was in this climate that the external PR consultant came into his own. The communicator in investor relations had arrived. Today, few finance departments of public companies would expect to carry on business without a specialist external PR consultant by his side, and those which do not retain a consultant turn to their director of public affairs or his equivalent for advice, especially in takeover bid or flotation situations. The ideal, of course, is both. However, in this case, there is a tendency for that function to be carried out by someone with a financial background. There are few people who are capable of handling the detailed nuts and bolts of, say, financial PR and yet can think in terms of the broader brush of corporate relations. Thus one part or another of the daily function has to be fudged. So, many directors of corporate communications paddle furiously under the water when either product marketing or the corporate strategy plan is needed for a repositioning of the total corporate identity. The skills are so specialist, and the range of abilities needed so technical and conceptual that they are too immense for them to be found in one person.

We arrive at a position therefore on organizational structure where we have to say there are three elements that *must* be made to fit:

(i) Multi-line management responsibility.
(ii) Acceptance that tactical communications skills are essential within the marketing, the personnel and the financial departments, as a basic requirement.
(iii) Tactical and technical execution that is separated from the strategic drive of the overall communications function.

We have already discussed the first item on this list. An example of the second was a finance department that wants to move towards a greater mix of skills and expertise within itself with the execution of communications activity being undertaken as part of the department. This argument applies as strongly in personnel and marketing as it does in finance. Within each department, there needs to be marketing communications, personnel communications and financial communications units, an integral part of their staffing.

It will be seen that the Communications Director has a direct responsibility for each of the specialist groups within the discrete departments as well as having a fully-fledged department of his own. His own department contains few surprises. The only possible one is the fact that a fully-fledged research capability is present within it. The days of loose public relations activity aimed, hopefully, at achieving editorial coverage in a selected group of newspapers and the rest of the time concerned with counselling on governmental affairs and print work for the AGM are past.

The communications department will not only gather importance over the next five years, but will become more and more disciplined in its approach. Each year a written communications programme will and must be demanded by the CEO. That demand has to be clearly stated in terms of its parameters and ultimate content and understood. The description of the message that is to be projected should quantify also the number of people who will be exposed to the message and evaluated in terms of possible effectiveness in changing attitudes over the period ahead. It should be noted that th ere is a clear differentiation between quantification of the number of people who will see the message and its effectiveness. They are not the same, although each must be measured in numerical terms.

These three layers – the written programme, the measurement of exposure and the evaluation of effectiveness are the minimum requirement. As market conditions intensify and the level of international competitiveness becomes tougher, there is a growing need for companies to establish for themselves some position in the marketplace that they and they alone will grow. This does not mean that the company will establish for itself a bland description which says 'We will become the authority, the industry standard for our sector, noted for quality, design and after-sales service'. That is fine if you can achieve all those things in such a way and to such a level that even your competitors will accept it – as IBM or DEC have done – but not much good as a positioning statement. After all, they should be the objectives of every company. It is like saying 'We believe that we should abide by ethical standards, work honestly and produce products that people want.' So what? If you do not aim to do these things the company will probably be out of business in a year.

A positioning statement takes months to evolve. It requires a careful analysis of a corporation's internal attitudes, hopes and ambitions. 'Where do you expect the company to be in five years' time?' the CEO is asked. 'Describe, in one paragraph, the company and its mission.' Then, when you are asked: 'How does that make you different from "X" company?' you should be able to say what makes you different without criticizing the competitive companies. It's only too easy to say, 'We're different because our products don't fall to pieces after you've used them once, like our competitors' '. Everyone knows that is not true. To say you want to grow or switch from one sector to another will not do. Some companies manage to create within their own ethos a belief that this or that competitor is either a crook, is badly organized, or that his products do not work. So instilled do some of these morale-boosting epithets become that after a while everyone actually begins to believe them. It becomes a great trauma of a lifetime when someone actually leaves to work for a competitor and then finds a rather well-organized operation making effective products.

We've written a great deal about corporate culture in this book. Corporate identity has not received parallel attention, even though it is to culture what cause is to effect. It is the outward and visible sign of positioning. It is not an image but the very heart and soul of an organization. It is about style, quality, personality, rather than reputation which is the image of the company or how it is perceived. If culture is the 'what' of a company, identity is the 'why'. Corporate identity is the focus for the corporation's identification – its positioning and competitive edge. It embraces business mix, management style, communication policies and practices, nomenclature as well as strengths (weaknesses) and market differentiation. Identity is vital because it is the symbol (literally and metaphorically) for building understanding, credibility and support in an intensely competitive and rapidly changing world. For instance, in the U.S. more than 2,500 corporate mergers, divestitures and acquisitions took place recently in a single year. Every one of these organizations had an identity challenge and opportunity before it. Some seized the chance to rethink, recast and re-present themselves more effectively. Most did not.

Nor is change being propelled only by the corporate restructuring phenomenon. Throughout the industrialized countries, quickening de-regulation, an almost irreversible decline in the industrial base, the rapid growth of service sectors, the emergence of new electronic technology and genetic engineering, a continuing world-wide population shifts and lifestyle changes, an increasing level of international trade, the emergence of design quality as a touchstone of consumer acceptance – all these and more make improved corporate and brand identification with communications to make a competitive imperative.

The fact is that, more and more, enlightened managements are grasping basic identity for what it really is: the comprehensive determination and orchestrated projection of what a corporation is and where it is going – its strategic commitments, core competencies, market presences and competitive differentiation. These same managements are, in turn, employing effective verbal and visual identification to focus and present each organization – in line with what it really is and is becoming – to each critical audience in as compelling, distinctive, significant and memorable a way as possible.

While attitudes, behaviour, patterns of belief, shared values are often observable, the motivation causality, the 'whys' of the 'what', if you will, are not readily apparent. This is particularly so in companies with a longer history, where the identity and its cultural consequences are a generation or more removed from the founders' influence.

By determining the special style, quality and character of a company, it is possible to position an entity in its marketplace and differentiate its capabilities against the competition with precision, clarity and greater impact. In other words, with the management's determination as to what the company really is, and how it can best describe itself it can signal the direction in which it is heading, and convey what most distinguishes it. The organization can then project a focus and commitment that wasn't possible previously. Like a laser beam, which focusses random light waves, a determination of basic identity crystallizes a company's essence and purpose with beneficial consequences, both within and outside the organization.

What are some of the benefits from this identity discovery process and what flows from it?

- First of all, top managements can discover or comprehend the central force that motivates the company and its employees to believe and behave as they do. With that knowledge, it is possible to adapt existing cultures with sensitivity and integrate new cultures following a merger or acquisition with less disruption.
- Second, strategic planners can provide insights concerning basic values, beliefs and motivation that could have as much

significance as financial results in selecting merger and acquisition candidates. They can judge what will be a good 'fit' from a cultural standpoint. This knowledge can prevent an unsuccessful attempt to mix one company's 'oil' with another company's 'water'.

- Third, operating and marketing managers receive clear signals on how best to convey corporate competence and distinctiveness across the range of divisional, business unit, product and service applications. At the same time, all marketing, communication, verbal and visual equities can be orchestrated, transferred and leveraged, as appropriate. In this way, reputation from the corporation or any of its parts can be used to enhance other parts to a fuller extent.
- Fourth, public and investor relations professionals will have a clearly defined, internally consistent, and competitively distinct story to tell about a unique organization. A story which also provides the platform for corporate advertising. These communications efforts become incrementally more effective as they build upon and reinforce each others' messages.
- Fifth, human resource managers and recruitment personnel can better understand the kind of people who would flourish (or flounder) in their company's particular environment. Such an appreciation can help attract needed talent and avoid costly hiring mistakes. Moreover, current employees will show greater pride in and support for an organization whose purpose, direction and specialness they understand.

The external benefits of comprehending basic identity – and of acting forcibly upon that knowledge – can be even more important:

- To begin with, by learning precisely where perceptions of the company are diffuse, shallow, inaccurate or even negative, senior management can take corrective action through orchestrated and targeted identification initiatives. Beyond that, the programme can position the corporation and project its core competencies in line with basic identity and strategic objectives. As a consequence, the corporation can present an integrated, cohesive picture of its current reality and intentions.

  In addition, with the aid of the more crystallized focus, the financial community can better comprehend the company and more fairly value its assets. Customers and prospects can become more aware of the organization's business capabilities, management strengths, product and service diversity, its competitive distinction; while governmental authorities – in the U.S., executive, legislative, regulatory and judicial officials at federal and state levels – can better understand the company, appreciate its contributions, bear with it (or even rally to it) in times of trouble. Other important publics, such as outside corporate directors, the news media, trade unions, suppliers, distributors, dealers etc. can with understanding speak more knowingly, supportingly and convincingly of the overall company and its mission.

It might be as well to mention some specific cases where the study of corporate culture and, with it, the ultimate deciphering of basic identity had profound effects on managements' view on their own companies and the way those organizations were consequently positioned by the outside world. Here we are indebted to Stephen Downey of Downey Week's and Toomey Inc. whose firm has forged frontiers in this under-utilized asset and its link into culture.

One example was a corporation that had long described itself as a large, diversified company in four major businesses: food and dairy, pharmaceuticals, industrial chemicals, and wine and spirits. Following a comprehensive analysis, the consultants presented management with some startling findings and recommendations. They said, among other things, that the organization was not so much a diversified company in four major businesses, but a unified company in four major markets . . . a company held together by a common thread of competence in distributing goods. It was a distribution company. Distribution was its basic, historical capability. That's why the company grew as it did, diversified (i.e. acquired other distribution-orientated companies) over a hundred-year period, as it did. In fact, however, the study also yielded other key insights. One was that in addition to providing professional distribution services, the company had built its ancillary services – like inventory accounting, market forecasting, administrative services etc. – which it was essentially not taking credit for. Over the years these valuable services had merely become 'part of the package,' taken for granted, hardly noticed by customers or management alike.

The central recommendation was to focus not only on the basic distribution competence, but on the 'added value' delivered as an integral part of the service. The positioning as captured in the competence statement developed by the consultant, became: 'Masters in value-added distribution'. Direct, descriptive, differentiating . . . and effective.

This distribution focus became the lynchpin for reaching and winning over three target audiences: the formerly sceptical financial community which became persuaded that here now was a cohesive company held together with a single thread of transferable competence; secondly, customers who came to appreciate the range of additional support services one company was providing that the competition was not; third, employees, once more orientated to their respective divisions, who increasingly viewed themselves as working for a larger, more unified company and thus looked for opportunities to realize further inter-divisional opportunities.

In many other instances also the search for identity revealed surprising insights that led towards action quite unlike that originally anticipated, for instance:

- A major corporation which was describing itself as 'A diversified management company' was persuaded to reposition the organization as 'A diversified energy company', insomuch as the large majority of its assets were expected to remain in energy-producing activities until well into the 1990s.
- A 'Big-eight' accounting firm that had always prided itself on being the largest company in its field, ultimately became convinced that a focus on quality and diversity of service was superior, yet a no less valid positioning, to reach newer, more enlightened, buyers of services who care less about who is biggest than who is best.
- A U.S. banking organization, being formed through the merger of two, culturally diverse, institutions accepted a recommendation for a new name and positioning. These not only surmounted former rivalries by, in effect, creating a 'new' institution that appealed to the employees' shared nationalism, but also helped pre-empt a large geographical home market from incursions by international money-centred financial institutions.

- An oil and gas retailer reversed an initial prescription against 'resurrecting' the company's original symbol that had been out of use for twenty years after being convinced first that the symbol still registered strongly across the range of key audiences; second, that a more recent design (employed since the early 1960s) had never been successfully 'seated'; and third, that the original symbol could better capture the past and revitalize the future if a more contemporary graphic presentation of it could be created. It was.

In many cases so-called corporate identity programmes don't work, or at least are not as effective as they could or should be. There seem to be several reasons for this:

First, an under-appreciation by many managements of the strategic value of identity, and positioning. In projecting a corporation and all of its parts as an orchestrated whole opportunities to convey competence, distinctiveness and reputation are missed.

Second, limited sophistication on the part of many graphic designers, who attempt to undertake complex identity programmes without sufficient business knowledge or strategic understanding of the job.

Third, a lack of discipline and will within many companies to follow through and execute an identification programme with the thoroughness and steadfastness required over a sustained period (up to three years).

Fourth, a failure to anticipate and address the 'cultural clash' that is all but inevitable in the wake of a merger or acquisition. There is also a tendency following a merger or acquisition to make identity decisions too quickly often without sufficient objectivity, and in an atmosphere of emotionalism and 'winner-loser' bias. In fact, because the combining organizations reflect multiple positions, cultures and personalities, considerable effort must be made to create a harmonious and valid identity amidst temporary dislocation and often bitterness.

What is most unfortunate, especially in the aftermath of merger or acquisition, is that the full synergistic opportunities arising from companies coming together are under-utilized or sacrificed. Instead, amidst internal bickering and external confusion, the added-value possible from combining – the 'goodwill' in both the financial and public relations sense – can be largely dissipated.

Finding a clear-cut position for a company requires some analysis of the corporation's culture, so that ultimately the external positioning is a natural extension of the internal life of the company. If we assume that, like people, a company has a personality (its culture), an identity (the external permanent appurtenances like graphics, buildings, packaging – the equivalent of a person's clothes), and it leaves behind from all that an image in people's minds, then it becomes obvious that the position taken in the marketplace must reflect all that. As the name implies, a corporate positioning is like a stance. It is a way of being seen that ensures onlookers will not muddle a particular company with any other. We talk about 'owning' a position. We talk about 'the difference that makes the difference'. Why is it so many corporate advertisements are so bland? What do we mean by that? Rather than say that a company is an authority in its field, producing high-quality products, we need to develop a concept or idea which has some meaning for the customer and an appeal that will draw certain target groups to it. Typical positioning statements might be: 'A company that always gives you the leading-edge of technology, so that you know you're ahead of the competition', or 'Technology you can feel at home with', or 'Safe, reliable, dependable, goes on forever'.

Now all these statements could apply to different companies in the same product group, yet they are quite clear and frankly each one has a sales minus as well as a plus. The final positioning is right for some customers, but on the other hand sunrise industries very quickly become sunset industries, and not everyone wants the latest before the products have been debugged. The rather comfortable feel of the second is not a good positioning for the young, who do not suffer from techno-fear and prefer something of a challenge. The last is ideal for certain users, but quite wrong for others. So a good positioning for a company brings with it disadvantages and it is for that reason that many organizations try to embrace a wide-ranging, over-bland positioning which they hope will not offend anyone. By doing this they run the risk of creating so inoffensive an identity that it becomes instantly forgettable. In many ways, such an appraisal spotlights the weakness of the marketing department's targeting when it comes to customer segmentation. Few companies, even in the packaged goods area, have a product that is all things to all people, and to attempt to do this only muddles the customer and leaves an indeterminate image behind.

An analysis of competitor positioning is an important element of the type of auditing procedure that is needed to arrive at a true positioning statement. The fundamental attitude of mind permeating the whole of this basic exercise is a view of the marketplace in customer terms. A positioning or identity for a company that does not take into account the rest of the market, and whether or not there is an open position to be taken up, is likely to lose many of the position's advantages. The whole concept of positioning is based on the idea that if a competitor can project a crisp, clear style and image that is quite different from other companies in the same area, customers are more likely to remember and retain the product message in the front of their minds. This should not be as difficult as it at first appears. Positioning is not a slogan. It is not some bright and attractive grouping of words that arise from a think-tank one afternoon in the advertising agency's office. If we consider that a company's character is its physique, its psychology, and philosophy, then its outward appearance is its style. This means that three quite individualistic elements come together to create something different. Just as every person is different. That difference does need to be articulated so that employees feel they are part of it. Consumers think in picture-postcard terms – part verbal, part visual, but always simply. A positioning statement must not only embody the physique and character of the company as personified in its style or clothes, but it must be portable too.

The heading or groups of headings in a typical positioning audit construct provide the flow for what are in effect a series of open interviews. Sometimes the questions may want answers in order of priority, but no respondent is expected to remain tightly within the parameters of the questioning if he or she wishes to expand. It is for this reason that we talk about topic menus and topic guides and avoid the use of the market research word 'questionnaire'. Audits of this type are not market research. They are a series of open-ended questions intended to create a dialogue and free-flow of responses between senior managers and an experienced public relations or marketing interviewer. The process can have a subjective element in it, and this might distort the final analysis. It is for this reason that interviews are normally carried out by senior practitioners, people who can bring years of experience in communication to bear on the discussion. All the time the audit questioning is going on an experienced public relations interviewer will be assessing the replies in terms of future communication gaps, and possible ways those gaps can be filled by certain types of action.

The work often undertaken by market research companies in this area, which after all is very close indeed to the normal surveys they would undertake, tends to miss out on that all-important commentary and action section. Whether it is in the provision of too much undigested data, or the fact that where a full commentary is given it is unlikely to edge into the area of communications recommendations in any detail, surveys carried out by market research companies do not always fulfil the needs of companies at a corporate level.

The audit helps create quality of leadership. It moves five or six steps down the line towards getting the show on the right road.

The final document when completed and discussed at various stages will have at its end a detailed set of recommendations, a timetable and a budget which arise directly out of the report. Quite obviously this is not enough on its own. The specialist areas mentioned earlier, such as marketing, personnel, finance and possible sectors within the corporate communications department itself, will all need their own sub-campaigns within the overall programme. Whatever happens, and whether the process starts with a programme developed for the departments or subsidiary companies first and the central campaign later or vice-versa, the various elements of the final programme *must* be seen as a whole. Here the relationship between divisional brand names and the corporate name is crucial. The various departments must take proper account of each other, not merely through bland statements and lip-service. The concept of the single company message need not be a straitjacket. It need not entail constraints from the centre and time lost in clearance, if the original document was based firmly on a detailed audit that included a close study of the company's culture. The idea of a company having a personality of its own, which is carefully developed because it creates a final image in the minds of the outside world, is a *natural* reflection of the corporation as it really is. If that image falls easily out of the company's life, everyone responsible for handling communication will have a natural feel and understanding of how a message should be styled and presented externally.

This may sound like a pipe-dream, something that is either too good to be true or requires a level of telepathy to achieve. This is only partly true. Certainly it can take years to arrive at a situation where the executive responsible for communications in a subsidiary company is so in tune with the corporate head of public affairs that everything he does and writes is 100% acceptable further up the line. Yet if a properly structured attempt is made, with regular three-monthly working sessions – not committees where everyone either pontificates against an agenda designed to fill the time allotted, or where each person presents reports in excruciatingly boring detail on what they have been doing in previous months – there is then a chance that by working together in a task-force atmosphere, a community of spirit. A commonality of attitude will be generated and a coherent corporate identity created.

At this stage we should consider the constant debate over the use, or not, of external consultants. In the advertising world, a structure of commissions and support functions has created a situation where every company that advertises must have some sort of agency. In general communication, however, whether it is called public relations, public affairs or corporate communications, there is a constant debate on the extent to which the technical – and indeed the strategic – aspects of the function should be carried out from within or by use of external consultants. There is no clear-cut answer and it is quite wrong for any company to make black and white decisions based on subjective attitudes which arose originally because of past good or bad experiences.

The advantage of an in-house corporate affairs or public relations department is that it is close to the central life of the company and its staff understand the business from the inside. Apart from those situations where a consultant has handled a client's business for many years, it is unlikely that any consultant can understand the detailed technical life of the company and its products as well as someone working on the spot. When something happens, that person is actually present and a decision can be taken quickly as to what response is needed. Equally, if there is a requirement for media relations or perhaps a heightened attack on the trade press as part of a market support exercise, then the in-house manager may well find it easier to prise out stories and new angles when he or she is constantly out and about in the company. A further plus-point is the fact that the senior members of the PR staff in-house are more likely to understand the internal politics and culture of the company. This can be very important when it comes to such matters as choosing a spokesperson or deciding who should be quoted in a press release. So in summary, the plus elements of the house-team appraisal are associated with an ability to know the company and its products, combined with speed of reaction.

When we look at the other alternative, using an external public relations consultant, there are a series of advantages that are quite different from those listed above. The consultant provides an objective overview, and can therefore see the company as others see it. As a result he or she can provide that market-related advice which is so valuable. Working within a company is very similar to living within a family setting. However difficult or wrong-headed the other members of the family may be, the fact remains that they are of the same blood and therefore must be loyally supported throughout any vicissitude. Equally, there is a tendency within a family to turn a blind eye to other people's failures. One of the toughest parts of any consultant's early relations with a new client are the meetings on product benefits. Time and again the response to questions about the plus-points of the product range are met with a rather pitying look as if to say 'Surely they are obvious; you don't need me to tell you.' Then, grudgingly or enthusiastically, depending upon his or her position in the company, the person you have asked will tell you that the plus-points of the company's products are quality, design, reliability and 'Of course, our outstanding reputation'. Everyone working for a particular company has to believe that it does things better than the rest of the market – why be in business if it does not? Thus, these statements of subjective opinion like 'best quality', 'wonderful service' come out as if none of the competitor companies is saying exactly the same thing about their products. The number one job of the consultant must therefore be to combine his or her own objectivity with the data that comes out of the market research, to provide a piece of reality to what can frequently become a fairy-tale world where hope triumphs over fact.

The second advantage of using a PR consultancy or adviser is that most such operations have a number of staff. Through that team and its network of contacts the client therefore has access to a wider range of skills. The underlying theme through so much of this book is that modern communications require a more diverse set of experiences and technical abilities than ever before. In some ways these are more broadly-based and more likely to be drawn from different types of people than would be the case with say, an accountant or a lawyer. How many public relations practitioners are able to say, hand on heart, that they have a specialist knowledge and skill in the handling of parliamentary relations and marketing communications, and can offer equal skills in corporate identity and investor relations. We suspect that very few can, yet there are not many companies operating successfully today who do not need a high level of expertise in each of these sectors. The sensible CEO will allocate sufficient resources for skilled communications practitioners to be employed in each sector. But is he or she experienced enough to be able to make the necessary judgements? We hope this book has provided some illumination on this understandable problem.

There is a balance therefore of advantages between the internal and external approach to public relations support. The most effective operations are always those that draw from both sides of the divide and ensure that each one's advantages are recognized and built upon.

The difficult element, however, is to bring a matching pair together. Not all in-house PR heads are enthusiastic managers who can develop all the advantages of the 'close to the scene of action' position. Neither are all PR consultancies such veritable universities of new ideas and creative thought that we have described. Even if both sides were such paragons, they may not necessarily make a good marriage. The chemistry can be wrong, and personal relationships can be sufficiently indifferent to make the synergetic effect non-existent. After all, there should be a creative bond that produces work finer than its parts, if the people working on the account can break out of the normal client-agency relationship. Once the client treats the agency as a sub-contractor, a supplier who must jump because the piper calls the tune, then many of the advantages of the external consultancy concept are lost. Objectivity is only possible if it can be used to give advice fearlessly. An atmosphere of creative ideas is of use only if there is an equal climate of encouragement to produce and argue through this new thinking. Equally, on the consultancy side there is unlikely to be any profit from a relationship where the agency staff look upon their clients as an annoying intrusion into the tranquillity of their everyday life. Too many PR consultancy staff make comments like 'public relations would be wonderful if it weren't for the clients!' But the client, as we said earlier, is the only reason for the agency to exist. A statement of the obvious perhaps, although you might not think so if you listened to younger staff, many of whom think they have all the answers to the world's problems because of the pressure-cooker atmosphere within which they exist. As the public relations business draws more and more on business-school graduates, we hope to see a steady improvement in the quality of advice and judgement within this whole area. To have spent three years at college gaining a business degree, then following that with an MBA, may not produce a genuis at the end, but at least through the process of case-study and analysis of the business decision-making process the people produced through that educational channel will have worked off some of their bad decisions and mistakes where it can do the least harm.

Having made the decision to develop an internal public affairs department that includes the control of advertising and all elements of the communications programme, it becomes that department's duty to select and appoint the advertising agency (if needed at corporate level – the product agencies should be appointed by the marketing communications departments) and the public relations consultancy. By taking this belt and braces approach it is possible to gain the best advantage of both worlds.

Significantly some of the latest handbooks of management which allegedly provides a single source of reference for every management skill and function fails to cover, except peripherally, the essentials of this book. For those companies which ignore this advice, it won't just be a cosmetic job they'll need, but plastic surgery!

10
The latch-key audit

'The practical questions for managers to ask about the next ten years are what changes can be expected in social values and how these are likely to affect work and employment, and what can be done today and in the future to maintain as close a correspondence as possible between working practices and external pressures for change.'

Technological Shock,
A report by
The Management Research Group of BIM
(1980). British Institute of Management.

There was a time when corporate PR was easy. A glossy brochure or two, some press lunches for city journalists, then if your luck was in, the chairman might develop a penchant for motor racing and you'd get the job of running a couple of big events at Brands Hatch. Of course, if the company was in a sensitive area like pharmaceuticals or the oil industry, things could get a little hairy. It was on occasions like that when the easy life called and the consultancy world seemed quite an attraction.

Today all is different. Most companies are concerned about the way they are viewed in the marketplace, both the financial and customer variety. The in-house head of PR is expected to sort out the intricacies of corporate identity programmes, divert awkward questions from MPs, build up relations with pressure groups and above all, steer the company's external persona through the labyrinthine maze of corporate strategy often without having been a party to that strategy in the first place.

Suddenly communication is the in-flavour and you can't spit in the forecourt of the London Business School without hitting some bright young MBA with the PR plans for a new Jersusalem in his hip pocket. Today it isn't enough to talk about corporate image and corporate identity. We have to delve deeper. We're expected to find out what really makes the corporation tick, take a judgement on how the new corporate strategy will be accepted by the world outside, talk to everyone down to the tea-lady and get a fix on what we now refer to as corporate culture and then arrive in the chairman's office armed with a fully-blown positioning statement.

What has led to this enormous lurch forward in the role of the corporate PR executive? Why has the job function changed? Why has it become sufficiently interesting for many consultants working on the fringe of our business like accountants, industrial psychologists and management consultants to start moving in on us with so called strategic units.

The reason is simple. It's called competition. In the sixties, which was the heyday of corporate identity, all the big companies launched into massive graphics programmes. Once the new colourful symbols were agreed enormous sums were spent on the application of these artifacts to every part of the company's life. Like the mystical signs laid out at the summer solstice they were raised to the status of religious icons. What Jung called 'The transcendant function of the pysche'. They became the means by which the contents of the corporate unconscious could enter the conscious mind.

Once these cultural changes had taken place it was the turn of the advertising agencies. They stepped in with their big budget commercials and every corporation worth its salt was telling the public that they were 'In business to serve you', were 'Ahead of our time', or had a 'Tradition of progress', or even surprisingly that 'What's ours is yours', surely the most unbelievable ad slogan of the century.

The problem of all this was that once the highly expensive TV commercials came to an end most people forgot the slogans. The reason was obvious. They had no root in the real being – the true psyche of the company. They were seen as no more than expensive pieces of couture draped across an ageing frame.

The purpose of a communications audit is to analyse the effectiveness of a company's internal and external communications.

In the process of making this analysis we compare the image of the company as perceived by the management with the actual image held by the public or specialist target audiences outside it. There is usually a divergence of such views and as a result of 'gap analysis' detailed recommendations can be made for bringing those views more closely into line with each other.

The communications audit also produces secondary advantages. By interviewing in depth senior and middle management as well as shop-floor staff where appropriate, it soon becomes apparent that even within the company there are divergences of opinion about fundamental issues. Quite explicit statements on corporate objectives are often shown to have been interpreted in different ways by different levels of management. As a result of this, the company is shown to be divided not only about the identity it should be projecting but even about the techiques to be used for communicating that image.

When it comes to analysis of the views held about the company by its external publics, divergences of opinion are usually even greater. They vary according to the groups interviewed – customers, 'City', or Parliamentary interests, consumers, local government – and also within each group itself.

It is our experience that unless there is consistency of attitude towards a company among those working in it, then we cannot hope to communicate effectively with the target audience outside. The audit, then, defines the inconsistencies and, more importantly, recommends action.

We usually divide the analysis into two parts – an internal and an external audit.

The Internal Audit

We first draw up a list of those who are to be interviewed by our audit team. The list normally includes the chief executive and chairman as well as divisional heads – marketing, production, finance etc. We would also expect to take a sample of middle managers in the departments which communicate with external audiences. If possible, we like to meet shop stewards, union leaders, and those in a position of influence at shop floor level. Quite naturally the list of interviewees will vary according to the ultimate purpose of the main audit. The questions we ask are structured and cover a wide range of subjects relating to corporate strategy as well as to areas directly impinging upon the communications needs of the company.

A secondary purpose of the internal audit is to analyze the channels of information flow and to assess how effective they are.

The External Audit

This is the more complex of the two sections, dealing as it does with different target audiences and a larger number of people. We do not attempt to carry out research into the total consumer market. This is the job of market research and if such research is available we expect to analyze it *after* we have completed the audit. To do so earlier would influence our questioning and the subsequent flow of discussions. But there is obviously a role for research of the 'statistically significant' variety.

Our prime purpose is to assess the views held by opinion leaders, especially those who are in the communications field such as journalists, TV/Radio producers, writers and academics. We term this latter group 'communications targets' to distinguish them from the ultimate sales target, the consumer, or from financial targets, such as shareholders.

If, for example, we needed to know how the trade in which the company operated viewed the company's image, we would interview trade journalists, officers of trade associations, and a sample of trade buyers.

When we are concerned with the views held by parliamentary and financial leaders then we would not only interview journalists writing for the media read by those groups, but also key people in such areas i.e. chairmen of relevant back-bench committees, officers of parliamentary groups, senior management in City institutions and members of those bodies which may influence the more immediate target audiences.

So far as the public is concerned we concentrate on the media read or viewed by the different groups the company hopes to reach. Our research on the impact of opinion leaders and on how attitudes are formed plays an important part in the selection of the media to be interviewed and other groups in this section. Sometimes it can be important to interview consumerist groups, leaders of social or professional organizations or leisure clubs and institutions. On other occasions it is sufficient to concentrate on the media alone.

We must stress that the audit is not intended as a substitute for market research. It does not fulfil the same function. Indeed, the questions, although structured, are open-ended and allow for quite extensive responses.

It would be impossible for this type of audit to be carried out by someone untrained in public relations, since it makes use of a different technique from that used in market research. For example, far from trying to create a sense of objectivity, we expect trained executives to be making informed but subjective judgements as the audit sheets are completed.

In the last analysis the audit is a complete examination of a company's communications needs by executives who are themselves experienced in planning and implementing programmes to meet such needs.

Thus, on completion of the questioning, we are able to analyze the communications needs and to prepare a detailed plan or public relations programme to help solve the problems we have isolated.

If a public relations programme is to be fully effective, it must be designed to meet a set of specific communications objectives. It is our belief that without an audit of the kind outlined, these specific objectives cannot be set with confidence.

External issues are now an important part of corporate strategies and as more companies are realizing the need to consult and influence the groups which shape those issues, we have developed disciplines and formulae that ensure we analyze these pressures and develop early responses.

How does a company identify which external forces are relevant to its corporate policy, and, once it has identified those forces, how can it best liaise with those groups of people who shape issues? Finally, which of those groups does a company need to influence early, before policies harden?

It is with this in mind that the 'Issues Audit' was created which works hand in hand with the positioning and communications audits. It is designed to identify and then qualify which issues are relevant now and in the future and which internal mechanisms should be created to take account of those issues.

Key personnel are taken through a highly structured series of open-ended questions to identify crucial areas of interest and questions of importance facing the company. The differences between the responses gives us a basis for analysis.

Today we are seeing the development of whole new methodologies whereby a carefully structured internal survey can be completed against clear topic menus. After much intellectual effort and many sleepless nights, a positioning statement emerges like white smoke from the papal court. Eureka, we're in business. This discipline grew out of what was called the Communications Audit. It was a bland all-embracing term. It allowed the consultant undertaking it to do as much or as little as he chose. Before considering a more modern up-to-date version of this technique perhaps we should consider its basic appeal.

Within this audit construct a topic menu is prepared and it is this that makes or truly breaks the ultimate success of the audit. The difference between a positioning statement and the sloganizing of old is that the statement is not only developed by natural parturition from the life of the company, but it is never made in public, or not in its literal form anyway.

Corporate positioning as a concept is now becoming the basis for all communication activity whether to customers, the City, government or even its own employees. The idea being that a corporation should seek to own one overall position in the marketplace. A position that is uniquely theirs. Trespassers will be prosecuted. A piece of ground that is so clearly owned by the company that if a researcher goes out among its target audiences they will, under interview, describe the company in a way that not only will all the right adjectives be used, but they will be different adjectives to those used about their competitors. This difference that makes the difference is what gives a company its competitive edge. What leads it to the front of the race.

When the positioning statement has been clarified and refined, it can be validated externally among a sample of the target audience. Once done it becomes necessary to find issues through which the corporate positioning can be given life. Positioning is strictly about message, not one message but many. All of them held together by the single thread that represents the one true faith of the company's corporate marketing strategy. A public relations programme based around a series of clear-cut issues and message strategies starts to take on a life of its own. All elements from product and marketing support to governmental relations and the response of pressure groups begins to have an internal logic and style that perpetuates the image left behind in people's minds.

Corporations that plan their public affairs over a longer time-span, setting up systems to ensure that they are ready to respond to changes in the business environment or possible attacks from environmental groups take the concept of the positioning audit one stage further. They launch into the more ambitious realm of the Issues Audit. Through the use of this methodology it becomes possible to prepare the ground for likely trouble in the future and set up response mechanisms.

The audit is a systematic investigation into the issues affecting the company, what mechanisms the company uses to manage those issues and how the issues are incorporated into the corporate planning process. It also identifies the external groups who affect and are affected by the company's handling of those issues, and how the company influences and is influenced by them.

Once the audit is completed the response to each question can be analyzed and qualified. Differences of opinion can be identified so that a chart and analysis of the company's mechanisms and responses can be drawn up.

When it is clear what elements are missing, a plan can be devised to correct those omissions. Equally, the analysis can be used to highlight areas which need attention, or those which can be modified or even dropped from the company's programme. From this we can make our own recommendations.

The audit is not statistical research, but a qualitative assessment carried out in a highly organized manner. The questions we ask invite opinion as well as fact, because people's perceptions in this area are often as important as the reality. In fact, perceptions *are* facts because people believe them.

The audit also helps the company examine its needs and position in the increasingly important area of issues management and to re-examine those needs in the light of an incisive independent analysis.

One thing must be made clear. The type of communications auditing procedure discussed here must never be seen as something apart from the basic public relations activity of the company. The data derived from the process should become the very core – the basic message strategy of each part of the PR programme. Speeches must be used to develop the themes, articles placed that will build upon it, and even the hardest of hard news press releases should find a place for some reinforcement of the message particularly at a time of major 'turn around' when cultures are adapting to fit new strategies.

The trend today is towards co-ordination of the communications message. This is to the good and means that the investment in time and money on a detailed initial audit, followed later by the more sophisticated Issues Analysis, is spread across the whole company.

Strategic planning is not an esoteric indulgence created for the intellectual satisfaction of business school graduates. It is the motor that should be driving the communications vehicles of European industry.

11
Corporate ecology

'This period of accelerated innovation we are going to see over the next five years constitutes for the information industry, and more broadly for our civilization a kind of climatic shift. The combination of new technologies, micro-processors, local area networks, satellite, fibre optics, and new kinds of software, expert systems, and artificial intelligence, is literally creating a different environment in which we are going to live, work and play.'

William F. Zachmann,
Vice-President,
International Data Corporation.

The word ecology, before it was absorbed by the conservationists and re-cycled for political usuage, meant the study of the inter-dependence of living things with their environment. In the same way that paradigm is a word which describes a confluence of attitudes and ideas, so ecology is concerned with that indescribable confluence of pressures and dependencies that ensures biological balance. It is for this reason that we use the word advisedly to describe corporate life and its responses to the world within which it is embedded. We go further than this however and attempt what is almost impossible. We look forward in this chapter to the pressures on corporate life – on its total ecology, in fact – that may well be experienced during the coming two decades into the twenty-first century.

To do this we follow certain clear threads. The first is an assessment of the changes expected at the workplace and the second is the impact this must have in personal and inter-personal terms. We make a cursory examination of the new channels of communication, of cable, of satellite, general de-massification of the media and how this will alter our normal day in the office. Finally, we describe the wired city and the life our children will accept as normal by the time they retire (assuming that 55 will be the accepted statutory retirement age for both sexes by the year 2000.) By that time the transition will be completed into a knowledge-based society driven by artificial intelligence, expert systems, and an unlimited data base for decision-makers. Our current period of living in transition between one age and another will have been completed. We will by then be accepting fast continuous change along tracks that will seem pre-ordained and to our children, normal. Our grandchildren and indeed our children, will see change as the mid-Victorians saw it. It will be an accepted part of life that brings few surprises and perhaps little wonderment.

Let us walk forward, therefore, and examine our children's working lives as they might appear in twenty years' time, possibly even sooner. We believe that CEOs need to think about this now as should corporate planning and human resource departments.

In the first place office buildings in the last decade of this century will probably be smaller and more domestic in their decoration and layout. Many will be as comfortable as first-class hotels, but most important of all we can expect them to be closer to the houses of the staff. Higher productivity will be the norm thanks to less time spent fuming in traffic jams. Indeed will there even be traffic jams?

Rapid decentralization of major companies will be taking place as they are forced to push more and more of their support functions out of the city centres. This will mean that good working conditions and high pay will be available in most towns. The domination of the office scene by information technology may not yet have moved along the lines of decentralized top management. The belief that satellite conferences and video-telephones will take away the need for meetings of managers is less likely than we believed five years ago. Intellectual functions are performed better in an atmosphere of constant inter-action. This is unlikely to be replaced completely by video technology. What it will do, however, is make it easier to move many more departments away from the high rent glue-pots that urban centres will soon become. Personalized transport is unlikely to be broken by any democratic government and even if it seems to be destroying many of our cities, step by small step, in a nightmare trudge towards Los Angeles, the Houston-type motorways, it is still likely to happen. The effect will be to deter more companies from operating within such a stultifying atmosphere.

City congestion may be the push but in parallel with it the surburban office centres will provide the pull by designing more attractive working environments. Strangely this desire to attract staff from the cities may lead to a more traditional or human scale to our buildings. We can expect more people to be repelled by the enormous high-rise office block, just as they were by the high-rise flats. Architectural symbolism may well go through a massive change as local firms and decentralized transnational corporations become more employee driven and less status conscious.

There is no doubt that senior managers, anxious to satisfy staff requirements will influence more strongly the architectural briefs that get sent into the office development companies. By 1990 it will not be a case of an isolated paradise here or there but the norm towards which all offices will strive when the time for refurbishment comes around. A visit to IBM's award winning offices in Havant or the equally attractive Digital Park factory and the offices of the Digital Equipment Company at Reading are symptomatic of the design that new corporate ventures will impose on themselves. Richard Roger's new U.S. headquarters for PA at Princeton, New Jersey, is a veritable system with all the waterworks on the outside to allow for human creativity and conducive environment on the inside. To say that a reaction to the hostility provoked by the flamboyant glass office boxes of today will take place during the next decade is to be unduly conservative. The new wave of high-tech companies anxious to appear forward and modern in their approach has already forced change. Strangely enough this will not be an artificial adoption of smart new clothes to impress the world. The smart new clothes won't seem like that to staff and management in the 1990s but only the norm to which they are accustomed. 'What other way is there to do it?' they will say. The British *Sunday Observer* (19.5.85) carried a piece by Laurence Marks, always a perceptive writer, in which he described a typical office of the 1990s.

> 'The new corporate image is of an almost eighteenth-century civility and reticence. Not that the facade is a weary pastiche of Georgian styles or cute Cotswold vernacular. On the contrary, its cast-iron balconies (decorated with patterns derived from micro-circuitry) and the crisp geometrical detailing of its ornamental brickwork proclaim a thoroughly modern building. Inside the

unobtrusive double doors, the immediate effect is theatrical: a deep internal courtyard, overlooked by balconies, rises wide, the full height of the building, to a glazed pitched roof which floods it with light. To left and right, each balcony on the three upper floors is occupied by unpartitioned space for eight people, the maximum possible without losing a valuable feeling of intimacy. The front and back of each floor is divided into five walled offices for single occupants, providing well proportioned space of Georgian elegance. The thickly carpeted ground level, with seats scattered about, doubles as coffee lounge and reception area. Colours are light and airy. There is a glass-sided wall-climber lift, iron staircases (more micro-circuitry), a small fountain, illuminated by an electronically programmed sequence of coloured lights, and rich planting cascading from the balconies.

The atrium, as this type of space is called, is one of the newest and one of the oldest architectural features. At Cambridge in the 1960s, Leslie Martin and Lionel March, challenging Le Corbusier's theory of high-rise building, discovered that the most efficient use of space on any given square footage of land was a low-rise courtyard.

In doing so, they confirmed what the designers of Oxford and Cambridge colleges had known without benefit of computer studies: that it permits the best distribution of natural light and the easiest movement from one part of the building to another.

In 1978, two other architects, Richard MacCormac and Dean Hawkes, demonstrated the energy saving benefits of putting a glazed roof over the courtyard and making it an internal space.

In the U.S., the new-style atrium was at first exploited as an extravagant showpiece with elaborate environmental controls. (The new Portman Hotel in Times Square has a breathtaking 40-storey atrium.) In Britain, architects quickly recognized that, if you got the proportion right, it provided enough natural light and ventilation to dispense with costly air-conditioning.

A famous recent example is the 1983 block in Basingstoke, designed by Peter Foggo of Arup Associates for the paper-makers Wiggins Teape. Window overhangs, external shades, and louvres in the roof prevent overheating, the curse of the glass tower. The absence of bulky air-conditioning ducts allows more comfortable ceiling heights.

But, besides being physically pleasanter, the low-rise atrium office has a profound effect on working relations among colleagues. At Micro-play, a striking sense of transparency pervades the building. The separate working spaces are uncrowded yet almost everyone can be in visual contact with everyone else.

Organizational paranoia, fed by forced physical isolation in small closed offices and by the numbing impersonal character of vast open-plan floors, has almost disappeared. There is a cheerful sense of community.

Micro-play's atrium has become the focus of social activities for the staff and, in the service of good public relations, the townspeople. A snooker tournament was held there last month. Next week, the local chamber opera group will give a concert performance of 'Alcina'. On Guy Fawkes Night, the last steel and glass office tower on the edge of town, long since declared an unsafe structure, was blown up by demolition men in front of a cheering crowd gathered from all over the country'.

What should be immediately apparent from this extract is the emphasis throughout on human values – what we call in other chapters 'soft management'. Unfortunately the role-model for managers – reinforced today by the J. R. Ewing sydrome of Dallas fame – is one of strength, hardness, and an almost total rejection of the need in management for emotion or human values. Throughout this book we argue that such days are past. Companies are about human assets, quality people and products rather than just price earnings ratio. Useful maybe for a company doctor moving into a troubled organization where fast, tough decisions have to be made immediately or the concern goes under. But for the future where values will have to change, the emphasis of Laurence Marks is probably an accurate reflection of how business life will be by the end of the century.

Interestingly enough, the signs of the changing values needed towards staff and their perceived convenience at first started coming through in the seventies and early eighties when Flexitime became the vogue. An article in *Management Today* (June 1980) called 'The Flexilife Future' was even then adumbrating this change. Still immersed at the time in old culture there is a hint in the writing of Norris Willatt of annoyance and irritation. His opening sentence began:

'The managing director's secretary rings to make an appointment with the general manager of one of the subsidiaries – only to find that the GM is on his educational sabbatical, studying relaxation in a Poona ashram. She puts the next phone call to the finance director, forgetting that it is Friday – the day he doesn't work. Next on the list is the chief executive of a competing company, an old friend of her boss: but the friend, though only 45, turns out to be in temporary retirement – and, since he is spending the time in Barbados, is not available for lunch. She then tries with increasing desperation, to fix a board meeting, which must take place before the end of the month. After that day, her boss, having completed his 200-day work contract for the year, will be off on a long, long holiday . . .'

A fantasy? At the moment, yes. But elements of the fantasy are real. The four-day week; the 19-day month; the executive sabbatical; leave to take further education; re-employment of retired executives; voluntary early retirement; all these and many other current developments are part of a world-wide change in life-cycles.

Now, in the closing quarter of the twentieth century, it seems possible that the rigid formula of the past may be slowly changing. Not that everybody is about to enter the ranks of the idle rich. But it may be possible for everybody to make richer use of their time. This is the aim of those advocating what has been called 'flexilife', which would offer the individual some degree of deviation from the traditional three fixed stages of linear living.

The flexilife concept is, in fact, a logical extension of so-called flexitime, the system which lets workers choose, within limits, when they perform their jobs in the course of the day, week, or month. Flexitime is already quite widely applied, especially among white-collar workers, in the world's leading industrialized countries. Its projection to the flexi-year would allow an employee to contract for a specific amount of work, which could then be completed during any hours he selects – and this idea is already the subject of experiment in various parts of the world.

The ideal, still a long way off, is the full flexilife, which would give individuals some choice as to when and for how long, they would spend their time on the three stages of preparing for work, working, and not working. A combination of schemes is possible, including opportunities for further study, at intervals, after starting work; sabbaticals for employees at all levels in business and industry, comparable to those that are routine in the academic world; and more flexibility in deciding when to retire; with, lastly, the opportunity to resume his working life once again after one or more intervals devoted to leisure.

Such revolutionary proposals are not just the product of sociological theory. The experiments already in progress seem likely to become more popular in the future. Work, for so long worshipped as a duty and a virtue, enshrined in the Puritan ethic and canonized by the Industrial Revolution, no longer exerts the same kind of mystical force. More and more people are willing to trade some of the material rewards of labour for more leisure.

Interestingly enough it had taken a science-fiction writer rather than a sociologist or main-stream scientist to extrapolate these changes in attitudes and values and the resistance to technological development by staff to explain what business life is likely to be about when those of our children entering primary school today start their first jobs around the years 2010 or 2015. Isaac Asimov described in his book *Living in the Future* an office where our sons and daughters will be able to answer any known question from their data base, give verbal commands to retrieve much of that information and be able to have so many organ transplants that our current fears of coronary heart disease or of suffering a stroke, will have by then almost disappeared. Assuming that our new executive who has joined a company training scheme towards the end of the century needs extra creative ideas or some form of education, then his wrist-watch radio with satellite link will enable him to talk more easily and quickly to colleagues in other parts of the world than through our static telephone or today's electronic mail.

Just as the internal combustion engine created a form of personalized transport (the horse always restricted its owners in terms of distance and comfort unless you were part of the wealthy aristocracy) because it freed people to move anywhere at will, so cordless radio telephones will change the level of mobility of businessmen and free them from the shackles of the desk. A small improvement in technology like that – i.e. size and totally personalized conveniences – makes the executive mobile on the one hand but more time effective on the other. The need to come into the office, to have papers, secretary, computer, all grouped around the telephone base disappear. It is too easy to say that the car telephone, the remote entry for automatic telephone answering machines, electronic mail enable this to happen already. The fact that it doesn't shows that anyone who believes this is living in a journalist's dream world. It is not always the technology itself that is so important but the attitudes towards it. And the unwillingness of so many people to change work patterns of a lifetime can be the true blockage to progress. Telephones in cars only work if your secretary also comes to work in a car that has a telephone, doesn't go out to lunch and is herself always at her desk. In reverse it assumes that the executive doesn't leave his car either or is constantly near a telephone, has all the numbers in his wallet, and doesn't visit a restaurant without telling his secretary where he is.

The sheer inconvenience of modern communications makes it easier in many cases to waste an extra hour returning to the office. Asimov is more sanguine than we are about the convenience of video telephones and networked computers. Certainly this whole army of technological soldiers will affect many people at most levels of executive activity. We suspect however, that the mark or insignia almost of the senior decision maker will be that he is the one that works face-to-face more than his staff. How else can he make use of the personal charisma –his innate skill in personal psychology – to ensure that he always gets what he wants!

We have found that something more important as a common denominator among business leaders we have interviewed which is their need to conquer the present. If they look to the future then five years is the maximum span. Some, a few who go under the media's description of being 'visionaries', do look ahead to a future point when their corporations will dominate this aspect of their market. They are too often men who ultimately fail because of their inability to handle the boring minutiae of the day-to-day running of their corporation. Those who succeed are the men or women who know how to pick people below them capable of holding the show together as they set visions and evolve future strategy. The purpose of this book, despite businessmen's resistance, is to look forward, but not so far forward that we lose sight of what is happening. Not perhaps to the twenty-first century but certainly to the trends that exist around us. If we don't pick up these road signs early we can stick unmoving in today's mud with wheels spinning. Or worse, carry the company into a sunlit cul-de-sac from which there is no exit. Somehow cul-de-sacs are usually the most attractive road on offer.

We mentioned earlier the problems of communication with secretaries in the year 2010. The role of the secretary may seem a little parochial in a book that claims to be analyzing the great business trends of the day. Yet within all these changing values, new motivations and technological aids, there is one overwhelming need, a central department or unit that feeds, adapts and preserves the information on which the new manager must act. Whether we continue to use the word secretary with its prostituted meaning – most secretaries today are human word-processors or find some new title – the job function is too frequently under-recognized. The real secretary, or administrative assistant, capable of maintaining order out of chaos, of reading and understanding all the memoranda and reports, of taking short-term decisions in the absence of the executives, are few and far between. The tendency for them to be women has acted as a block to men taking up the role. But, as more and more intelligent girls move into university and management roles, there are fewer women available to fulfil the key function of running the decision-makers' back-up service. Because change usually takes place in business by evolution rather than revolution, it is likely that the secretarial function will divide into one that is primarily automatic and repetitive – the working and typing onto word-processors – and another which is in effect an executive or administrative function possibly going under some such title as Administrative Assistant or Personal Assistant reporting in to a general manager who controls the total unit and works to the senior decision maker. Trade Unionists Clive Jenkins and Barrie Sherman writing in *The Collapse of Work* argue that the secretarial function as 'typist' (the U.S. meaning of secretary tends to describe a more lowly function than it describes in Europe) will become no more than the modern equivalent of a factory worker operating a lathe. The new type Secretarial Assistant will become a true interface between the decision-maker and the rest of the company. Even if she has to take dictation – modern managers by the end of the eighties, will have at least dispensed with such old fashioned methods and learned to use a microwriter or their own WP terminal, only re-shaping needs to be done in the support unit – the secretary will by 1989 be using spelling check software automatically and deciding when to draw upon her Kincaid or Flesch indices to calculate word density. If the words or phrases used by the manager are too difficult to understand by a low I.Q. reader, the software will automatically rephrase the sentence into simpler words and syntax. This is not such a fanciful idea as it may sound. Work undertaken in this field has shown over and over again that failures to communicate between management and factory workforces breaks down not because of the use of unfamiliar words, but because the workforce, brought up in a different environment (both in schools and at home) also have difficulty in coping with abstract concepts. It is the combination of subject and explanation systems that cause the incomprehension, not just one element on its own.

Having completed the typing and transferred it to electronic mail – signatures for internal distribution can be done away with if the secretarial function is fulfilled by people sufficiently intelligent and well trained to check all outward going mail without further reading by the executive – the secretary will sign any external mail on behalf of the boss. Need we really continue the fiction at meetings of 'I'm going now, I need to get back and sign my mail. There's urgent stuff which must go off'. Why do we continue this pretence? There are two reasons, one is because we do not employ sufficiently intelligent and involved people to be our secretaries, thus failing to give them full responsibility for checking and sending mail; secondly, we have a convention of good manners going back to Dickensian times that it is somehow unfriendly to have a letter signed p.p. We've dropped Esq., in the U.K.; perhaps it is time we accepted the fact that correspondence is no longer always a private communication between two gentlemen.

Sue and Colin Suter, respectively executive secretaries to the chief General Manager of the Anglia Building Society and senior lecturer in management studies, New College, Northampton, in the U.K., described the typical administrative unit that would replace today's secretarial function, in an article in *Management Today,* back in October 1983. They said that the executive secretary will become one of the elite assistants to senior management. Below that assistant will be the traditional secretarial services. This department will be an area comprising operators of word processors and other hardware from electronic mail and copiers to Fax machines and voice receiving machines. The best operators will eventually be assigned to assist the executive secretaries and learn that work. This upwardly mobile group will be office juniors, mature female (or male, if the prejudice can be broken down) graduates who have trained both within the company or at day-release colleges. 'Their tasks include not just the personal activities of welcoming visitors, but also doing spreadsheet calculations, research, and the representation of statistical and financial data.' In the Suter article they go on to describe a typical set of operations by the management assistant and the junior.

> 'The period between coffee break and lunch is taken up by preparation of an electronic flipchart on videotape. Her boss is giving a presentation to board members on a new product. He has briefed her on certain facts and figures. Some information is on file, and she uses her work station to search and retrieve various statistics, still pictures, text and digital images. These she 'splices' electronically on videotape, allowing the manager to produce a voice-over later if he so wishes. The video recorder she uses is not standard office equipment, and has been specially hired for the demonstration. It has been adapted to take the information she has displayed upon her VDU. The electronic flipchart concept has taken over from the blackboard, the overhead projector, and the paper flipchart in most demonstrations. It also has the advantage that it can be duplicated for directors who require a copy to study.
>
> At lunchtime, the secretary calls an adjacent secretary of another senior manager and asks for her calls to be intercepted, promising to cover for the other girl on her own return from lunch. Before eating lunch, she goes to the company gymnasium for a game of badminton. In this, she is encouraged by the company – not only for general health, but because the exercise of her eyes in co-ordinating with the shuttlecock is believed to relieve strain from narrow focusing on a VDU for too long.
>
> Lunch is followed by a visit to the executive secretaries' lounge (as employee numbers fall, office blocks will have more space for those remaining), where a quick run-through of the video disc apprises her of the Japanese visitors' etiquette and behaviour. Playing safe, she orders an office junior to buy a bottle of Scotch and a packet of jasmine tea on her authorized expense account.

Returning to her work station, she finds that her sister secretary has stored more voicegrams and some electronic mail, which is passed between them using the standard local area network operating in the building. The arrival of her boss and his guest takes some time, and she is on call to provide data to both of them. The manager uses his intercom to ask for information to be displayed on his flat-screen VDU. The information is on teleconferencing, not yet widespread as a method of communication in 1988. The videophone, although a child of the 1960s, has still not arrived. Video conferences are only available at specific studios in the main city centres and most executives reject telephone conferencing even with facsimile transmission.

When the guest leaves, the manager calls in the secretary and asks her to prepare a short report on a 'What-if' scenario. He suggests that she can do this while he scans his mail, both electronic and hard copy. The secretary forwards the mail to the manager's VDU and starts her task. On her (standard) keyboard she has not only the typewriter QWERTY, but also a calculator layout, which she now uses to punch in figures and to calculate. Data is called up from the company librarian; information already on store in her own and others' work stations is accessed and merged. Having been trained in basic book-keeping, she uses a spreadsheet to extrapolate figures.

On a more advanced report, her boss would normally manipulate the figures himself, with his secretary feeding the data to his terminal VDU as required, but in this case, he is happy to use her skills. The report takes the rest of the afternoon for the secretary, while her manager checks that mail, dictated to the audio, occasionally asks for data to be flashed onto his VDU and contemplates a corporate strategy. He is happy to do the job he is paid for – taking decisions based upon relevant information fed to him by his secretary.

At the end of the day, the secretary quickly uses her work station to check the new 'All Weather News' channel on the cable TV system which has recently started in her town. It is snowing. As she grimly drives home, she ponders upon the possibility of commuting, as predicted by Alvin Toffler in the *The Third Wave* so long ago. What will the next ten years bring, she wonders'.

She may well wonder. By that time we suspect that business, as well as society generally, will have become more forward thinking and adaptive than it is today. In earlier chapters we mentioned how the Japanese programme the population to think about change and be ready for it. In Europe, especially in the U.K., we live on a pride in our past. This hinders our minds when it comes to the acceptance of change. If we love to read and think about the past, the present seems very modern. The present should seem old-hat for the forward thinking manager who plans for change.

It is this driving towards the future with one eye fixed on the rear-view mirror that causes rising levels of stress in so many managers. Unless we can remove this disease of epidemic proportions we have little hope of enjoying the future fruits of change.

In Britain alone, stress accounts for 23 million lost working days. It is being blamed on the quickening pace of information technology and the need to break existing work patterns. An extra factor that is frequently forgotten in this disease is that computerized control systems now allow managerial performances to be monitored faster. One British occupational psychologist, Dr Chris Ridgeway, claims that the spread of accountability is 'more than some people can cope with. It's like being in a glass pressure cooker. It used to take weeks or even months to produce accounts and an analysis of performance. Managers knew they had the time to react, adjust or prepare excuses. But with modern information technology there are no hiding places'. Earlier we mentioned the secretary slipping off for a lunchtime game of badminton which cleared her head and relaxed her eyes from staring at the VDU. The need to train for stress and learn how to handle it will have to become part of everyday business school degree courses if it is not to be a critical danger factor for the future. Not only does a heart attack or a stroke by a senior executive reduce the efficiency of that company in competitive terms but it affects the total culture around him or her. While staff claim overwork and say there is a danger of their becoming workaholics, there are likely to be problems in management terms that will seep through the whole company. In fact most people work at only a quarter of their possible speed and potential. They take more sleep than they need and generally never get into top gear more than once or twice a month. The collapse of a senior manager is seen as an example of 'what might happen to you too if you don't slow up', rather than a case of someone's inability to handle what is really a disease. Fortunately, new groups such as Dr Ridgeway's 'Psychological Consultancy Services' are now being set up and early signs of stress can be noted and help or advice offered. The giveaway sign of trouble for managers to watch for is early morning wakening with the mind already seething with activity as if it hadn't stopped all night. The need then is to get the executive to take a few days off, but in most cases the stress sufferer won't, as he normally fails to see that he needs to take such a decision at all. We tend to brush off words like 'challenging' when we consider change and new technologies as being positive. So it can be, but it can also mean stressful to people unable to adapt fast enough or who feel insecure. A manager who feels hemmed in by his or her immediate superior, who want a change from them, and those younger executives below who seem to thrive on it, create a feeling of being squeezed dry like a lemon in a squeezer. Unfortunately the rate of change we can expect in the office and managerial environment is likely to rise exponentially. Worse is to come.

Paul A. Strassman, a Xerox Corporation V.P. who was a key figure in a 1983 White House seminar which looked into different ways of how productivity might be improved, wrote in his book *Information Pay Off: The Transformation of Work in the Electronic Age*, that industrial economies were unlikely to see per capita incomes in Western countries rising to more than $10,000 (he was using 1979 dollars so some allowance is needed for inflation). Whereas service economies that use or disseminate information will soon be generating yearly incomes of $40,000 to $100,000 in the U.S. because of an annual productivity increase of at least 3% compound for the next fifty or more years.

To do this, however, and here is the point in relation to the impact we can expect on staff, there has to be a massive streamlining of office work. We must not 'automate obsolete patterns of how people work' he says. He attacks the banking and insurance industries, two of the most automated industries in the world, saying 'The efficient processing of a typical bank loan now involves 50–80 internal communications' and that some offices use many more times that number. He even coins a new word – 'micromyopia' – because he says too many people, when automating, analyze each little movement, each little activity and find how these can be automated.

Micromyopia is the bane of rising productivity because it reinforces inefficient work structures.

He expects and hopes to see far more sweeping changes than those described in this chapter. 'The essence of the service economy', he says, 'lies in customized responses and in adaptive handling of a client's wishes. A broad range of adaptive behaviour thus becomes a pre-requisite for delivering services without referring every new question to another speciality.' As he says 'Secretaries, for instance, live by a routine little changed in this century'.

Picking up the same thread, or a part of it, that was argued in our chapter on 'Corporate De-schooling', he believes that the generalist must now come into his own. It will require extensive re- and pre-training for the job but this must be done by blurring the boundaries between jobs – see our example on how communication is to become part of strategic thinking in our chapter 'A Positive Stance'. Leadership becomes an important skill in itself because it should be concerned with thinking in broad terms and its ultimate effects on the corporation. Donald Norfolk, osteopath and well-known health writer, sums it up neatly. 'With immense technological ingenuity we seem to have created a mechanically sophisticated paradise, whose only asset is that it enables us to be miserable in comfort.'

The pressure therefore on today's middle and senior managers will grow and the need to handle and treat the stress it creates will become paramount. If we don't carry our current managers across the bridge into the new territory we may not get there at all.

The signs are there that the generations falling in behind us are quite able and willing to walk across the bridge on their own. A news story in the British *Daily Mail* on September 4th, 1982, called 'High Tech Princess', may have been pandering to the appetite for royal stories but it highlighted a wider event when it said 'Seven-year-old Peter Phillips (the son of Princess Anne) will meet his first school computer this week, along with three-quarters of a million other children who are also starting junior school . . . computer-aided learning is now part of the curriculum at most schools, but teachers and parents have not yet realized the important issues the computer raises'. Thus wrote *Daily Mail* journalist, Ray Hammond:

'In schools across the country the question must be asked "Is the child programming the computer, or is the computer programming the child?" '

This journalist quite rightly asks whether the computer is being used with Strassman's micromyopic vision or is it opening up new vistas. He questions that in some schools the computer is being used as a mechanized form of the drill, and practises teaching methods that were bad even when followed by human teachers. When delivered by machines they can be worse. As he says, despite the initial £9m spent by the Government in putting at least one micro into every secondary and primary school, boosting it in 1986 with a further £20m, teachers generally have failed to understand the importance of the whole operation. In some schools, says Ray Hammond, the obligatory computer is kept in the stationery cupboard while scared teachers try to forget it exists. It is not only managers and businessmen who find it difficult to cross the bridge then, because he makes a useful comparison in his *Daily Mail* article when he says:

'If your child comes home in the next few weeks and tells you that he's been learning timetables on a computer or that he's had a computer spelling test, you'll know that the school has yet to realize the power of the computer. If he comes home and is excited about a robot he's been controlling or about a drawing he's made on the computer, you can count yourself and your child lucky.'

The general outlook then for smooth transition into the office of the future will be some sunshine with frequent bouts of rain. After a short and snappy start we're going through that unfortunate patch where sales promises, advertising hype, and over-enthusiastic press editorials, have led businessmen to expect far, far more than can be delivered.

Michael Bywater, associate editor of the British journal, *Punch*, writing in the *Observer* Business Section, had much to say in a timely article headed 'The Promise of Micro Revolution is Fading'. We quote it here in full because it sums up so many of the factors we are adumbrating in this chapter:

'I suppose that our honeymoon with the microcomputer is over. Things are certainly starting to look rather dreary.

If you want to know the signs, they are all over the place. Computer manufacturers are having a tough time at the moment. Dealers are increasingly separating into the successful sheep, which sell a few well-tried and well-supported lines, and the gloomy goats whom bankruptcy stares in the face.

The computer magazines are also getting fewer and duller, which is a shame. I have frequently berated them for being venal and wicked and wilfully obscurantist; but at least their obsessions demonstrated a manic enthusiasm.

Now they seem to be finding it difficult: difficult to survive, and difficult to think of new things to write about. It's all too often the same old thing – a review of a new computer which is exactly like every other computer, or a treatise on a word-processing program which does nothing that word-processing programs can't do already.

The fault, of course, is not simply in the writers. In the microcomputer business – both hardware and software – not a great deal is happening at the moment. The businessmen's cliché is that the industry is 'in a shake-out phase', but that has always seemed to us a bit like saying 'Act of God' or 'Dunno' in the belief that one is talking sense.

If the market is in trouble it cannot simply be blamed on external economic forces ('All new industries face this problem') or dud oracles ('We over-estimated the pace of market development'); you either have to assume that the total potential demand is becoming sated, or that manufacturers are not providing what potential buyers want. I find it hard to accept that so revolutionary – and open-ended – a tool as the microprocessor can have reached its near-maximum market penetration in so short a time.

The problem could just be that we have now institutionalized or expelled the first wave of entrepreneurial innovators. It is certainly true that this has happened. A couple of weeks ago, I met Bill Gates, one of the founders of the microcomputer industry, for the simple reason that he wrote an operating system – MS-DOS – which enabled a non-specialist to work a microcomputer. Gates's software corporation – Microsoft – is now prodigiously large and successful, and he himself now speaks, not of innovation, but of development of existing software concepts, of market analysis and of corporate growth.

Similarly, with another pair of folk heroes, Apple founders

Steve Jobs and Steven Wozniac. Wozniac, one of the most brilliant and original engineers the business has produced, effectively distanced himself from the subsequent corporate culture that cares with Apple's success; Jobs bought himself a range of Savile Row suits and remained at the sharp end of the company until last month, when he became what can only be interpreted as a sort of institutional guru. Jobs subsequently 'resigned' after a bitter battle with John Scully, the ex-Pepsi Cola marketing man whom Jobs himself brought into Apple.

These people and their peers were responsible for developing the first wave of microcomputer hardware and software; the micro itself, its peripherals, and the four major categories of software – databases, word-processors, spreadsheets, and graphics programs.

Since then, we have seen refinements of all these, but what has appeared which is really startlingly new, innovative and exciting? You could say that Job's Lisa and Macintosh computers fitted into that category, but the concept is over ten years old and the applications, although legendarily 'user-friendly', fall into the same four classes.

What of the great hope for the future – artificial intelligence? Yes, it holds out great promise. Yes, it is new. But, at the moment, it looks as though real A1 applications are going to run on mainframe computers even more complex, and probably even more expensive, than they are now.

So far as it concerns microcomputing – that great development which was to put the freedom of information on every man's desk – real A1 is unattainable.

Of course, none of this is necessarily bad, except that it reduces the adrenalin flow which has, until recently, been one of the great things about the micro industry and its implications.

But for me at any rate, the great principle of the microcomputer has been freedom – freedom from repetitive drudgery, freedom of information, and most important, freedom from the stultifying rigidity of the post-industrial corporation.

The orthodox corporate model is vertical and hierarchical in structure. It derives from military chains of command; and new technology, with its ability to propagate and manipulate information, has rendered that structure obsolete. Yet the rigidly structured corporation thrives as never before.

What worries me more than anything else is that this last potential freedom does not seem to have materialized. The global electronic village may be open for business, but you cannot visit it because you are still locked in corporate HQ worrying about the cut of your jib and the size of your desk. The microcomputer is here to stay, but the power has returned to the corporate data processing manager.

The major developments under way at the moment will not fit on your desk, but must reside in the mainframe machine which only the corporation can afford, and to which it will restrict your access.

This jeremiad could continue at will, but the central thesis is this: the microcomputer offered an alternative to the corporation. That alternative has not taken hold. Instead, information seems to me to have become a tool to support the traditional corporate structure. The choices have not widened as they might have done'.

We don't want to sound negative about the very forces we consider will drive change over the years ahead. But sound management theory is about getting the right answers not too fast, not too slow, not all projects, but at least some of them. Stasis must be avoided at all costs. This means Bywater's article should be seen as a summing up of attitudes, not a single voice shouting in the wind.

A survey carried out by PA Technology by MORI (published in Brussels on May 3 1984) made the point that the majority of companies interviewed were using technological innovation to move into related or new fields. The survey, of more than 500 company directors, from manufacturing concerns in West Germany, U.K., Belgium, the U.S. and Australia, showed also that British companies came bottom of the five-country league table in terms of application of new technology for the creation of fresh products. The dangers of moving too slowly in this area were highlighted by Dr Peter Hyde, a director of PA Technology, when he was reported in the *Daily Mail* (16.5.84) as saying that British managers 'Are living on borrowed time if they think they can hold their position without a major change in the emphasis they place on applying new technology'. He went on to accuse British firms of 'Being complacent about their competitiveness in world markets. Companies needed a major change in the emphasis they placed on technology.'

The theme set by the PA Technology research was picked up in that same week by Bill Johnstone, writing in the London *Times* (8.5.84), when he commented on another piece of research, this time by the ECC in association with the journal *Futures*. The study was a strategy to help the Europeans improve their high technology R & D record. Talking about the £850m Esprit project (European Programme for Research and Development in Information Technologies) he quoted the report as saying that similar massive inter-country budgets must be set aside for areas such as robotics and, above all, the relationship between man and machines. 'Although we are inundated with speeches and hypotheses about man-machine relationships, about the grand global vision of their transformation and their future, the knowledge actually available on the nature of the new machine, the new systems, and the new networks remain fragmented, and limited to a few privileged circles. The vast field of research which goes under the title of industrial relations is equally in need of a profound renewal.' Here we are back full circle to the blockages that can slow our progress towards at least getting the hardware right for the next office revolution. Peter Marsh writing in the *New Scientist* back in April 1982, complained that despite massive studies launched by the British clearing banks on Electronic Funds Transfer (EFT), the Banking, Insurance and Finance Union representing 150,000 staff in the U.K., had not been consulted. Intermittent talks had taken place with the Retail Consortium, but in general the banks were accused by Jeremy Mitchell, Director of the National Consumer Council, of a 'conspiracy of silence' on electronic payments. Since that time the silence has become a little noisier, but it is nonetheless a symptom of the crucial need to integrate human relations into decision-making, not as an add-on, but as a part of 'open' discussion.

It may sound like an over-simplistic statement but we are prepared to argue that a failure by any corporation to accept this need for open communication, both internal and external, will mean a failure by that company to move forward more than a few short steps.

The explosive changes now upon us have created a media environment of unparalleled abundance and choice. Because it is possible for every thought, experience and event to be stored, transmitted and retrieved at will, staff and public alike expect the systems to be used. Some corporations are taking the hint. In the U.S., it was reported in the *Harvard Magazine* as far back as 1979 that 300 U.S. firms outside the media industries had developed major video capacity for in-house corporate newscasts – some with film, video-tape and computerized editing facilities that rival those of the national networks. In an outbreak of what they called 'media fever' these corporations were buyers into the business of mass communications.

What of the people at the receiving end of this technological Meccano set. Opening the sluice gates of information may result in more and more people drowning in data they don't know what to do with. It's called 'Information Overload' in the jargon, something President Carter suffered from. One of the largest computer companies in the world was audited by one of the authors of this book early in 1985. In the section of that audit concerned with what we call the 'cultural artifacts', a number of questions were asked about information flow – 'Were you, as a manager, satisfied with the amount of information you were receiving about the company?' Almost without exception, every one of the 25 senior managers interviewed complained about the overburdening of paper, reports and memos they received. 'Look at this pile', one said, pointing to a foot-high bundle weighing down and bending his in-tray, 'This lot arrived this morning. Heaven knows when I'll read it.' He actually used a more descriptive expletive than the word 'Heaven'. What had happened was that two to three years before, the company had been close-lipped and secretive in its communications, letting people have information only on a need-to-know basis – as little as possible was the rule. A new managing director came in, keen to bring the company into the twentieth century in communications terms. Quite rightly, he wanted to move towards a more participative form of management. From one extreme the company had lurched to the other. Improving information flow doesn't necessarily mean pouring undigested data over the heads of already overworked staff. Skilful monitoring is needed. A department or unit needs to handle internal communications just as it handles the external variety. What is the objective, what are we trying to say, and is this the best way of saying it? Are questions to be asked before another report goes on wide circulation and the photocopier overheats?

Before we sum up the changes and attitudes we can expect to see in the next two decades, let us scan quickly the values and attitudes we can expect to see held by businessmen and the public by the year 2000. Remember 'The Public' is not some target group of consumers 'out there'. It is the world, the ecology within which our companies, great and small, are embedded. What they, the public, think will be what we, our staff and management think. If we don't understand that we can forget our grand designs for better communications.

The U.K. Henley Centre for Forecasting has done some of our job for us and the results of its 'Consumer in the Year 2000' study can be said to be the ground-rules for how we intend to handle the human factors in management during the years ahead. The Institute for the Future in California have undertaken similar studies. First, we must accept that managers talking to their employees must no longer think that by the end of the next but one decade – i.e. the year 2000 – that the family as we know it will continue to exist. Half of all women of marriageable age will have experienced divorce, remarriage and single parenthood. This in itself produces a totally new attitude, style and set of values which are often termed those of the 'divorcynic'. Women who have had to fend for themselves are less likely to respond to the classic emotional messages which, by implication, imply that the prime objective of female life is to be an efficient housewife. In fact, by the year 2000, a quarter of adults will be living as single people – helped along by an increased life expectancy which will mean that one half of a marriage will outlive the other by longer and longer periods. As money becomes less and less of a factor in an increasingly wealthy society, convenience, choice and flexibility will become more important than price – hence snacks and fast food will take over from family meals – providing a less hemmed-in family unit. The impact of ordering by home computer will strengthen the role of the home and of do-it-yourself pleasure. It will become considerably more convenient to have food and entertainment sent in than to journey out looking for it. This in itself provides new opportunities for corporate communications.

There will be a growth in the 'me' generation concept as people become more and more independent and look to a greater control over their own environment. The report made a useful summary of the values that each generation or age takes forward with it into later life. By looking back at their formative years we can make a useful judgement of how each age group that works in the post year 2000 company will think and act.

The 65-year-olds (children of the 1950s) will be:

(i) Conservative and cautious
(ii) Give-and-take makes the world go round
(iii) Basically secure and content, almost resigned and complacent.

The 55-year-olds (children of the 1960s) will be:

(i) Radical
(ii) Unconventional
(iii) Iconoclastic
(iv) Utopian.

The 45-year-olds (children of the 1970s) will be:

(i) Cynically conservative
(ii) Pessimistic, cautious and thoughtful
(iii) Hedonistic

The 35-year-olds (children of the 1980s) will be:

(i) Feeling rejection
(ii) Hopelessness
(iii) Rebelliousness
(iv) Confusion.

What stands out from this study is the need to provide for the employer and consumer, greater choice within an increasingly discriminate and fragmented market. By market we refer to the labour market also. It will no longer be satisfactory to have machines working night and day to produce popular staples. The consumer or retail market, however, will be dominated by smaller brands appealing to the mass of identities which will appear by the year 2020. Machines by then will have to be capable of being switched three or four times a day to produce different and distinct brands. Cars will become bespoke, or made to measure. The role of simple robots that can be quickly reprogrammed – probably linked to the normal personal computer – will be important to the manufacturer.

To close this chapter which has sought to lay out across the management floor some plans for the business environment at the end of the century, we turn to the Hudson Research Company in Europe. Hudson Research was founded by Dr Edmund Stillman and has built a high reputation for its work in long-range political and economic forecasts. We believe that no better summary, or road map, can be laid out for the next two decades than to quote *in extenso* Hudson Research's views on Europe in the year 2000.

'What will Europe look, feel and act like in the year 2000? First of all, it will be still recognized as Europe. This statement is not a simple-minded tautology but rather an antidote to the fatuous idealism that still promotes the vision of a "United Europe", in whatever form. If any lesson is clear from the past two decades, it is that the national and cultural obstacles to wide-ranging European integration are just too deeply implanted. Frenchmen will not vote for German officials; Italians will not drink English beer; Danes could not care less about the Spanish Catholic school system. There are more distinct, sophisticated cultures on the continent of Europe than there are in any other advanced region in the world. It is useless to hope that these cultures and national identities will disappear merely for the sake of economic efficiency and political compromise.

This said, however, it should not be supposed that the diversity and pluralism of Europe constitutes a long-term disadvantage. Today's pessimists put forward one basic explanation of the general European dilemma: they maintain that the fragmentation of the European Markets prohibits the economies of scale needed by large European companies to compete with American and Japanese ones. There is some truth to the charge but, critically, it underestimates the strengths inherent in diversification – and smallness. If the British textile industry is now floundering, modest-sized Italian firms are going strong. Small may not be beautiful, but it is the small enterprise that creates most of the jobs – and a rapidly increasing proportion of GNP – in both Europe and the United States. The continued emphasis on bigness is sadly misplaced even if it is understandable: large firms, to be sure, command more attention and thus are generally seen as the creators of national wealth. Yet more and more, it is the local supplier, attuned to local demands, who is making the quickest stride.

Even so, glaring inefficiencies of the European marketplace cannot be ignored. If the European Common Market is to have any meaning in the year 2000, it must become precisely what its name signifies: a common market. Painstaking piecemeal reforms – most of them promulgated by dusty Brussels bureaucrats – will be the order of the day. The net effect will be to reduce the cost of doing business in Europe, especially for those small entrepreneurs who cannot afford high-priced lawyers for the reams of national paperwork. Whether the lowering of non-tariff barriers to trade will also result in lower consumer prices remains an open question, but at the very least profit margins will be improved. Progress in this domain will be laborious, involving as it does the gradual harmonization of varying national standards and practices. To many, the entire effort will appear unglamorous. But sometimes modesty is the best policy: better to concentrate on the tangible gains than seek an ephemeral glory.

So no 'New Europe' is on the horizon. What, then of the loss of normal European? A first point to remember is that he is rich and will remain so. In terms of purchasing power, most West Europeans (with the notable exceptions of Britain, Ireland, Southern Italy and Iberia) enjoy standards of living not much inferior to the American norm; vis-à-vis the Japanese, there is still a gap in the Europeans' favour. Two to three per cent growth per annum may sound uninspiring, but Europe cannot 'catch up' forever. And it certainly remains to be proven that the American economic 'miracle' of the past two years – coming, it should be recalled on the heels of one of the developed world's worst post-war recessions – will be an enduring one. Yet the question for the future is not so much how to inflate expected growth rates: borrow $200 billion per year and you too can be rich. Rather, it is to assess how a return to an historically more normal pace of economic expansion will affect working habits, life-styles, and political expectations among post-war Europeans. Clearly the changes from the go-go years of the 1960s will be pronounced, and they will generally be somewhat sombre ones.

It is an inescapable fact that most European countries will suffer a period of protracted high unemployment, probably until the early 1990s. Demographic trends, technological mutations and poorly conceived government policies dictate that this will be so. But this does not mean that the very fabric of European society is threatened like it was, for instance, during the 1920s and 1930s. Social security, like national security, need not be an empty phrase; the social programmes now in place, while often too costly and overly generous, will cushion European societies during the coming troubled period of transition. Of course, the argument is well taken that the European welfare state impedes economic adaptation and hence perpetuates employment. Certainly the generous schemes on offer in countries like the Netherlands, Belgium and France cannot be said to encourage a competitive, job-seeking instinct. But neither can they be held responsible for over 10% unemployment rates.

Perhaps the greatest tragedy of the unemployment dilemma will be the effect on European youth. Already the youth unemployment rates in several countries have reached alarming proportions, with no quick remedies in sight. In a sense, Europe can be said to be paying the price for its exclusive educational systems, which throw too many young people onto the labour market at too tender an age. It is a telling fact that, at the last count, fully 58 per cent of 20- to 24-year-old Americans were enrolled in a programme of higher education; the ratios in Europe were 28 per cent for Germany, 27 per cent for Italy, 26 per cent for France and merely 20 per cent for Britain.

Today's unemployment problem, combined with probable trends over the coming few years, should produce a markedly different attitude toward work by the year 2000. It is not that the work ethic *per se* will be in decline; on the contrary, competition for good jobs will be as stiff, if not more so. Instead, there will probably be less tolerance for single-minded careerism; greater emphasis will be placed on 'personal satisfaction'. For one thing this means that the trend to a shorter working week will continue – a trend reinforced by the probability that virtually all households will have two income earners. For another, it implies that work will become more task-oriented than time-oriented.

Homework will take on a new (actually old) meaning, spurred on also by the elaboration of telecommunications and computer networks and the growth of information services. And finally – although potentially much less salutary – the reduction of the working life seems bound to proceed. Early retirement policies are now being assiduously pursued by numerous European governments; their potential effect on the quality of the workforce, not to mention the financing of public and private pensions, should not be underestimated. It is not inconceivable, given the constant lengthening of life expectancy, that the typical European in 2000 will face twenty years of 'retired' life.

Should this be so, there will very likely be a burst of self-employment. Already the new information technologies make this possible; further refinements allowing greater recentralization of work, even probable. While Europe may now seem laggard in producing the hot-selling, high-tech hardware, nothing suggests that its people will be unable to make good use of that equipment. Despite the elitism of European university systems, educational standards as a whole are high, and this, of course, is a key criterion for any information business. Knowledge has long been something of a European speciality – particularly in its cross-cultural form – even if it has sometimes been poorly acted upon.

European society 15 years hence will have suffered no cataclysmic upheavals, but neither will it experience a politics of ecstasy. Europeans certainly will not be starving, but neither will they be living at the Ritz. The average European of 2000 will be a decidedly middle-class creature: materially comfortable, socially tolerant, politically stolid.

This portrait is admittedly a rather staid one; will not some external development – a war here, a revolution there – mess it up? Firstly it is necessary to put to rest two favourite European bogeys: the prospects for North-South confrontation and for another OPEC-like cartel. To put the matter cruelly, the so-called South has no essential unity and little meaningful leverage, political or economic, to use against the North. Some Third World countries, in fact, are not just under-developed; they are undeveloping, literally unravelling, in parts of Africa. The sight is not a pleasant one, but at least it suggests that visions of impoverished Third Worlders storming rich Europe's gates are wildly unrealistic. Power works the other way around.

As for the threat of another OPEC, the short answer is: most improbable. Oil is the only commodity of such high intrinsic value to Western economies for which tradeable reserves are concentrated in a handful of culturally similar countries. (Today, with Mexico, Britain, Norway and others producing oil, even the Middle East's role has greatly diminished as a result.) Conditions that would permit a cartel to be formed by other materials of significant value simply do not exist. If they did, other OPECs would already be with us; as it is, OPEC itself is now in trouble.

Wars and revolutions there will inevitably be in the Third World, as there have been constantly throughout the post-war era. A short list of candidates for turbulence would probably include India, Saudi Arabia, Libya, Chile, the Philippines and Indonesia. No matter what happens in the Middle East, it will remain a highly unstable region. Yet even the most unthinkable development – revolution in Saudi Arabia, for instance – would have little enduring effect on Europe's prospects. After all, few people give a second thought to Iran these days despite its unsavoury Islamic extremism. The future of Europe will assuredly not be determined in Tehran or Riyadh.

More problematic for Europeans would be the emergence of a jingoistically nationalist United States or an aggressively mercantilist Japan. To some extent, both of these traits will become more visible in coming years, but the trilateral damage should be controlled. Despite perpetual European fears about American isolationism, the fundamental bonds that seal the transatlantic relationship are strong and lasting. And while Japan in the future may be tempted to be more militant in its economic diplomacy, the only notable impact would be in Far East Asia. Such a policy, however, would run the risk of a costly reprisal; Japan has a large stake in maintaining access to European markets, whereas the reverse cannot be said to be true.

There are two other potential trouble spots; the Soviet Union of course, but also Europe itself. The greatest threat to West European – and, it might be added, world-peace and prosperity, lies in Eastern Europe. The risk is not of some Soviet-led blitzkrieg through the Fulga Gap, sweeping up West Germany and the Low Countries. The Soviet Army has no historical record of offensive genius, and there is no reason to suspect that East Germans will fight West Germans, or Poles attack the French, merely at Moscow's bidding. The NATO countries should not become complacent or relax their defence efforts, but they should develop a more realistic appraisal of actual Soviet capabilities and intentions.

Those capabilities and intentions are under serious strain in Eastern Europe, and the pressures will continue to grow. The

> simple truth is that the 'Soviet model' has nothing to offer the East Europeans – and they know it. Living standards are miserable compared to Western lifestyles; there is little prospect of dramatic improvement. Goods are of shoddy quality and in short supply. More fundamentally, Russian culture, derived from a Byzantine and Orthodox heritage, is profoundly at odds with the Western cultures of Poland, Hungary, Czechoslovakia and East Germany. There are sharp differences between Russia and its satellites over traditional styles of government, religion, and individualism that even forty years of occupation have not quashed. The Soviet Union may sit on its empire for many more years but, like the Hapsburg Empire, it grows progressively weaker.'

If the true meaning of ecology is the study of inter-dependence in nature, then corporate ecology is concerned with the inter-dependence of business, politics, society, and the people who flow between corporations and the world in which they are embedded. In this chapter we have tried to plot how that ever-changing flow will affect companies and their managements over the two decades ahead. If ever there was proof of the death of the currently structured corporation, this look into the future should have proved it. Judging from the inertia of *some* senior managers to the changes, they embody the living proof of life after death.

12

Paradigm paralysis or revolution?

'Information is the answer, but what is the question?'

Professor James Halloran,
Leicester University.

Why did America sleep, given the extraordinary amount and quality of intelligence available about the likelihood of a Japanese attack on Pearl Harbor? Was it confusion, conspiracy, incompetence or design? Warnings were received from the Navy about possible attack, there were reports of a change in Japanese codes (evaluated as very unusual), Japanese ships were sighted in Cam ranh Bay, Japanese Embassies were observed destroying secret papers, and Admiral Stark in Washington issued warnings. Yet the fleet remained a sitting duck, the island was not air patrolled, the emergency warning centre staff were 'off duty', and the army were not notified as they should have been. Had the key decision-makers been rational and in possession of the requisite information on which to base a judgement? This sorry saga represents more dramatically than is usually the case, standard outputs of an organization function according to very established routines. Organizations are blunt instruments, not susceptible always to the leader's direction, but to what are known as standard operating procedures (SOPs).

In the near Pearl Harbor-in-reverse situation in Cuba, President Kennedy believed he was President and that, his wishes having been made clear, they would be followed, and the Turkish missiles which were provocative to the Soviets removed. Yet they were not. This is because there were so many players all dealing with different information, with different motives, and standard operating procedures, that the desired output did not occur.

Some call it the science of muddling through with inadequate information on which the proper judgements are not made. Does this ring any bells?

This final chapter will review a number of ways of looking at the changes taking place and its discontinuities through a series of conceptual lenses. It is a paradigm paralysis of excessive, confusing, and too little information.

The word paradigm was given a new dynamism by T. B. Kuhn in his book *The Structure of Scientific Revolutions*. It is a conceptual framework, a way of looking at the world, a set of assumed categories into which we file the facts. When Copernicus suggested that the earth was not at the centre of the universe, he became a paradigm revolutionary. But it was the minds of men that changed, not the motions of the planets and the way in which they now viewed that same universe which had a profound impact on their beliefs, values and behaviour.

Social paradigms seem to change when a new technology coincides with a shift in values or priorities. The new paradigm then needs its articulate exponent to spell out and legitimize the new assumptions on which we can begin to build a new era of continuous change. Capitalization and the concept of money, not land, as the key form of prosperity, needed the two technologies of mass production and limited liability to make it work. It required Adam Smith to articulate it and make it credible. The result was the rise of the merchant or managerial classes plus all the values and social changes to which it gave rise, not least economic growth. Could it be that the new technology of the 'micro chip', with all the implications now apparent, will combine with a new value system to give us a new paradigm, a paradigm only awaiting its prophet?

The irony is that with the new technologies, leading us inexorably to the post industrial 'knowledge'-based society, the pace of change is so great and the quantity (not the quality) of information creating so much overload, our basic assumptions have run out of steam. We appear unable to order the information on which to make intelligent judgements about the present, let alone have a confident basis for predicting the future. Social and even moral change always lags behind technological and economic change. Certainly the politicians who tend to concentrate on the waves rather than the tides have failed to provide the necessary leadership to explain the changes, which have led to unemployment and the long-term transformation in the nature of work.

Leaders can't lead us on to the new paradigm however, unless they have open minds and the right information. Both are lacking. It seems to us that business leaders not only need to allow old ways to die and new ways to grow in their businesses but play more of a role in the debate, moulding society to satisfy its current needs and requirements. It will never be forthcoming from the financial community or the politicians and the clergy and academics who are locked in their ivory towers. Why not from business men? Without of course, expecting them to totally reform society? Yet as the providers of society they should be in a more powerful position than they are to move us forward. They appear defensive and hesitant. They appear to have neither the will nor the way, due to the wrong skills, information base and vision. Organizations have to be the mirrors of our societies however much management may regret that fact and yearn for other times and other places. The Chinese ideogram for crisis combines the signs of danger and opportunity. We need to see both signs clearly when we look into the future, lest we are carried away by enthusiasm into extravagant experiments or by dismay into dogged reaction. Of two things we can be sure, corporations of some shape and size will still be needed and people will still be people however we present them.

We are now entering a condition which has been variously described as discontinuous change, a paradigm shift or even the realm of catastrophe, and we are totally unable to predict, because of our data base, our education and training. Above all our attitudes have failed to keep pace.

According to Charles Handy in *Understanding Organisations* (he was, incidentally, Warden of St George's House, Windsor Castle, until he joined London Business School) there are four common assumptions now in need of reconceptualization:

1. That concentration plus specialization equals efficiency.
2. That hierarchy is natural.
3. That labour is a cost.
4. That an organization is a form of property.

The first is still partially valid but when one of the cogs in the organizational machine seizes up, the whole machine grinds to a halt. Various groups of specialists have an opportunity to hijack the whole organization, whether unionists or professionals. Imaginative leadership and skilful communications can do something to help but, says Handy, this form of organization can only survive when productivity exceeds inflation. When costs exceed benefits, then the concentration plus specialization formula will self-destruct. Try digging a plot where there is concrete all round and one foot down, it becomes alienating. This has been demonstrated in the rise of absenteeism and demands for more variety in work.

Hierarchy is natural, says Handy, it has been around a long time, but the worm, as we have seen, has begun to turn. Individuals are less prepared to accept impersonal authority from those over whom they have no control. The advent of hijack power has meant that those at the receiving end have negative power at least equal to the positive power of those at the other end. To call this 'industrial democracy' is to risk losing the point in a label. The point is that authority has to be earned. Title or role no longer necessarily means power and as with the true meaning of authority, it must be based on consent. This does not necessarily mean participating in the decision. The implication of this is small groups and a leader who is known, is close enough to be touched and to be respected.

That labour is a cost, to be laid off when they were no longer producing a surplus, has been turned on its head. It still happens, but in future it will be treated as an asset to be disposed of only after proper thought has been given to its use. This puts tremendous pressure on recruitment and selection and on producing the right products for the market.

The idea that organizations are property to be disposed of by those who provide the money is another assumption gradually being eroded. Does it really make sense, comments Handy, for shareholders who are principally institutions representing thousands of anonymous individuals who have no way of knowing what part of the company they own nor any way of representing their views, to regard them as owners? Far better to regard them as providers of finance with privileges proportionate to their risk. As we've discussed throughout this book, stakeholding is a new concept, implying that there are a number of interested parties with rights and duties appropriate to their interest. Surely a company is a community rather than a property? After all a community belongs to no one, instead one belongs to a community, where the whole is greater than the sum of its parts.

Paradigm shifts are uncomfortable. It is understandable that those in the centre with the most privileges and power resist changes in their assumptions. New assumptions derive from the young, from outsiders and from newer organizations. The problem is that many are dreams and rash experiments but one never knows which ones. The current problem is that many of our so-called leaders are fighting the current war with the strategies of the last. The stubborn insistence of the French that warfare was combat between knights blinded them to the potential of the longbow, leaving them prey to the English for a hundred years. The reluctance of the generals in the First World War to acknowledge that the machine-gun had altered forever the tactics of war, wiped out a generation of Europe's manhood. What are the reasons for today's organizations persisting in fighting the challenge of tomorrow with today's methods and assumptions?

Before developing some new frames of reference for management, it is worth pausing a moment to look at how corporations function from a number of different perspectives, based on some work, undertaken in the foreign policy field by Graham Allison (*Essence of Decision Making – the Cuban Missile Crisis*).

Professional analysts of foreign affairs think about problems of policy in terms of largely implicit conceptual models that have significant consequences for the content of their thought. Incidentally this does not imply any satisfactory, empirically tested theory, merely a conceptual framework. Most analysts explain (and predict) the behaviour of national governments in terms of one basic conceptual model, known as the Rational Actor Model. The assumption therefore is, as in the case of Cuba, that happenings in foreign affairs are the more or less purposive acts of unified natural governments, implying aims, options and logical action. If this is so for governments, it should be even more so for corporations. But as Allison has argued, there are two alternative models which give more emphasis to the organizational processes and political actor involved in the policy and decision-making process. The implication that important events have important causes, that monoliths perform large actions for large reasons, must be balanced by the appreciation that monoliths are black boxes covering various gears and levers in a highly differentiated decision-making structure.

Large acts result from innumerable and often conflicting smaller actions by individuals at. They usually operate various levels of bureaucratic organizations in the service of a variety of only partially compatible conception of organizational goals and political objectives.

Recent developments in organization theory provide the foundation for a second model, which emphasises the processes and procedures of large organizations. According to this Organizational Process Model, what the first model characterizes as 'acts' and 'choices' are thought of instead as outputs of large organizations functioning according to regular patterns of behaviour. Faced with the problems of Soviet missiles in Cuba, a model II analyst frames the puzzle – from what organizational context and pressures did the decision emerge? He then fixed the unit of analysis, namely organizational output. Next he focusses on certain concepts such as the strength, standard operating procedures and repertoires of organizations. In other words all organizations, whether corporations or governments, can be viewed from the perspective of organizational process. The more bureaucratic the organization, the more complex the structure and inter-relationships, as we have seen in earlier chapters, the less adaptable and flexible it is and certainly the less rational. This is particularly so when the government or corporation or military are not working from the same information data base. There are still many corporations (despite IT) which fail to report quickly to the centre, that employ different criteria in different bits of the business and above all do not have enough relevant information of a marketing or competitive nature.

This felony is compounded by Allison's third model – the Governmental Politics Model, which views foreign affairs events as neither rational choices nor outputs. What happens is characterized as a result of various bargaining games among players in the national government. The unit of analysis here is the perceptions, motivations, positions, power and manoeuvres of the players. It is amazing to us as advisers to corporations how much time is spent on internecine warfare and feuds between fiefdoms, particularly where the company is a loose federation with a faceless board. The real enemy is out there in the marketplace. These bargaining games are expected of politicians but somehow not of businessmen. Perhaps it is a trait of all human beings. As in the rational actor model we assume, when looking at corporations, that the action is chosen as a calculated solution to a strategic problem. Failure to achieve goals cannot be laid at the feet just of the pace of change, but of these other factors entering the play. In our view corporations, like governments, could benefit from more research building on case studies on organizational practice at business school. We need to look at how boards really function, the role of the outside or non-executive director, the relationship between organization chart and practice, and between the centre and division.

Coca Cola, Mars, Sony, Seiko and Toyota are producing standard products for a worldwide market rather than producing and marketing their goods for each local market as multinationals do. Even worse they may sometimes be producing products for the domestic market and expecting to export them to other countries without adaptation. Globalization has arrived but few companies have the structure or the management to cope with it.

To delve deeper into the organizational process model is to realize why some corporations in some situations do not act in a rational way. Problems are so complex that only a limited number of aspects can be attended to at any one time and then usually by different bits of the organization, each with their own vested interests and perspectives. In some instances, organizations find a course of action which merely 'satisfices'. Stopping with the first alternative that is good enough or avoiding risk are typical examples of this pattern of behaviour. Policy manuals which assume there is no change are another.

The overriding fact about large organizations is that their size prevents any single central authority from making *all* important decisions or directing *all* important activities. Factored problems and fractionated power are two edges of the same sword. Organizations perceive problems, process information and perform a range of actions in a very introverted way, with little outside inputs.

All of this not only has implications for the future flexibility of organizational structures but rather for the way in which the CEO's vision is translatable into action, given the constraint of standard operating procedures (SOPs). Now we know why America slept, because organizations are blunt instruments, information is incomplete, and people in power spend more time in power-broking and bargaining games than fending off the potential predator. In the

White House this is called 'The President in Sneakers'.

The leaders who sit on top of organizations are not a monolithic group. They focus not on a single strategic issue but on many diverse problems, players acting in terms of no consistent set of strategic objectives but according to various conceptions of organizational and personal goals. Issues emerge piecemeal over time and hundreds of issues compete each day for attention. Foul-ups occur because choices are not made, because they are not recognized, or are raised too late. They are misunderstood because the relevant information wasn't there or if it was the manager suffered from information overload. The gap between academic literature and the experience of participants is nowhere wider than at this point. The science of muddling through is still very much apparent. Compromise, conflict, and confusion of managers with diverse interests and unequal influence is the order of the day, summed up by Allison as 'Where you stand depends on where you sit'. Corporations like governments, increasingly in the goldfish bowl of public opinion find themselves even more blown off course than before. Hence the issues and changes discussed in this book make it all the more urgent that further study is undertaken on the question of misperception due to imperfect information and miscommunication. The pace and the noise level merge with propensities of perception to make accurate communication difficult. In the electronic communication era this should make all chief executives and senior managers pause for reflection.

The different perspectives on how corporations function (obviously there are many more conceptual cuts, which could be undertaken) described above, hopefully give insight into why corporations and their managers have failed to switch from their current assumptions, concepts and propositions that were more relevant to an earlier era.

What assumptions will emerge to take the place of the outworn ones. What new schools of thought are in the offing? The future is already here but we are not soothsayers, so all we have are clues.

The communications revolution is the first. Just when it is getting more expensive to move people and things around it is becoming cheap to move information around. This is a revolution of assumptions. The second clue is *fees not wages*, which is a shorthand way of saying that the contract between man and organization may be due for a change. This reflects the changing attitude of individuals, particularly knowledge workers, towards selling their asset, and the sensitivity of corporations to large overheads and employment costs. The third is *tools not machines.* As Schumacher in *Small is Beautiful* pointed out, a tool is something which extends the capacity of the man rather than making him the servant of the machine. This relationship is changing. Robots are the tools of modern man and this could signal a return to a sophisticated network pattern with the organization providing the tools and the individuals using them at home.

The fourth and final clue is *the economics of quality.* Economics is the study of value-added, but there are signs that the premises which underline the economics of quantity may no longer be so valid, because in states of relative prosperity, there is a built-in limit to material growth. There are only so many rooms with a view, and as publisher Robert Maxwell once said 'You can only eat one steak a day'. This trend is reinforced by the shift in values towards non-materialistic goals, particularly if happiness is not always the outcome of more money, and people may trade money for discretionary time. If economic activity moves back to the household we may well see a big switch from the economics of quantity to the economics of quality. For organizations the consequences are clear. They will no longer rely on the wage-packet as the panacea in issues of motivation, control and authority. When people only have to work a little to satisfy their material needs you will need to rely on other parts of the calculus to get them to work marginally smarter (if not harder) to extract quality performance.

According to Charles Handy, the changeover in assumptions opens up a Pandora's box of opportunities for the federal organization (combining the autonomy of individual parts with the economics of co-ordination). The pressures we have described will push organizations towards a smaller size of operating unit, say 500 people, depending on the nature of the technology and the products or services. The key to co-ordination however is having the right information at the right time. Federal organizations will rely on a small nerve-centre co-ordinating a range of small, nearly autonomous operations which can be disposed geographically. The concept of a holding company will begin to mean more than just a financial and legal entity, more of a knowledge-based task force of senior managers, each with different skills and a broader, more global, perspective than individual operating units. This also has implications for ownership among stakeholders and of course, corporate culture.

In addition people may look forward to more varied work or a spliced career, with a mix of employment, self employment and a rotation of that with sabbaticals. As L. F. Otters, head of product innovation at Philips, put it, 'Quality and speed are principles that must be applied to all activities and must be met if we want to be better than our competition'.

In becoming more marketing driven, one must realize that the main purpose of business is not to generate sales but create satisfied customers. Every company must become more research orientated, even if it is in a service or non high-tech area. R & D also applies to new ways of doing things, improving product service or a methodology that enables lower-paid people to carry out an intellectually based service. There is a need to understand better the psychological barriers to communication and customers' frames of reference. Images exist whether or not they are planned. Every company must decide where it fits into its industry and define its objectives and direction. Above all, it needs to become different from its competitors. Rarely is a company intrinsically interesting. It's how people feel about it. An image should be the truth about a company. What it is and what it does. Hence the need for research to determine the attitudes of various segments of the public towards the company and its competitors. There's nothing more important than finding out the perception people have of you, because people purchase symbols as much as products, hence the need for concentration on corporate identity.

Few companies have a truly sophisticated design management system in which each product and brand relates to the other and the whole projects a coherent idea of the corporation. As corporate designer Wally Olins has said, 'Design has to be managed'. Are you a management-company, a conglomerate, a personality company, federal or holding, centralized or decentralized, or a bland faceless company? Just as it is important to 'know thy customer', so too will it be necessary to evaluate the effectiveness of communications programmes. This doesn't only mean activities that are tangible and numerically measurable. (Arriving at a clear position for yourself in the marketplace is as much a matter of communication as of product.)

However, despite what stockbrokers and bankers would have us believe, success cannot be measured in terms of quantifiable phenomena, such as the bottom line alone, but in terms of management philosophy, style and context. Qualitative data is as important as quantitative. Dealing solely in money is distorting. It's worrying how much influence financial institutions wield over corporations when they represent only one group of stakeholders. All the more important therefore to develop broader-based communications programmes, which in turn have a positive impact on the financial community. We cannot stress enough the importance here of developing a corporate identity as an umbrella for programmes directed at specific audiences. That provides the philosophical underpinning theme running through all promotional programmes anywhere in the company.

After all, information is giving out, communication is getting through, and the whole is only as strong as the weakest link. Management can no longer afford to see its role merely as putting its head down and making profits. It needs to do that while accepting that life is not risk-free. There is a greater need to explain what the board is doing in terms of wealth creation in a mixed economy and a democratic society. It's about contribution. As Sir Geoffrey Chandler, Chairman of Britain's Industry Year 1986 said 'Industrial decisions should be made public rather than private, particularly when they affect the broader community. Industry must be seen to be reasonable, especially in what it contributes to the community. Management is not only a social and human, but a moral and intellectual challenge. Leadership is partly about proselytizing, as well as trust and commitment'.

With the greater application of information technology to business efficiency and productivity, of computer-aided engineering, to the smokestack industries, the growth of service industries and the information industry itself, plus closer links between academea, financial institutions, government and industry, so senior management's ability to assess and articulate its contribution will be critical. You can't just manage well, you have to manage differently. Many managements know what to do, few how to do it. It's not merely about inflexible organization structures, or anti-technology cultures, or turning risk capital into opportunity capital, it's about WILL.

Why can't people put together the best of the U.S. and Japanese methods? There needs to be more social action, not just lip-service to social responsibility, more communication of technology's benefits to staff for example, and more 'social auditing' which would help motivate employees and make management aware of negative social consequences of certain economic actions. In any management process there's nothing more important than people, a truism, but the business community still talks about corporations as if they are inanimate. How many employee reports do we read which talk about the finances in a vacuum, without involving people in the process. A whole culture change should be put in hand, but it won't happen without management retraining. A classic example of this is British Airways' use of the term 'emotional labour' in its 'Managing People First' training programme, which emphasizes clarity, feedback and teamwork.

Dealing with the media is not something management have been trained to do. It's high risk but it's essential. No longer can management afford to wing it. It needs an investment in time to avoid the conflicting signals from too much, as well as too little, talk. Where else would management not be prepared? Candour works in media relations, so does the growing tendency to fight back when the press get it wrong.

It can no longer be considered a game. It is about knowing your audience and the media. 'If the true source of power in an information age is knowledge, then the media, or chief disseminators of knowledge, have a particularly responsible role to play', asserts Geoffrey Goodman, industrial editor of Britain's *Daily Mirror*. They need not act only as mediators between politicians and the electorate, but between experts and the public. He hopes, as do we, that the fourth estate will also act as an integral part of a new and more enlightened system of education and communication. Working with information will become the central activity of modern society, so the public relations departments of large corporations will have to become the foreign office or state department of the corporation. The fact that there are so many different names for the public relations departments attests to the lack of comprehension as to its boundary definition. Communication is now all-pervading and the CEO should be its trumpeter. Gaining share of mind (and heart) isn't easy. As Margaret Thatcher's Press Secretary Bernard Ingham once said, 'You have to get your point over 999 times and then you find that 999 people haven't heard it.'

The new paradigm will create a change in the time span of the media to longer-term issues, to arguing the case for industry, while management readily accepts its responsibilities in the employment and environmental areas. This means early warning radar, intelligence gathering, building a nucleus of support and action/adaptation programmes as well as monitoring progress. In this, management must set the agenda and build bridges with government and pressure groups. There need to be more interchange. No one has satisfactorily explained or built into policy the impact of information technology on our lives and on the concept of work. The IT revolution knows no class distinctions and it seems certain to see a rapid expansion in the numbers of professionals working untraditional hours.

IT is breaking down the traditional barriers between night and day, management and shopfloor worker. If we can understand this shift, we can create more jobs. We shall share our leisure time over a longer time span and, above all, fill that leisure time, not in front of the TV alone, but in learning and re-learning pursuits. We have of course tended to forget the information side of information technology. Communication skills will be built into job specifications along with personnel, training and development matters.

In the future managements must also review the relationship between outside directors, and the executive directors, particularly as so many of them are recycled. Equally there is a need to re-define the boundaries of communication responsibility in broad as well as narrow terms between chairman and managing director. Who does what and to which audience. Succession issues need to be resolved early but so rarely are. The fine balance between the corporate H.Q. and the divisions needs to be reviewed as we move towards less rigid structures and there is a blurring of line-management responsibilities.

While the status of Fortune 500 leaders is low in public opinion polls, young anti-establishment entrepreneurs can be very influential, particularly among their own age group. Baby Boomers will make up half the U.S. electorate by 1988, the problem being that they defy conventional pigeon-holes, being neither liberal nor conservative, democratic nor republican. Without drawing the parallel too closely, this pattern is reflected in the rise of the Liberal/SDP Alliance in Britain. What the people tend to be are libertarians –

maximizing personal liberties, minimizing government controls. Free marketeers but with social concern. They are at last rediscovering the marketplace, something which is slowly happening in Europe, but without the educational and organizational infrastructure to support it. Politics too will need to come to terms with the pressure to reconcile their divergent hawkish economic attitudes and dovish social views. This and more, must be taken into account by senior and aspirant senior managers. We have covered the question of corporate culture and entrepreneurship and the likely impact of more joint ventures with Japanese and European MNCs. We have also discussed whether classical conglomerates can maintain coherence without the individual geniuses of Harold Geneen or Lord Hanson at the top.

Articles in the *Harvard Business Review* continue to blame European and U.S. companies for failing to comprehend global competition and the globalization of markets, so ably exploited by the Japanese. They call for new concepts of competitive analysis and organizational structure. For instance, country organizations are important for good local citizenship, but there is conflict between the need for a global strategic perspective which may vary for manufacturing marketing or distribution industries. Companies will have to be sliced in different ways. Senior management must have the capacity, argues Gary Hammel of London Business School and Professor Prahald of Michigan University, 'To think and act in complex ways.' New analytical concepts and new organizational arrangements must go hand in hand. The concept of 'usable knowledge' is relevant in the context of screening or prioritizing strategies that will work. Adapting the culture to suit. The most important item for managements to address is the need to find a mission and build a bridge between themselves and their line operations. One of the advantages of the founder owner as opposed to the professional manager is that he is orientated toward creating, achieving and taking risks. He is intuitive with a long-range time horizon and to some extent able to see the total picture, whereas the professional manager isn't. More of these values need to be instilled in the modern corporation without necessarily embedding all the dictatorial aspects that come with entrepreneurship. Equally in a company of disparate cultures it makes it all the more important to internalize certain core values, such as integrity and the need to take holidays to avoid emotional burnout. As someone once said 'We're a long-timehorizontal'.

Talking of that word but in another sense, we cannot stress enough the need for more horizontal networking, cutting across the vertical functions and compartments as a way of promoting cohesion.

In order to bring about some of the changes we've argued throughout this book, there must be a change in the underlying assumptions about the relationship between education and industry. This is particularly important in the retraining area, as a result of technological change and new skill priorities.

This book has tried to stimulate ideas about how top managers will need to be managing and leading, how corporations will function and the link between that and communication. It does not provide an academic survey, yet we have tried to point the way in this chapter towards a new philosophy.

Tomorrow's corporation will be very different from today's, and tomorrow's leaders will need to have very different skills and expertise to operate in a looser more dynamic environment. A number of books have dealt in the macro, a number with the changing fashions of successful managerial styles and cultures. In reviewing these, we've attempted to create a bridge to the future, the interrelationships between the internal organization and the external community the link between culture and strategy and the resultant positioning of corporations in terms of image and identity.

We make no apology, as professional communicators, to address this theme. Because most communication is reactive, tactical 'feast and famine' based on inadequate information, it tends to be dispersed among different departments. It tends to be confused with advertising which is just one facet of communication. Most senior managers neither communicate themselves other than via a chain of command, nor relate culture to strategy or culture to corporate identity. Without assigning blame, we've tried to diagnose and suggest solutions. In our role as professional advisers to senior management and as the voice and conscience of our organizations, we should be in a pivotal position to foster winning values and beliefs.

One of the best statements we've seen on the challenge to us as professionals runs as follows: 'The true public relations professional is an analyzer and evaluator of the socio-economic and political environment in which his corporation or organization operates'. In fact, he is adviser, counsellor to management and communicator to various publics, including his management. He is also an evaluator of results.

But ultimately communications experts won't be listened to unless we develop an intellectual basis for what we do and talk the language of management. We are in a position to help management but like them, we too are on trial and are unlikely to help if they won't listen. Communications theory needs to be built into a new management philosophy. Discontinuous change makes planning difficult, if not impossible. Yet a changing approach to the future is imperative if companies are to avoid being bypassed by their competitors. More of the same means the death of the corporation as we know it today.

There needs to be a shift to risk and reward, which we've discussed under the innovations/entrepreneurship headings. Oil companies bidding for exploration contracts in the British North Sea understood this concept. Estimates, scenarios and careful monitoring are fine, but on a walk into the fog a light is of little use. Loose-linked organizations help contain the risk and provide the flexibility for experiment. The general contractual organization may well be suited to discontinuities but will senior management adapt? Have we thought through the implications for strategic planning, issues management and early-warning radar? It is to be hoped that the paradigm paralysis will be replaced more by evolution than revolution. The acceptance of death as the prelude to new life is an age-old recipe for the survival of nature. It also applies to organizations. We shall see if the slowness of corporations to adapt will force a revolution.

In summary, European companies in particular need loosening up to narrow the gap with the U.S. and Japan. Eurosclerosis needs to be replaced by entrepreneurialism. The dogma and sacred cows should be laid to rest. Companies should be less bureaucratic. Decentralization doesn't necessarily mean less bureaucracy. They should be market- not product-driven. Decision making needs to be speeded up, while introducing a much greater development of co-ordination between geography and product market niches.

Above all the corporation needs a leader, with the courage to take action, who will put the question that Nestlé's CEO, Helmut Maucher, asked: 'Are you part of the solution or part of the problem?'

The British magazine, *Chief Executive,* in a survey of managers found that 85% of managers think that advances in IT will have significantly changed the role of the CEO by the year 2000, and demand more professionalism. As we commented in our opening chapter, 62% think that the spread of IT will encourage a more open style of management, but there was ambivalence on the role of women, corporate citizenship, the need for outside activities, and the balance of skills needed. Public relations was quite low on the list, as was personnel, two of the most important skills required. It is vital that CEOs should have a clear mental picture of the qualifications and experience that will be needed in fourteen years' time. After all, they have a role in recruitment and personnel development.

There will need to be a clear vision on where the company is going, how it will get there and the communication required to ensure it happens. The implication for information systems, intelligence gathering and communication channels is enormous. Alliances with foreign partners are inevitable. Robb Wilmott, formerly head of Britain's computer company ICL, complains justifiably that many European CEOs are 'nationally myopic'. Companies must improve the sophistication of their marketing via product differentiation and customer segmentation.

Many European executives still lack the ability, as Herbert Hezler of McKinsey & Co. put it, to 'synthesize functional thinking'. 'In many companies you can do ten excellent things but be hanged if you make just two mistakes', says Professor Herman Sunar of USW, Germany's leading executive education centre.

The balance between loose-tight controls needs to be carefully checked in a flexible era. The British and the Americans manage ambiguity better than the French and the Germans. Change needs to be made at the top level, the attitudes of the CEO himself towards his goals, job, employees, media and stockholders. How he runs his day and priorities must change. The stumbling blocks are corporate culture, lack of strategies, communication, outdated structure, attitudes and lack of relevant information as well as the much-needed process of learning and re-learning.

There are a welter of factors increasing the complexity and diversity of business management and pressures under which companies must operate. Inter-dependence, globalization, intuition not just rationality, outward not inward, the balance between specialization and broad vision, qualitative versus quantitative managers versus leaders, co-operation not just conflict. Technology push and market pull are all part of the new paradigm on which change can happen in an instant. We live in an emotive visual era.

Europe's past success has been concentrated on stable predictable industries. Will there be awakening giants to close the gap, the industrial all-rounders, the hybrid companies. Under whose type of leadership will the new company fall, corporatist or personal? Will the new generation of management be tortoises or hares, and will they be able to break the mould to enter a new paradigm? Will we find the new transactional leaders and thus avoid managerial ulcers in the short term and corporate extinction in the long term? Will we have yet another 'Peptic ulcer generation?'

We have tried, albeit imperfectly, to provide different answers to different questions. There will be some CEOs, senior managers, and advisers to CEOs, who will say after reading the book that they know all this, or that it's all at best, nonsense, at worst, heresy. We hope not too many, because that's what this book has been about, opening hearts and minds. We are not arrogant enough to believe we know all the answers or even asked all the right questions, simply to help responsible business people readjust the compass to find their way through the corporate maze with the new route map.

Appendix
Top management check list

Although it is impossible to reach any general conclusions about what senior managers should do about technological change, the following is a check list of the main points that may at least be relevant to many:

Personal

1. Have you examined your own attitude to changing technology?
2. Are you familiar with the mainstreams of technical change as they may affect your organization?
3. Do you know enough about computer and microprocessor technology to understand the expert?
4. Do you know how to obtain information and advice?
5. Do you intend to initiate change?

Strategic Planning

6. Is your organization keeping pace with your industry's technology?
7. Are competitors more efficient in such areas as cost, design and product characteristics? What is your market share and is it increasing?
8. Are new technologies likely to undermine your own competitive position in U.K. and world markets?
9. Are you investing sufficiently in R&D and product development to provide product and market leadership opportunities?
10. Is the response of your organization to marketing opportunities fast enough and sufficiently resourced to maintain or improve market share (U.K. or world)?

11. Are financial policies restricting growth and enterprise?

Organization

12. Is the right priority being given to the interests of customers, employees, shareholders and the community?
13. Is there resistance to change in your organization, and are the problems sufficiently isolated and controlled?
14. Is management receptive to change and practised in its implementation?
15. Is development work sufficiently closely related to markets to provide a focus and sense of direction?
16. Do all employees get informed about, and participate in, decisions affecting them directly? Is the participation genuine or contrived?
17. When introducing technological changes do you think them out in terms of the needs of people, or mechanistically?
18. Is there scope for implementing change in smaller rather than larger units?
19. Do you evaluate technological projects solely in terms of cost benefits to the company, or do you consider the benefits to the other interests involved? What value do you give to the experience of change and to being up-to-date?

Industrial Relations

20. Have you consulted your work force and trade unions about likely changes, and invited their co-operation?
21. Do your negotiating procedures facilitate or retard the rate of change?
22. Are your employees sufficiently flexible in the variety of work they are prepared to undertake?
23. Have you given sufficient consideration to the questions of security of employment and to changes in the status, responsibility and skill content of jobs?
24. Are you sufficiently sensitive to change in the moods of individuals and groups of people to anticipate and prevent outbreaks of militancy?

Education and Training

25. Does your organization aim to develop fully the potential of individuals throughout their careers?

26. Do you encourage young employees to undertake higher and further education, or are they just 'dumped' in jobs?
27. How do you assess employees for retraining?
28. Are your contacts with schools (headteachers, careers staff and students) sufficiently close?
29. Do you maintain sufficiently close contacts with universities, colleges and research organizations?

Social

30. Are your organization's value systems compatible with a more educated and less socially divisive society?
31. Is there scope for a relaxation of some of the traditional habits of employment (e.g. more flexible hours, part-time work, and phased retirement)?
32. Is the perpetuation of privileges and distinctions at different levels of the organization generally acceptable?
33. Are technical staff encouraged to take part in activities outside their own organizations to broaden their range of experience?

Source: *Management Research Groups, British Institute of Management Foundation*

Index